ELEMENTS OF THE WRITING CRAFT

ELEMENTS OF THE WRITING CRAFT

ROBERT OLMSTEAD

STORY PRESS

CINCINNATI, OHIO

Elements of the Writing Craft. Copyright © 1997 by Robert Olmstead. Printed and bound in the United States of America. All rights reserved. No part of this book may be reproduced in any form or by any electronic or mechanical means including information storage and retrieval systems without permission in writing from the publisher, except by a reviewer, who may quote brief passages in a review. Published by Story Press, an imprint of F&W Publications, Inc., 1507 Dana Avenue, Cincinnati, Ohio 45207. (800) 289-0963. First edition.

Story Press Books are available from your local bookstore or direct from the publisher.

01   00   99   98   97   5   4   3   2   1

Library of Congress Cataloging-in-Publication Data

Olmstead, Robert.
   Elements of the writing craft / Robert Olmstead.—1st ed.
     p.   cm.
   Includes index.
   ISBN 1-884910-29-7 (alk. paper)
    1. Authorship—Handbooks, manuals, etc.   I. Title.
PN147.044   1997
808'.02—dc21   96-50165
                                               CIP

Designed by Clare Finney

Just for Emily

ACKNOWLEDGMENTS

For their shrewd readings and valuable contributions, I would like to thank Lois Rosenthal and Jack Heffron at Story Press and Judy Gill at Dickinson College. For their commitment to my education as a teacher of writing, I would like to thank my students.

CONTENTS

INTRODUCTION

It is often said that writing is like driving at night. You only have your headlights, but you still manage to get where you're going. As writers, we have our destination in mind: novel, short story, essay, memoir. But as we write our attention is focused on those areas our lights wash across: how to begin, how to end, how to switch from narrative to dialogue. These small concerns along the way can make the trip sometimes difficult and confusing.

This book teaches you how to write better fiction and nonfiction by focusing on these small concerns, so that you can master the craft one step at a time. For example, rather than offer a lengthy discussion on how to create vivid characters, I focus on the "micro" elements that make up characterization, such as gestures and mannerisms. We will watch the sentence and the paragraph and not so much the page. We will take, if you will, a close look at the trees instead of at the forest, where too often writers get lost or feel completely overwhelmed.

I offer this "close look at the trees" in more than 150 lessons. The premise behind these lessons, and the book, is simple: To learn to write you must master the small aspects of the craft, and to master them you must learn to *read like a writer*. If a writer doesn't read with an eye toward noticing specific, technical strategies, development is almost always slow and torturous, an endless cycle of trial and error. By reading insightfully, a writer improves more quickly, develops a sense of what good writing sounds like, and how it works. The stories, essays, novels and nonfiction books of masterful writers can, and should, act as guideposts.

You may claim, of course, that you don't have time to read all the necessary writers who might help you improve. Time, in our world today, is at a premium for all of us. But I have solved this problem by offering in each lesson a short excerpt, usually only a paragraph long, from great writers past and present, ones I have found most useful in my workshops and ones my students have found most inspiring. These excerpts will save you a great deal of time while providing a solid foundation on which you can build an understanding of the craft. The excerpts appear at the beginning of each lesson and can be read and reread in just a few minutes.

After each excerpt I provide a brief but detailed analysis pointing out the techniques at work within the passage. I explain in simple, practical terms exactly how the writer is creating the effects the reader feels. The analyses are specific, accessible and, I hope, fun and surprising. Above all, I hope they inspire you, that they spark new ways to approach your own writing.

In the third and final part of the lesson, I help you hone your craft with writing exercises. These suggestions, based on the methods you have just studied, allow you to apply your new awareness, sometimes through imitation, sometimes through simple practice, and always with the goal of making this strategy your own.

Use this book the way you would use a field guide or a map, but not a flat map, more like a map of topography, handy and functional and practical for traveling mountainous terrain. Use a notebook to collect the writing possibilities, or maybe use the back of an envelope. Implicit in every entry is that you should continue with your own good work. The best writers have already written the best short stories, novels, memoirs and books, until you write one better. Here is where you begin.

PART I
STORYTELLING

OPENING WITH THE STORYTELLER

READING

Call me Ishmael. Some years ago—never mind how long precisely—having little or no money in my purse, and nothing particular to interest me on shore, I thought I would sail about a little and see the watery part of the world.

FROM THE NOVEL *MOBY DICK*, BY HERMAN MELVILLE

LESSON

Melville begins *Moby Dick* with the character Ishmael talking to the reader. Imagine that Ishmael has come up to you and has begun to tell you this story. At the outset, his presence is commanding. He tells you what to call him, not what his name is. He makes it clear that when the story happened is not important, that he had no money and no interests on shore. He is denying you this information. He is directing your curiosity, but he makes up for it by saying, in so many words, that he is a thinking sort of person and capable of being precise and particular. He gives and he takes, all for the purpose of spinning his yarn. He entices you with his appearance of honesty.

WRITING POSSIBILITIES

1. How do people introduce themselves? How do they say their names and also let you know what they want to be called? Perhaps a nickname? Here are four examples: My name is; My friends call me; I am called; Her name was.

Open a story of your own this way. Write a paragraph in which you introduce a character to begin a story.

2. Sometimes we introduce ourselves by saying who and what we are not. Listen for these. For example: My name is John. I'm not what you'd call rich; My name is Hemingway, but no relation to the writer; My name is Jane. Not much of a name really.

Now try an opening paragraph in which the character introduces himself by saying who he is not.

3. Think about how we meet and greet each other. What do we do in those small instances? We shake hands. We wave. In the military, people salute. In Europe, people kiss cheeks. The distance between people is important. As you open with a character, think about how intimate you want that voice to be to the listener, about the relationship you want between your character and your reader. Is the reader sitting across the table from the character? Is the character whispering to the reader? Do you want your character to have an arm around your reader's shoulder? Don't forget—Ishmael does not tell us his name; he tells us

what he wants to be called. Write a paragraph in which characters meet and greet each other and try to characterize the relationship by the type of greeting.

4. Without taking the time to think, can you say how you usually introduce yourself to a stranger? Can you answer such a question on the spur of the moment? Now think back to the last time you introduced yourself. Have a character use your method, introducing himself to another character, a stranger. Write a few lines of dialogue for each character. Then, in a new scene, have a character use a method completely different from yours. Create a dialogue for this set of characters as well.

OPENING IN ILLNESS, NONFICTION

READING

It starts in my sleep, a partly dreamed memory of being young and about to wake to the life of a young man. This morning I was playing basketball with Michael Jordan, and I was as big as he was, or bigger. What a mass of roles, of personae, is mixed in when one is ill, alongside the self-loathing and self-protection, the recurring simplicity and the terror. My identity is a raft skidding or gliding, borne on a flux of feelings and frights, including the morning's delusion (which lasts ten minutes sometimes) of being young and whole.

FROM THE ESSAY "THIS WILD DARKNESS," BY HAROLD BRODKEY

LESSON

To be a writer and to know the imminence of your death . . . Where do you turn? What do you do? You take up your pen and address the impending darkness. Somewhere in the ink is a cure, or at least something akin to meaning and purpose to hold in your head. These are the questions we as writers are often most curious about: What is it like to die, to be born, to take a life?

Brodkey begins *It starts in my sleep. . . .* He is talking about this particular half-dream of being young once again. But consider the phrase. It is bold and old-fashioned and mythic, demonstrating the writer's prerogative always to say where a story begins and ends. This quote is an opening into a life, a mind, a youth, an illness. In these few lines he remembers, he speculates, he declares, he recounts, he reveals, and he makes wisdom. In these few words we have indication of what is to come: a mind, however afflicted, still urging itself to make sense where there is none. Harold Brodkey died January 26, 1996.

WRITING POSSIBILITIES

Start your own personal history. In the following exercises, let's work down through the sentences in Brodkey's essay, maintaining similar word counts within the parentheses.

1. Where might it start for you, the thinking on your life? Use the following frame to begin: It starts _____, a partly (dreamed, imagined, made-up?) memory of _____.

2. In the second sentence, Brodkey makes a simple declaration. Use the following frame yourself: This morning I was _____.

3. Sentences one and two are the foundation. From the basis of these two sentences, the writer is poised to comment, to make wisdom. Continue: What a _____, of _____, is mixed in when one is _____, alongside the _____ and _____, the _____ and the _____.

4. The fourth sentence returns to the intention of the second sentence. This declarative sentence takes flight and then returns to itself as it concludes. Note how a reference is made to the dream and also how there is a parenthetical comment as to its duration. Fill in this sentence: My identity is a _____ _____ or _____, borne _____, including (make a reference back to the experience in sentence one) of being _____ and _____.

5. As you have been working through the exercises, you have been learning your own opening. Combine exercises one through four, and as you do, make the rewrites you feel necessary, including those that bring the words closer to your own. Perhaps one rewrite is to exchange the word *begins* for the word *starts*. Maybe you'd like to change the first sentence to past tense. Make these changes. You now have a beginning.

OPENING IN CRISIS

READING

We fought. When my mother and I crossed state lines in the stolen car, I'd sit against the window and wouldn't talk. I wouldn't even look at her. The fights came when I thought she broke a promise. She said there'd be an Indian reservation. She said that we'd see buffalo in Texas. My mother said a lot of things. We were driving from Bay City, Wisconsin, to California, so I could be a child star while I was still a child.

"Talk to me," my mother would say. "If you're upset, tell me."

But I wouldn't. I knew how to make her suffer. I was mad. I was mad about a lot of things. Places she said would be there, weren't. We were running away from family. We'd left home.

Then my mother would pull to the side of the road and reach over and open my door.

"Get out, then," she'd say, pushing me.

FROM THE NOVEL *ANYWHERE BUT HERE*, BY MONA SIMPSON

LESSON

This novel begins with a two-word sentence—a subject and a verb. It tells what has been happening between the narrator and her mother from the narrator's point of view. These two words give conditions. They create a complicated dynamic, yet one that is easy to understand. It is not a drama taking place before your eyes, but still a drama that was and is constant. The word *would* maintains the past tense. *Would* is the past tense of *will* and indicates habitual action, in this case, the relentlessness of the fighting.

In the second sentence we find out their car is stolen. But this information comes to us through an adjective inside a prepositional phrase inside a clause. That the car is stolen is made to be much less important than that they are fighting. Nevertheless, we are told the car is stolen, and it isn't mentioned again in this passage. Simply put, this information is revealed in an adjective, not in a statement of fact, as the fighting is.

Another statement of fact is *I was mad*. Notice how each time the narrator makes a statement of fact, she follows it with an example, reason or detail. The thinking is personal and childlike. Sometimes it doesn't make sense. But more important, it *appears* to make sense. The narrator's strength is in her thinking. This is why the mother's behavior in the fourth paragraph is so striking. It has consequence. Knowing the car is stolen now comes back to haunt us. The crisis is enlarged. However dangerous we thought the situation, we find we misjudged.

WRITING POSSIBILITIES

1. Open with a two-word sentence. Come up with ten possibilities. For example: We argued. We left. He cried.

2. Choose a two-word sentence from exercise one to open your story and follow it with a paragraph in the conditional, using the word *would*. Give the customs of the action defined in your two-word sentence. For example: We argued. When the bills came, I would tell him that money was the problem, or I wouldn't tell him anything at all. But money was the problem, at least one of them. . . . (Continue.)

3. Hide an adjective inside a sentence the way Simpson does with the word *stolen*. For example: She lied. When she and I went to bed in her boyfriend's apartment, I stared at the wall and wouldn't talk.

OPENING WITH A HISTORY

READING

This is the saddest story I have ever heard. We had known the Ashburnhams for nine seasons of the town of Nauheim with an extreme intimacy—or, rather, with an acquaintanceship as loose and easy and yet as close as a good glove's with your hand. My wife and I knew Captain and Mrs. Ashburnham as well as it was possible to know anybody, and yet, in another sense, we knew nothing at all about them. This is, I believe, a state of things only possible with English people of whom, till today, when I sit down to puzzle out what I know of this sad affair, I knew nothing whatever. Six months ago I had never been to England, and, certainly, I had never sounded the depths of an English heart. I had known the shallows.

FROM THE NOVEL *THE GOOD SOLDIER*, BY FORD MADOX FORD

LESSON

The narrator opens his story with a simple truth: This is the saddest story he's heard. Telling stories is a casual pastime, and most of our daily conversations are filled with the histories and happenings surrounding people we know. We love to hear about people's pasts, and so we love stories that divulge these pasts. Such stories are often filled with superlatives: It was the saddest thing, the nicest thing, the most generous man. The narrator opens his own story like a friend or a family member might, and we trust him for this; he seems honest and direct.

In the next sentence he implies the story is not about himself, but about a couple he knows well. However, his confidence of just how well he knew them seems to slowly slip through his fingers. He goes from having *an extreme intimacy* with them, to *an acquaintanceship*, to knowing them *as well as possible*, to knowing *nothing at all about them*. This recession lends the couple a sense of mystery. The narrator had known the shallow, surface parts of these people's lives, but not the depths.

But as the novel develops, we learn that the story is very much about the narrator—Captain Ashburnham and the narrator's wife have had an affair. The opening line distances the narrator from the events. It is a sad thing he's heard, not a sad thing that happened to him. However, we learn that, as the affair developed over this nine-year acquaintance with the Ashburnhams, the narrator knew absolutely nothing about it. Mrs. Ashburnham tells him the story, which she was privy to the entire time, only after Captain Ashburnham and the narrator's wife have died. Confused? That is one of the pitfalls of introducing history early in a story—you must always be precise.

WRITING POSSIBILITIES

1. Follow Ford's example and open a story with a simple truth. Come up with ten lines like these: This is the sweetest story I have ever heard. This is the longest story I have ever heard. This is the scariest story I have ever heard.

2. Now choose one of your opening lines and tell your story from the outside, as Ford does. Stories can be about people our own lives barely touch, or people our lives are deeply entangled with. Think of the constellations of people that you might come across in a single day, and then tell how long you've known them. Write a paragraph beginning with a line like this: Susan and Les had been my best friends since college; My parents have been married for twenty-seven years; The Seymours had lived upstairs since Christmas; I passed the woman every morning in the elevator for nine months and never knew her name.

3. Decide, as you begin your story, that you are discovering something you have never known about these characters. What are the phrases that Ford uses to draw out this effect? What other phrases might you use? Continue your paragraph from exercise two using Ford's phrases and your own to create the feeling of discovery.

OPENING AFTER A DEATH

READING

This time it was a girl Halverson knew, halfway eaten and her hair chewed off. She had been awake in the night; she'd been afraid and whimpering as the great bear nudged at the side of the nylon tent like a rooting hog. She held to the other girl's hand, and began to scream only when the long claws ripped her out of her sleeping bag, continuing to scream as she was being dragged away, the feathery down from the sleeping bag floating above the glowing coals of a pine-knot fire. This time it was someone he knew. . . .

FROM THE STORY "WE ARE NOT IN THIS TOGETHER," BY WILLIAM KITTREDGE

LESSON

One of life's marking events is death. Kittredge uses our fascination with death to draw us into his story. The first two words of his story indicate the history that precedes this event: *This time*. Without saying so, the writer lets us know there have been others. Halverson has experienced these feelings before. The writer begins not with the first death, but with the one that is the breaking point for Halverson. The second half of the sentence sends home the horror of what Halverson knows.

Then Kittredge takes a breath, for his own sake as well as the reader's. The narrative is direct and vivid and imagined by the character. The horrifying event is made more so by the contrasting details: The bear nudged, the feathery down floated, and the coals from the fire were glowing. Kittredge makes the action seem ongoing by using the -ing form: *whimpering, continuing, being, floating, sleeping, glowing*. And finally, as if to reaffirm what is already known, a version of the first sentence is repeated.

WRITING POSSIBILITIES

1. Begin a story with the very same words Kittredge does: *This time*. Talk about your own version of a literal or figurative death. Write at least two paragraphs, beginning with a sentence like one of these: This time was not so easy. This time it was his mother's house, sprayed with paint and a note in the mailbox. This time she knew the girl, a friend from high school.

2. Most often, we are not direct witnesses to death. Our firsthand experience comes from knowing a person who has died, not from watching him or her die. Allow a character to imagine how something might have gone. Move right into it, and use verbs that allow the action to be ongoing. For example: This time was not so easy to take. He imagined them riding up in their cars and trucks, drinking beer and laughing, a little afraid.

3. Consider description that contrasts the event you are telling about. In a paragraph, use delicate words to describe something harsh or horrible in order to reveal something unexpected. For example: This time it was his sister's house, a cross burning in the front yard, warm and incandescent and casting sparks into the grass.

OPENING WITH AN ENCOUNTER, NONFICTION

READING

Summer, ninety-five degrees. The residential unit for chronic schizophrenics sits dead and silent in the heat. I ring the bell and a fat sweating boy, his face a mash of pimples, answers. "I am here to see Dr. Siley," I say, glancing down at the job advertisement in my hand. The pimply-faced boy stares and stares at me. I can tell, from his fatness and sweat, that he is a patient. He reaches out and touches my neck. I flinch.

FROM THE MEMOIR *WELCOME TO MY COUNTRY*, BY LAUREN SLATER

LESSON

The writing begins by efficiently establishing time and place, something we expect of all writing sooner or later. The first person comes forward in the third sentence, but because it's a memoir, we expected that before we even began to read. In our lives we like to know where we are, when it is, and who is talking to us. A writer must fulfill or at least address this need. This writer is taking us into a very difficult world. It's important that the reader be guided through as clearly and artfully as possible. The writer rang that bell some time ago and now she is reenacting it on the page so we might make this entry with her and experience what she has experienced. Keep in mind, also, she is an expert and the reader is not. She takes special care of the reader because she understands how very different this world is. She returns to the moment so we are entering with her.

WRITING POSSIBILITIES

1. Do you have a job or a life experience that someone might want to read about? A time worth revisiting? It is strange how bad we are at recognizing the significance of our own experiences. We tend to see them as being more or less important than they really are. What makes an experience worth telling? List ten subtle clues. For example: When you are in a group, there is a particular story your friends want you to tell; there's a story your children want to hear again and again; there's an experience a group of you had together and years later you still talk about it.

2. As we work through these next two exercises, use an event from exercise one or feel free to write fiction. Let's begin by filling in the following frame based on Slater's passage: (Season), (temperature). The _____ for _____ sits _____ and _____ in the (heat, cold, wind?). I (ring the bell, knock on the door, let myself in?) and a _____ answers. "I am here to see _____," I say, glancing down at the _____. The _____ _____ at me. I can tell, from _____, that (he/she) is a _____. (He/she) _____ and _____ my _____. I _____.

3. Imagine you are taking your reader into a place of delight. Begin again: (Season), (temperature). The _____ for _____ sits _____ and _____ in the _____. I ring the bell and . . . (Continue.) I smile.

4. Draw Slater's text away from its original construction. Begin: (Year). Summer and ninety-five degrees. The (barracks?) for (new recruits?) sat dead and silent in the heat. . . . (Continue.)

5. Draw it away even further. Begin: 1997. Winter and twenty-three degrees. The water for the livestock froze block solid in the cold. I called the plumber and a fat bundle of a man arrived, his face a . . . (Continue.)

OPENING IN AFTERMATH

READING

The other victim the summer my wife left me was my dreamlife, which, like a mirage, dried up completely the closer we came to the absolute end of us. In the fourteen years we were married, I had been a ferocious dreamer, drawing all I knew or feared or loved about the waking world into my sleeplife.

FROM THE STORY "DREAMS OF DISTANT LIVES," BY LEE K. ABBOTT

LESSON

Often the unpleasant events in our lives are most dramatic, most suited to story. But unpleasantness is difficult to talk about. A good place to start might be once the dust has settled. Abbott begins in the aftermath of a broken relationship. But the narrator is finding a way to tell about the pain of something large and incomprehensible by talking about the pain of something small and inconsequential, the strange loss of dreamlife. Our minds find a place where they can endure what is unendurable. The first sentence likens the dreamlife to a mirage, which is the central part of the sentence, and the relationship begins and ends the sentence. The second sentence with its *fourteen years* sharpens the breakup; the word *ferocious* sharpens the dreamlife. This story goes on for many paragraphs recounting the demise of the dreamlife before the narrator finally settles into the story he wants to tell.

WRITING POSSIBILITIES

1. Abbott enters this story, in a sense, at the end. He invokes the chain of events that precede the breakup of a marriage with the phrase *my wife left me*. He doesn't need to give the details at this point, but knows he can depend upon the reader to realize the size of what came before. Start a story of your own this way. Write at least two paragraphs. A perfectly good word to begin with is *after*. Two examples: After the house burned down; After my mother broke her hip.

2. Open a story with a tragedy and some small parallel event. Perhaps a death is accompanied by a profound loss of appetite, a bankruptcy by a dying lawn, a loss of faith by forgetfulness. Write at least two paragraphs in this vein.

3. Open a story in the aftermath of a joyful occasion. Something new has come into a character's life, a success of sorts. Let a small good thing accompany this occasion too. Baseball players on a hitting streak have all manner of superstitions they follow. Maybe your character is a traveling saleswoman who has a lucky charm. Write a few paragraphs to open this story.

STORYTELLING IN NONFICTION

READING

". . . She ran the forty feet. There was no tree for me to climb. You can't fight a bear. They are so strong. She wrapped around me. I tried to put my stuff sack in her mouth so she wouldn't bite me, but it didn't work. She came at me seven times. I looked her in the eye. People say you shouldn't look a bear in the eye, but I wanted to tell her: 'Don't do this to me.' But she wanted me.

"She lifted me off the ground by my elbow. I'm what you call a six-foot woman. I weighed 160 pounds then. I weigh less now, after the operations. I don't really know what happened. I hope to remember some day. It was so quick. The next thing I knew I was on the ground and she was gone. It was almost like a dream."

FROM THE BOOK *KAYAKING THE FULL MOON*, BY STEVE CHAPPLE

LESSON

Chapple is retelling a true story, and he lets the victim recount the drama of the attack. This is an extraordinary personal experience—not many people have been attacked by bears and survived. Often the best way to tell the story of something many people have never experienced is to carefully detail the action: *she ran, she wrapped, she came at me, she wanted me, she lifted me.* The victim then also tells her reactions just as clearly and simply: *you can't fight a bear, I tried, I looked her in the eye.* The intensity of the moment is revealed in these short sentences, like gunshots or breathlessness. The woman gives an idea of her injuries when she says that she weighs less now after the operations, and as the passage continues she points out the specific damage the bear caused to her body. These are the marks left behind. The woman says she really doesn't know what happened, but now she has these injuries like a map of the event on her body. Remember, as a writer of nonfiction you must seek out your stories. You must adhere to the facts.

WRITING POSSIBILITIES

1. What are some unusual, survivable dramatic experiences that you can report? Make a list of ten. For example: being struck by lightning; waiting out a hurricane; being trapped in a car wreck, in a snowstorm, under ice.

2. Now find a person who has had one of these experiences, a friend or a relative. Interview him on precisely what occurred. What was going on around him? What was happening to him? What was he feeling and thinking? You can use this material in either fiction or nonfiction.

3. Find some detail left behind by the disaster, like the bear victim's injuries. For example, in a hurricane, there could be a board driven through a palm tree. If a person falls through ice, there is the hole that freezes over. Details like this can shape your story. Use this key detail in a descriptive paragraph or two.

4. Decide whether to tell the story yourself or let those who experienced it tell their own story. Chapple lets this woman tell her own story because she is a good storyteller. Base your decision on the information you've collected and write your story.

REPORTING IN NONFICTION

READING
Kazmann got into his car, crossed the Mississippi on the high bridge at Baton Rouge, and made his way north to Old River. He parked, got out, and began to walk the structure. An extremely low percentage of its five hundred and sixty-six feet eradicated his curiosity. "That whole miserable structure was vibrating," he recalled years later, adding that he had felt as if he were standing on a platform at a small rural train station when "a fully loaded freight goes through." Kazmann opted not to wait for the caboose. "I thought, This thing weighs two hundred thousand tons. When two hundred thousand tons vibrates like this, this is no place for R.G. Kazmann. I got into my car, turned around, and got the hell out of there."

FROM THE BOOK *THE CONTROL OF NATURE*, BY JOHN MCPHEE

LESSON
Sometimes we need to get facts across to our readers in the quickest, most efficient way possible. This is reporting, not storytelling, and this is the technique McPhee uses. Nonfiction also depends upon people to carry its message, just the way a story would. Except for a word or two, this passage from McPhee could easily be mistaken for a story excerpt, and Kazmann for a character in that story. Facts are precise and places are named. McPhee recounts Kazmann's sensation of being on this dam. We rely on our characters, real and fictional, to share their impressions as well as their knowledge. Whether you are writing fiction or nonfiction, it is done the same way, except one is supposed to be true.

WRITING POSSIBILITIES
1. Rewrite this McPhee quote as a piece of fiction, perhaps the opening to a story. Rename Kazmann. Make up all your places, states and cities. Create a structure to put your character on such as a bridge,

a dam, a skyscraper; make up its dimensions and your character's perceptions of those dimensions. Think about the third sentence. Does that work as fiction?

2. How do you have a character tell his feelings in his own words? You just do it. Settle your character in the position of a storyteller. Here are some examples to get you started: He sat down and lit a cigarette. "That whole building was on fire by the time I got there," he recalled years later. . . . She sat back and put her feet up on the hassock. "I don't really know how it all started," she said to no one in particular. . . . He flew into Charlotte, landed in a fog and walked away. "It was the smartest thing I ever did," he said, years later. . . . Now try it yourself. Briefly describe a character and then launch him into his own feelings in dialogue.

3. Description by the numbers. The dam is 566 feet. It weighs 200,000 tons. Think about size, distance and weight as ways of describing. Be precise. If you have a car rolling over on the highway, how much weight is tumbling through the air? How far is it from Concord, New Hampshire, to Charlotte, North Carolina? How long does it take to bake a meat loaf?

4. Look at the first sentence of the reading. Put someone in a car. Send him across a river on a certain bridge, have him turn in the direction of his destination. Fill in the blanks: He got into his car, crossed _____ on _____ at _____, and made his way _____ to _____; She walked down _____ to _____ where she turned up _____ and crossed _____ to _____.

HIGH DRAMA IN NONFICTION

READING

. . . Pat is in the chair now and guards are moving quickly, removing the leg irons and handcuffs and replacing them with the leather straps. One guard has removed his left shoe. They are strapping his trunk, his legs, his arms. He finds my face. He says, "I love you." I stretch my hand toward him. "I love you, too."

He attempts a smile (he told me he would try to smile) but manages only to twitch.

A metal cap is placed on his head and an electrode is screwed in at the top and connected to a wire that comes from a box behind the chair. An electrode is fastened to his leg. A strap placed around his chin holds his head tightly against the back of the chair. He grimaces. He cannot speak anymore. A grayish green cloth is placed over his face.

Millard says, "Father forgive them, for they know not what they do."

Only the warden remains in the room now, only the warden and the man strapped into the chair. The red telephone is silent. I close my eyes and do not see as the warden nods his head, the signal to the executioner to do his work.

I hear three clanks as the switch is pulled with pauses in between. Nineteen hundred volts, then let the body cool, then five hundred volts, pause again, then nineteen hundred volts. "Christ, be with him, have mercy on him," I pray silently.

FROM THE BOOK *DEAD MAN WALKING*, BY HELEN PREJEAN, C.S.J.

LESSON

This is the moment before a death, an excerpt from Prejean's nonfiction account of her correspondence with a death row prisoner. She tells exactly how Pat is placed in the electric chair, how he is strapped down. The careful details build tension. Prejean wants us to be intimate with this process. The guards and the warden and the silent red telephone that would bring a last-minute pardon are all details of inevitability. They highlight the feelings of doom. Prejean closes her eyes and does not see the actual moment of execution. She finds no refuge in her mind, however. She knows exactly what is happening as the switch is pulled. Her solace is prayer.

The telling is straight subject-verb. In the face of this most extraordinary event, the writer has removed herself as much as possible, letting the facts speak for themselves. But not quite. She has decided to use the present tense, making the events immediate. It seems Prejean is telling the story in a straight chronological order, but she isn't. She is also accounting for simultaneous actions, or actions completed. Few events happen one at a time. The second sentence is an action already completed. Reportage has its own difficulties being precise with time, place, and event.

WRITING POSSIBILITIES

1. The present tense is a way to create immediacy, a sense that the drama is unfolding before your eyes. Rewrite Prejean's passage in the past tense. What do you do with the words *now* and *pause*? Which draft is better?

2. In the third paragraph, Prejean seems to tell of actions without actors when she writes *a metal cap is placed, an electrode is fastened.* But not so. In the first paragraph it is established that the guards are

doing this work. Write a set of sentences describing a process without an actor. Use this technique to describe actions that are bringing doom and drama.

3. Prejean uses the phrase *I close my eyes*. Given the situation, we have every reason to believe she did close her eyes. Try opening a story with a phrase like this. What are other examples? Perhaps *I cover my ears*. Write two or three paragraphs in which a character has purposely closed off one of her senses. This effect heightens the drama of the event. Remember, however, that at some point the character must undo such an act so narrative might continue.

DAILY DRAMA IN NONFICTION

READING

. . . "I slammed the door on her finger," Colleen said sorrowfully as she set Cara down on the counter and took off her blue mitten. Then I heard her scream. "Her finger came off! The top of her finger came off, Don!"

It was more than the bills for the emergency room and the hand surgeon that carried me back to the house to ask for a job. It was the memory of me just standing there in the kitchen inside my fears, taking all that time to feel sorry for myself while Colleen zipped Cara inside her down coat. . . .

FROM THE ESSAY "WINTER WORK: DIARY OF A DAY LABORER," BY DON J. SNYDER

LESSON

Too often we are taught that essay is about idea. It is discussed in terms of logic, argument, theory and delivery. Yes, essays are about ideas, but the writer is telling the story of that idea. Based on what you learned in school, you would not know this is an essay even if you read the whole piece. This is an essay about a man who has been out of work for eighteen months and finds a job as a carpenter building a mansion. He has just moved to Maine with his wife and four children, and he is really not qualified to be a carpenter but needs the work. This essay is about the risks we take when we're in need. It's about being out of work and desperate.

Notice how the word *as* in the first sentence efficiently creates simultaneous action. The word *then* moves us forward within the small drama of the moment. The trip to the emergency room, being there, and coming home all happen offstage. After the word *coat*, thirteen more words get us out the door and on the way to the hospital. A line break ends the movement. The true drama of Cara's injury is what lingers in our minds. This is the use of dense dramatic narrative.

WRITING POSSIBILITIES

1. People are always getting hurt. Remember a real situation where someone you cared about was suddenly injured or suddenly discovered he'd injured someone else. Rewrite the beginning of the quote. Use the following frame: "I _____," _____ said sorrowfully as (he/she) _____ and _____. Then I heard (him/her) _____. "_____."

2. Continue with the second movement, the one that references but does not tell all that followed. You can change subject matter or actually continue with exercise one. Notice the movement of Snyder's *in . . . inside . . . inside*. Try to replicate this as you write, perhaps with another set of prepositions. Use the following frame: It was more than _____ and the _____ that carried me _____. It was the memory of _____ in the _____ inside _____, _____ while . . . (Continue.)

3. Now either combine exercises one and two or complete each one separately. Consider combining them even if you were thinking about different subject matter when you wrote them. You will probably need to change some words of fact, but change as few as possible. You may have arrived at something interesting.

4. Move to fiction. In exercises one, two and three you were working with real events. Do the same exercises again with made-up events.

STORY INSIDE STORY

READING
. . . It was with these feelings that he heard the uncle's suddenly solemn voice. What was this voice, this tone? What story?

It was in the dark afternoon on a November day of sleet, told the uncle. We waited and we waited for Louetta to get home from her trip into town. The darker it got the scareder we got.

FROM THE STORY "HAD I A HUNDRED MOUTHS," BY WILLIAM GOYEN

LESSON
Often we wish to tell a story inside a story. The problem is how to move gracefully into this story. Goyen begins with the boy hearing his uncle's voice as if it were coming from a strange place. Goyen is moving both the reader and the listener within the larger story. The movement is gradual and inexorable, as if sliding under water, falling under a

spell. The first move is the solemn sound of the voice. Then the question, What voice?, then a reference to tone, then, What story? Before an answer is forthcoming, the story commences, yet we are not sure until we too are already under its spell and read the words *told the uncle*. The story thus is begun.

WRITING POSSIBILITIES

1. Storytellers inside your stories, in all likelihood, will sound different from the narrator. They will tell their story in a way that is unique within the larger story. Begin with the sound of a voice. Make a list of ten phrases that describe a voice. A few examples: his father's voice was but a whisper; her voice like a reed.

2. Use questions to move into your story. Choose one of the phrases from exercise one and add three questions to move into your story. For example: her voice was like a reed. What was this sound? Was this her voice? Her story?

3. Now begin your interior story, and once inside, understand you have a new storyteller. For example: His father's voice was but a whisper. Why so quiet? Why such a whisper? What story?

It was sunlit in December. Snowfields and cold, said my father. We walked and walked and walked. . . . (Continue.)

MEMORY

READING

. . . The way I always see her is the way she used to be on a Sunday afternoon, say, when the old folks were talking after the big Sunday dinner. I always see her wearing pale blue. She'd be sitting on the sofa. . . . Maybe somebody's got a kid in his lap and is absent-mindedly stroking the kid's head. Maybe there's a kid, quiet and big-eyed, curled up in a big chair in the corner. The silence, the darkness coming, and the darkness in the faces frighten the child obscurely.

FROM THE STORY "SONNY'S BLUES," BY JAMES BALDWIN

LESSON

More often than not, storytelling is the act of bringing forth memory onto the page. As we remember, so do our characters. But not so fast. Memory on the page is an act of storytelling in all its fullness. In these passages from the same paragraph, the narrator tells the story of his memory. He sees his mother in a time and a place. But note the use of the word *say*. It is used the same way we might use *maybe*. When he uses the word *say,* he is calling upon you to agree with him. In the second sentence he repeats the phrase *I always see her.*

Later on in the movement the word *say* becomes *maybe.* So that his memory might include as much as possible, he writes the scene as if it were held immovable in time and place. He writes the scene as if he, too, is trying to hold it in place. He makes for the possibility of a child curled up in a chair; then in the next sentence he evokes that child as if it were really there and carries that through the paragraph and into the next one. His repetition of words is like the cupping of photographs in his hands. He is seeing with his eyes closed, conjuring up the past.

WRITING POSSIBILITIES

1. Perhaps it's time to go after that one memory you have always wanted to commit to the page. Maybe it changed your life for the good or bad. Maybe it's a small special memory you have always carried inside your head and don't quite know why. Write down this memory in loose phrases and words. Be as precise as you can about what you remember, but don't worry about making good sentences.

2. Use the words Baldwin used to translate that memory onto the page. Begin:

The way I always see (person, place, event) is the way (he/she/it) used to be. . . . I always see (him/her/it) . . . (He'd/She'd/It'd) be . . .

Maybe somebody's . . . Maybe there's . . .

3. With the exception of the word *silence*, this memory is all visual. In a few paragraphs, describe a memory in terms of another sense: hearing, smell, taste, touch.

FACT TO FICTION

READING

. . . It is known that Muhammad composed the Koran after attacks of epilepsy. Black Elk experienced fits before his grand "buffalo" vision. Joan of Arc is thought to have been a left-temporal-lobe epileptic. Each of these in a terrible flash of brain lightning was able to pierce the murky veil of illusion which is spread over all things. Just so did the scales fall from my eyes. It is called the "sacred disease."

But what a price. I rarely leave the house anymore. To avoid falling injuries, I always wear my old boxer's headgear, and I always carry my mouthpiece.

FROM THE STORY "THE PUGILIST AT REST," BY THOM JONES

LESSON

One of the reasons we read is to learn. We are drawn to small bits of knowledge, and we trust writers who speak with authority. Jones begins this passage by citing the lore of epilepsy. Notice how each example is focused on a different aspect. The writer then sums up by saying what is common about them: *Each of these. . . .* Then the narrator explains why he is telling us this, because he, too, is subject to seizures. Then he backs away for a moment, letting this information sink in, strikes a new paragraph and begins his own story.

WRITING POSSIBILITIES

1. Think of a condition that afflicts us, such as epilepsy. Find out its claim to fame, its subtlety, its nuance. Come up with a page full of these facts.

2. Describe in a paragraph how a character might live with one of your afflictions. Your lore doesn't have to be encyclopedic. Make it up, if you like. For example: It was known that my Uncle Phil often went to the mailbox in his sleep. Aunt Rose would rise up from her naps and walk about the house in broad daylight. My grandfather is said to have gone to the barn and milked cows in his sleep. Just so do I wander my own house, walking in my sleep.

3. Now follow exercise two with a new paragraph that moves away from the lore of your character's affliction to the personal experiences of it, the day-to-day life. For example:

. . . Just so do I wander my own house, walking in my sleep.

But it's okay. Before I go to bed, I lock the doors and windows, hide the keys. I padlock the cellar door and, for some reason I don't know, I wrap the knives in towels.

PERCEIVING

READING

"I have a headache," Jane says.

Milly nods. Her expression seems to indicate how unimportant she finds this, as if Jane had told her she'd already got over a cold or something. "They're in the garage now," she says.

"Who?"

"Teddy, Wally, Martin. Martin conquered the world."

FROM THE STORY "THE FIREMAN'S WIFE," BY RICHARD BAUSCH

LESSON

Notice how Bausch depends upon Jane's perception to tell us the nature of Milly's response. Imagine how difficult it would be to give Milly's nod the action required to gain the desired effect. Milly does not act out her feelings. She simply nods and the reading of that nod is placed inside Jane's head.

WRITING POSSIBILITIES

1. Make a list of a dozen simple acts. Some examples: John smiled. Mary shook her head.

2. Now make the next move and let another character interpret one of your simple actions. Depend upon Bausch's words to get started. For example: John smiles. His expression seems to indicate . . .

3. Pick another simple action but have your other character interpret this one negatively. For example: Mary shook her head. But her expression did not seem to indicate she was against the idea. . . .

CONFLICT

READING

. . . I used to imagine it wasn't the 'flu that killed my mother, but a broken heart at the death of her beloved.

But the truth of the matter was he'd moved into a logging shack a year before he'd broke his neck, and only showed up to our house at twilight on Saturday nights to have at my mother, then to attend church the next morning, his black hair slicked back and shiny with pomade.

FROM THE STORY "TWO STORIES," BY BRET LOTT

LESSON

Conflict in this case is not so simple as a disagreement, not so simple as the tug and pull of opposites. Lott writes of the conflicted mind. He calls on the imagining of a broken heart, the fact of 'flu, the truth of abandonment, and the reality of a broken neck—all in four lines. The conflict occurs within a contentious mind, a mind that has to face up to the differences between imagination and truth. Also he explores the way the imagination can still operate in the face of what it knows to be a fact.

WRITING POSSIBILITIES

1. Make two lists, one for phrases similar to *I used to imagine* and a second list for phrases similar to *But the truth of the matter.* Do five phrases for each. For example: I used to think, but to tell you the truth . . .

2. Try several sentences like Lott's first. Use the frame: I used to imagine it wasn't _____ but _____. For example: I used to imagine it wasn't the meanness that broke us up, but the long cold winters in Wyoming.

3. Select one of your first sentences and now make your second move. Use the frame:

I used to imagine it wasn't _____ but _____.

But the truth was _____.

For example:

I used to imagine it wasn't the meanness that broke us up, but the long cold winters in Wyoming.

But the truth was she used to break things and slam doors, and one time she slammed a door on my hand, saying it was an accident.

DECIDING

READING

. . . Then it occurred to him that by taking a dogleg to the southwest he could reach his home by water.

His life was not confining and the delight he took in this observation could not be explained by its suggestion of escape. He seemed to see, with a cartographer's eye, that string of swimming pools, that quasi-subterranean stream that curved across the county. He had made a discovery, a contribution to modern geography; he would name the stream Lucinda after his wife.

FROM THE STORY "THE SWIMMER," BY JOHN CHEEVER

LESSON

Stories are about change. Sometimes what brings about change is outside of us: an act of man or nature. Sometimes what brings about change is inside of us. Sometimes we decide a change is in order. The decision in Cheever's story finds a place in the character's being, specifically his eye. It is something seen. Cheever illustrates the decision making with references to a cartographer, a string, a stream, a discovery, geography. The decision becomes a vision. This all begins when it occurs to the character that between him and home are backyard pools. It's a simple thought he stitches together. The change in paragraphs allows the character to step back with his fresh idea and let it come into his life.

WRITING POSSIBILITIES

1. Let a character make a decision at the outset of your story. Examine the passage above and find Cheever's phrases that describe the process of deciding something. Write a new and different decision of your own character's making for each of the phrases you find. To get you started: It occurred to him that _____. The decision took hold. She could _____. He'd made a discovery. He could _____.

2. Place the decision within the character as Cheever does in the second paragraph, only depend upon another sense. For example: He took in this feeling . . . ; He seemed to hear a clear message. . . .

3. Cheever uses an extended metaphor to illustrate his character's decision. Try making one of these yourself. Start by listing a group of associated words. For example: aviator's eye, elevation, jet stream, wind shear, cloud cover, visibility; weatherman's mind, fronts, systems, precipitation, accumulation, heat wave. Now write your paragraph, but be careful. These can get silly pretty fast.

REVELATION

READING

Monday morning an answer—or at least a possibility—was waiting for him, as though it had actually chosen to enter his mind now, with the buzzing of the alarm clock. He got up quickly and stood in a shaft of sunlight on the floor. Maxine rolled away from the clock and was still asleep.

FROM THE STORY "THE DOCTOR," BY ANDRE DUBUS

LESSON

A revelation is a momentary occurrence, like being awakened or shaken by the shoulders or slapped in the face. Dubus gives his character such a moment coming out of sleep. He pairs opposite actions. The sleep is quiet and calm and dreamy, and the revelation is quick and pulls him to his feet. There is stillness and then sudden motion, much like the way a revelation comes. It's as if the answer were waiting for him to uncover it. The buzzing of the alarm clock is almost synonymous with the thought in his head—jarring and loud and clear as the shaft of sunlight he stands in. A revelation, too, is a personal thing. The character's wife is still asleep. She rolls away from the clock, does not participate.

WRITING POSSIBILITIES

1. Make a list of ten times when your mind is not paying attention to itself. For example: staring into space, driving on a long highway, petting a dog.

2. Write a paragraph in which you give one of these activities to a character. Now bring her out of her quiet with an opposite action accompanied by the idea she's been waiting for. For example: I was driving through the desert when I slammed on the brakes. I knew what to do . . . ; He was stroking the cat in his lap when the possibility came over him and he got to his feet. . . .

3. Now create a new paragraph in which you give your character an unaffected companion. For example: He was stroking the cat in his lap when the possibility came over him and he got to his feet. Lydia heard him slam the front door on his way out.

INTENTION

READING

. . . He was ready to hang up when she answered.

"Hello?" she said.

He couldn't move. The voice went through him like ice. He could feel it even after she stopped speaking.

"Hello?" she said again.

He heard noise in the background, the TV going, and a man saying, "Who is it?" over the sound of the TV.

"Who is this?" she said.

He hung up the phone gently.

He sat there for a long time, dazed, not feeling a thing.

FROM THE STORY "LIVING THROUGH THE WINTER," BY MARY BUSH

LESSON

Often we set out to do things with the best of intentions, but the outcome is not what we anticipated. Sometimes our intentions are not clear; nevertheless we are moved to act. It is the same way with our characters. A young boy makes a phone call. He intended to talk, but now he can't bring himself to do so. The scene is filled with sound. The voice that goes through him is *like ice*. The TV is going in the background. The image is of sound coming through a TV screen, which reminds us of a voice through ice. Also in the background is a man's voice. The boy's intentions are thwarted. Bush accounts for that moment of defeat by telling us the character is left *dazed* and *not feeling a thing*.

WRITING POSSIBILITIES

1. Instead of a phone call, imagine the intent is to mail a letter, to stop for milk or gas or to see someone. List five things you intended to do in just the last few days.

2. Consider the interior of this quote. Imagine it's not a phone call, but a face-to-face encounter, a dialogue where a question goes unanswered. Try writing one of these. For example:

She couldn't speak. She intended to tell her brother, but the sight of him made her want to hide her face.

"What?" he said again. "What is it?"

She could see how innocent he was, and behind him were his children and his pretty wife.

"What?" he said. "Tell me."

She shook her head and he turned and walked away, his family following behind.

She sat. . . .

3. What about the opposite, an intention realized? Even when we intend to do something and carry it through, things don't always turn out as we anticipated. Sometimes the opposite of what we expect occurs. Perhaps we are still left dazed or defeated or turned away by our own unmet expectation. Write a passage in which a character does precisely what she intends to do.

PREMONITION

READING

He bought the paper and some cigars and drank a Coca-Cola or two before he went in to breakfast with his father. After breakfast—out, out, out to attend to business. The getting out had in itself become the chief business. But he had realized that he could not keep this up much longer, and today he was afraid. He was aware that his routine was about to break up and he sensed that a huge trouble long presaged but till now formless was due. Before evening, he'd know.

Nevertheless he followed his daily course and crossed the lobby.

FROM THE NOVEL *SEIZE THE DAY*, BY SAUL BELLOW

LESSON

Sometimes in life we have the feeling that the future is sneaking up on us. It comes to us exactly as Bellow evokes it. We realize. We become aware. We feel a change in the air. There is little we can do about this. When it comes over us, it is still only a feeling. Call it intuition or premonition. It is that sense we are being followed by what is to come. And like Bellow's character, we go on with our lives, convinced for reasons not yet apparent that change is coming.

WRITING POSSIBILITIES

1. Make a list of synonyms for *realize, aware, presage*. Keep this list handy.

2. Imagine you have a character who senses a change coming. Begin with two small acts. Rewrite Bellow's text, using this frame: He bought ____. After breakfast, ____.

3. In Bellow's third sentence, a fact is established. This becomes the foundation of the premonition. Try sentences like these: The showing up for work had in itself become work. The driving had in itself become a reason not to make the trip.

4. Now, from your list of synonyms, complete the movement into premonition. Fill out your paragraph by completing this frame: He realized ____. He was aware ____, and he sensed ____. Before evening, ____.

5. Now move back to narrative. Bellow starts a new paragraph to make this move. Try the same technique yourself.

ACTION TO INTERIOR

READING

. . . I will not defend myself. I was experiencing a peculiar revenge towards my sister. But I intended this familiarity to stop; I fully intended to control its limits.

Later, when he drove onto the dirt road which led to the graveyard, saying that he had left something, I knew that my revenge had conjoined with his and that we would very soon prove uncontrollably, weakly submissive to our instincts.

He parked behind the white shed, leaving the door of the truck yawning open.

FROM THE STORY "SHED OF GRACE," BY MELISSA PRITCHARD

LESSON

The narrator has reasons in her mind to betray her sister. Her sister's husband has reasons of his own. Their mutual ambitions become one. In the middle paragraph, Pritchard follows action with her character's interior. These thoughts interrupt the action, allowing it to take place without being narrated. This character is able to make these moves for several reasons. The most obvious reason is first person license, the first-person narrator's ability to make quick moves in and out of thoughts because of an intimate relationship with the reader. This character expresses a need to be understood by the reader, a need to explain her actions. She is self-conscious. She is the subject of her thoughts and deeds.

WRITING POSSIBILITIES

1. Make a list of the phrases particular to a character expressing his or her own interior. For example: I was experiencing . . . ; I fully intended . . . ; I was aware . . . ; I knew . . .

2. Create a sentence in which you move from the action of the story to the interior thoughts of a character. For example: Earlier, when she went to town saying she needed groceries, I knew that my distrust of her would only grow with time.

3. In the first two lines of the passage, the character explains herself. Create a small movement where one of your characters does the same thing. For example: I will not lie. I was enjoying what was happening to my town. But I intended to put a stop to it. I fully intended . . .

REALIZATION

READING

I let the lamb go. It just lay there awhile. I had to kick it gently a couple of times before it stood up on its own. It cried to its mother. The old ewe came running, letting it hide under her body. I tipped my hatbrim up and let the wind cool my forehead. I tasted blood on my lips, spitting, already feeling tired. I looked around. There were a lot more undoctored sheep than it seemed. My face and eyes burned from the Sioux's holy sun. I knew at that moment this was not my future—not this farm, this labor, not this whole sphere of human toil. I would do anything I had to do to get away.

FROM THE NOVEL *LEAVING THE LAND*, BY DOUGLAS UNGER

LESSON

Characters are like us in that they come to moments where they see the writing on the wall or, in this case, what's written in the sky, lit by the sun. The narrator catalogues his actions, step by step, and they clear his mind, prepare him for a realization, a decision that will beget decision. Beyond that this will not be his future; he turns on himself and confesses he will do anything he has to do to change his life's course. But before all that, see how the moment is built. The acts are small and can be witnessed. The first imperceptible act is the wind cooling his forehead. Then he tastes, then he feels and then he turns inward, toward the realization.

WRITING POSSIBILITIES

1. Think of a job or task that you know well, such as weeding a garden, paying bills or washing dishes. Write five succinct, precise sentences that lay out the sequence of the procedure. For example: I fill the sink with water. I let the dishes slide to the bottom. I squeeze out more soap and stir the water. It foams and bubbles at my wrist. The phone rings, but I don't dry my hands, don't answer it.

2. Now describe what cannot be seen. Start with one of the senses. For example: The water is too hot for my hands. I feel them redden and swell, but the phone has stopped ringing. I knew then he would not be coming back. . . .

3. Continue, telling what your character would not do. For example: . . . because I would not answer his call, would not say, I forgive you, would not open his letters, would not even remember he'd ever been a part of my life. I would do anything to not ever remember again.

INTO DRAMATIC MOMENT

READING

I saw him many times, caught glimpses of his truck, of him, but only once in thirty years did he look back at me, last summer when Costin's old place caught heat and burned and everybody gathered there. The barn was still burning, but the house had gone. People shone flashlights over the ash pile, but there was nothing left to see but charred wood and one lone teapot on a blackened stove. Across the ashes that had been the house, against the blaze that was the barn, stood Call.

FROM THE STORY "WHAT THE THUNDER SAID," BY JANET PEERY

LESSON

This passage comes toward the end of the story. Peery shoots forward thirty years to this moment, a last contact between characters who were lovers when we last saw them. Phrase by phrase she moves us into this drama of their final meeting, into the feel of events unfolding before our eyes. *Thirty years* becomes *last summer, last summer* becomes *was still burning*. Another way she makes the moment large is simply by widening our view of it. She moves from words like *glimpses* and *flashlights*, to small details like the *charred wood* and *lone teapot,* to *the blaze that was the barn.* The light grows big, and Call becomes as enormous in our eyes as the fire around him.

WRITING POSSIBILITIES

1. Rewrite Peery's first sentence. Go from ten years to last week. For example: I saw her often, caught glimpses of her car, of her, but only once in ten years did she look my way, last week when a wind brought down trees along the highway and everybody came out of their houses.

2. Rewrite this as a reunion. For example: I didn't see her after that, not for six years did our paths cross, until last weekend when the sun was hot and everybody headed for the park.

3. Think about the way we see, the way we focus. Reread Peery's last three sentences. Write three sentences that make the same move. An example: The six-story building was mirrored glass and held the sun. People passed in front of it, and it was hard to see but color or shape, tall man, short woman, boy in a blue T-shirt. Then across the way, against the light of the building, was my father, waiting for me.

OUT OF DRAMATIC MOMENT

READING

We shall come back, no doubt, to walk down the Row and watch young people on the tennis courts by the clump of mimosas and walk down the beach by the bay, where the diving floats lift gently in the sun, and on out to the pine grove, where the needles thick on the ground will deaden the footfall so that we shall move among trees as soundlessly as smoke. But that will be a long time from now, and soon now we shall go out of the house and go into the convulsion of the world, out of history into history and the awful responsibility of Time.

FROM THE NOVEL *ALL THE KING'S MEN,* BY ROBERT PENN WARREN

LESSON

This is the final paragraph of *All the King's Men.* In the first line, the narrator speaks of an eventual return to the places the novel inhabits. However, look at the verbs Penn Warren uses: *walk, watch, lift, will deaden* and *shall move.* These are all very easy, gentle verbs. They give the mood of a stroll, of slipping quietly away, of a fade-out on a movie screen. Even as Penn Warren is speaking of action, he is moving us slowly to rest.

The final sentence begins *But that will be a long time from now.* This also transports the reader away from the drama of the novel. A return is a long way off. The motion of this sentence is similar to the flight of an eagle over some dinner he wants. There is the descent, almost a glide so that you might even think the bird means to land on the water, but then he snatches the fish, his wings beat, and he and the fish take off in another direction. Penn Warren sends his narrator out of the house and into the world. It's as if he were a parent bundling up a child and sending it forth, telling that child to go ahead, but be careful. But of course, Penn Warren is speaking to all of us.

WRITING POSSIBILITIES

1. Let's look at this, not as an ending, but perhaps as a middle, something that might precede a line break. Try to rewrite this passage, saving its essential movement. Your story may not have the space for such large issues as time and history and mankind, but what if a character is moving or has lost a job, or a flood has come through? On such occasions, we may wish to allow for what has been and look toward what will come. List five more of these turning points in life. Begin: I will come back. . . .

2. Penn Warren's first sentence conveys what has been by telling what will be. He does this by making inextricable movement and place: *to walk down the Row and watch young people on the tennis courts by the clump of mimosas. . . .* He does this several times. Try another sentence: Ben thinks he will come back to swim in the creek and watch the trout rise in the deepest holes, and walk. . . .

3. Now turn to what stands in the way, something Penn Warren does in his second sentence. Continue: . . . But that won't be for some time, and now he will get in his car and find the highway, drive west. . . .

PERSONAL EXPERIENCE

READING
One of my favorite examples of bureaucratic understatement has long been the commercial airlines' decision to refer to the horror of motion sickness on their official barf bags as "motion discomfort." "Discomfort" describes the internal upheaval of motion sickness the way that "neck ache" describes hanging. The specific feelings that attend a full-fledged case of motion sickness are probably impossible to describe, but what the hell, let's try.

It begins subtly enough with a flickering sense of ennui.

FROM THE ESSAY "MY LIFE WITH THE HORROR," BY DONALD KATZ

LESSON

It's safe to say that just about anything can make for a good story. If ever you had your doubts, go find this essay by Donald Katz. In the last line of the excerpt included here, the antecedent of the pronoun *It* is—you guessed it—motion sickness. This essay is about all manner of motion sickness. The narrator begins in grand and high-minded style, speaking of *bureaucratic understatement*, going at the English language and its abuse by way of euphemism, something he feels further exacerbates the condition of his own weak stomach. This umbrage, this pique, sets the tone for what is to come. He goes on to make an analogy, *"Discomfort" describes the internal upheaval of motion sickness the way that "neck ache" describes hanging*, the boldness of which heightens the indignity and in turn raises the level of importance of his subject. This accomplished, he settles into narrative with the naturalness of a true storyteller. In the last two sentences of the quote, he uses tried-and-true methods to enter the narrative.

WRITING POSSIBILITIES

In exercises one, two and three you are asked to make lists. Keep them separate and number each entry.

1. The sentence *"Discomfort" describes the internal upheaval of motion sickness the way that "neck ache" describes hanging* heightens the subject and its importance to the storyteller. List five more like this. Use the following frames to get started: "_____" describes the _____ of _____ the way that "_____" describes _____. To say "_____" in describing _____ is about like saying that "_____" describes _____.

2. The phrase *but what the hell, let's try* signifies a marked casualness, perhaps the necessary attitude to assume when one embarks on an odd topic. List five more of these. For example: but who cares, let's give it a shot.

3. The phrase *It begins subtly enough* takes us into narrative, the beginning of a story. List five more of these. For example: It starts out quietly enough . . . ; It commences with barely a flicker.

4. You now have three lists of five each, fifteen beginnings or turns of phrase or openings to a story. Play some games with your lists. Try the following: (a) Pick, for instance, the third entry on each list. With some imagination, can you make them work together? (b) Your lists are created in the order the phrases/sentences appear in the quote. Can you rearrange them and find combinations that work? (c) Find a set of three that seem to click for you. Write them down in the order you want and keep going.

ENDING QUIETLY

READING

So we kept on with it. His fingers rode my fingers as my hand went over the paper. It was like nothing else in my life up to now.

Then he said, "I think that's it. I think you got it," he said. "Take a look. What do you think?"

But I had my eyes closed. I thought I'd keep them that way for a little longer. I thought it was something I ought to do.

"Well," he said. "Are you looking?"

My eyes were still closed. I was in my house. I knew that. But I didn't feel like I was inside anything.

"It's really something," I said.

FROM THE STORY "CATHEDRAL," BY RAYMOND CARVER

LESSON

A story can come to a quiet, peaceful ending in what is learned or changed or accomplished. We can render this change with small, incremental moves. In Carver's ending, the narrator is up late with his wife's houseguest, who happens to be blind. The narrator has his eyes closed, pretending to be blind, and the blind man is guiding his hand in the drawing of a cathedral. The moment is defined in the declaration *It was like nothing in my life up to now.* Purely and simply put, but still extraordinary to this man's life. The narrator keeps his eyes closed even after they are finished with the drawing. He gives us small truths in small sentences as entrances to his mind: *I was in my house. I knew that. "It's really something. . . ."*

Notice, too, the small deceptions involved here. The narrator comments as if he really is looking at the drawing, when in fact his eyes are still closed. These are white lies that recognize the difference between the two men, but also express a desire for some mutual understanding, the common ground of the cathedral.

WRITING POSSIBILITIES

1. Your narration has come to the moment of conclusion. You wish for movement to become poised. Carver does that in the first sentence of this passage. Create five more of these moments. Some examples: So we kept driving. So we continued down the path we were on. So she went on with what she was saying.

2. Choose one of your sentences and complete the paragraph. For example: So we kept driving. His fingers held the steering wheel as my hand rested on his leg. It was like no place else in my life I'd ever been.

3. Try this. In several lines, Carver has the narrator affirm what he has told us: *I thought I'd keep them that way for a little longer. I thought it was something I ought to do. I was in my house. I knew that.* Follow your paragraph in exercise two with three statements your character makes and allow him the three sentences necessary to reaffirm these statements.

ENDING WITH INEVITABILITY

READING

. . . There is every possibility that my baby will be loved and cared for and will grow up to be like any of these people. Another contraction, and I reach out for Oliver's hand but stop in time and stroke it, don't squeeze.

I am really at some out-of-the-way beach house, with a man I am not married to, and people I do not love, in labor.

Sven squeezes a lemon into the pitcher. Smoky drops fall into the soda and wine. I smile, the first to hold out my glass. Pain is relative.

FROM THE STORY "GIRL TALK," BY ANNE BEATTIE

LESSON

Often what you do not write is as important as what you do write. In this story, the reader knows what has begun. The narrator tells of a contraction, creates dramatic distance, and then tells us she is in labor. Consider the sentence where she reveals this: the third sentence. The subject and verb are the first two words: *I am.* She then holds the sentence, raises it, suspends it the way a singer might hold a note, and finally she tells us. Beattie's sentences hold to something that is patternlike. They have a fluid rhythm created by two- and three-word phrases. There are three reference points for the narrator—what she thinks, what she feels, and what she does—and she is their only connection. What is not written? The birth itself. It is not necessary. It will come of its own accord. The reader is left to imagine it.

WRITING POSSIBILITIES

1. Imagine an event like childbirth, an event that is out of our control. Perhaps a fall, perhaps the course of a sudden illness, a car wreck. Name five more of these.

2. Choose one of these events and rewrite Beattie's third line. Use the past tense. For example: I was standing on an icy sidewalk in New

York, with a woman I just met, and friends of hers who were strangers to me and I was falling.

3. The narrator is moving inside of herself and outside and back inside. She is in a place and is narrating the action of that place. All the while, she has something very important on her mind, and she is narrating that also. This is one way of rendering a character's interior. The events inside this woman's body and mind are powerful, and they will not relent. The action inside your character may be less determined, but you can still use these same alternations to make that move. Write a paragraph that mimics this inside story and outside story narration. Alternate your description, sentence by sentence, interior then exterior.

ENDING WITH CONSEQUENCE

READING

. . . He jumped up and ran to his room, to kiss him, to tell him that he loved him, that he would never fail him again.

The light was on in Norton's room but the bed was empty. He turned and dashed up the attic stairs and at the top reeled back like a man on the edge of a pit. The tripod had fallen and the telescope lay on the floor. A few feet over it, the child hung in the jungle of shadows, just below the beam from which he had launched his flight into space.

FROM THE STORY "THE LAME SHALL ENTER FIRST," BY FLANNERY O'CONNOR

LESSON

Sometimes our characters make mistakes. They set in motion events they cannot control. In this passage, Sheppard runs to his son's room to tell him he loves him. He has been neglecting Norton because in his capacity as a counselor he has been paying attention to another boy. The first sentence in the quote comes at the end of a long passage when Sheppard realizes his mistake. He wants to make it up to Norton. But, of course, it's too late. As readers, we knew of the boy's growing distance from his father. Like Sheppard, we were concerned, but not alarmed. We discover the boy just as his father does, and as we think back, we see the chain of events leading to this act.

WRITING POSSIBILITIES

1. Write three sentences like O'Connor's first. Notice how the sentence grows. For example: He jumped down from the truck and ran to the house, to kiss her, to tell her that he loved her, that he would always stay by her side.

2. Move to the second sentence. Notice how O'Connor pauses here, achieves some distance. Select one of your sentences from above and continue with a sentence like O'Connor's second. For example: The light was on in the kitchen, but she wasn't there.

3. Continue. You must decide how this will turn: for the good or the bad? The cliché in writing workshops is that you have to earn such moments. Sometimes clichés are not so far from the truth.

ENDING WITH KNOWLEDGE

READING
And after *that*, it was all over. And I did not want that to happen to me—did not, in fact, think it ever would. I knew what love was about. It was about not giving trouble or inviting it. It was about not leaving a woman for the thought of another one. It was about never being in that place you said you'd never be in. And it was not about being alone. Never that. Never that.

FROM THE STORY "SWEETHEARTS," BY RICHARD FORD

LESSON
Sometimes we would like a character to be so bold as to tell us what he has learned. Think of an actor who comes to the front of the stage and talks to the audience, acknowledges its presence. Ford ends here on the tight urgency of something realized that must be said before such clarity of mind is lost. He repeats the words *and, that, it, was, about, never*. The word *it* takes on several meanings. *It* and *that* refer to the same thing; they are joined in that way in the first sentence. *It* begins three sentences, and *And* begins three sentences. The last two sentences echo Poe's "The Raven."

WRITING POSSIBILITIES
1. Make a declaration. Take Ford's line: *I knew what love was about.* Challenge yourself to be bold about a dozen of life's most important bits of knowledge. Rewrite his line twelve times. Some examples: I knew what hate was about. I knew what happiness was about.

2. Pick one of your dozen declarations and craft the five or six conditions you know about it. Begin as Ford did: It was about . . .

3. Now claim this for your own. Start by switching to the present tense. Ford's passage would read: I now know what love is about. It's about . . .

4. Find a single word to change in your paragraph. For example: I knew the truth about love. The truth is, it . . .

PART II
CHARACTER

CHARACTER BY SOUND AND APPEARANCE IN NONFICTION

READING

... His wife was sitting on a platform under one of the chickees, piecing together another shirt with a sewing machine. She had on a long dress. "My daughters wear shorts and miniskirts, but I don't want people to see my legs," she explained. She wore the traditional twenty or thirty pounds of beads around her neck, threaded on separate strands. She had received these for birthdays and earned them for acts of virtue. Later in her life she would begin to give the strands away one by one until only the first one remained. This she would wear to the grave.

FROM THE BOOK *FLORIDA RAMBLE*, BY ALEX SHOUMATOFF

LESSON

Think of this piece in terms of its composition. Shoumatoff is an artist crafting a life on the page. He describes the woman and uses that occasion to give her a voice. He is a reporter. Is what she said in response to a specific question he asked? Probably. The writer is conveying her to us in appearance and by the sound of her voice. He is finding a way for her to tell us about herself. No doubt the information in the last four lines was also solicited. What he knows and what he tells is based upon what she has told him, not just the quoted words, but in all probability, also the words that follow. This is the creation of narrative to avoid a question-and-answer format. The journalist is creating a piece of prose that tells a true story.

WRITING POSSIBILITIES

1. Consider doing what a journalist does, actually talking to people for purposes of telling their story. No doubt, there is someone whose path you cross on a regular basis whom you might engage in a conversation. What are some possibilities? Make a list of ten. Perhaps: your boss; your tennis instructor; your neighbor, who is a circus clown.

2. After you decide whom to interview, keep in mind the challenge ahead. You must compose the picture, must reveal them in their world. Let's say you've just had dinner with your neighbor, the circus clown. What did he cook? What's his living room like? What does he look like? If you asked him nicely, would he put on his makeup and costume for you? Write an imaginary descriptive paragraph for practice. Begin: His wife was sitting on the couch under a cage full of _____, sewing together ...

3. Returning to the quote, take note of the thread, no pun intended, that runs through the writing. She is sewing. *She had on a long dress.*

She explains clothing. Shoumatoff observes her beads and tells us of their tradition. Now, as you write your profile, look for the thread that runs through your information. This is what both fiction writers and journalists do on the page. Maybe it is something of sound or appearance, a hobby that seems to have found its way into the nooks and crannies of the subject's life.

CREATING A CHARACTER BY ACTIONS

READING
. . . The other girl, Daisy, made an attempt to rise—she leaned slightly forward with a conscientious expression—then she laughed, an absurd, charming little laugh, and I laughed too and came forward into the room.

"I'm p-paralyzed with happiness."

She laughed again, as if she said something very witty, and held my hand for a moment, looking up into my face, promising that there was no one in the world she so much wanted to see. That was a way she had. She hinted in a murmur that the surname of the balancing girl was Baker. (I've heard it said that Daisy's murmur was only to make people lean toward her; an irrelevant criticism that made it no less charming.)

FROM THE NOVEL *THE GREAT GATSBY*, BY F. SCOTT FITZGERALD

LESSON
The first time we meet Daisy in *The Great Gatsby*, we come to know her by what she is doing: she attempts, leans, laughs, speaks, laughs again, hold hands, looks, promises, hints, murmurs. And each of these actions has an effect on the storyteller. He leans and laughs and listens and holds her hand. There are people we meet every day and we know them more for what they do than for who they are. What people do is apparent to the world. There is a kind of mystery to not knowing a character's thoughts or inner feelings. The way we behave is as particular to us as the way we look. Behaviors are like fingerprints; every one is different.

WRITING POSSIBILITIES
1. We all fancy ourselves to be people-watchers, but we are quick to come to a conclusion based on behavior and appearance. We overlook the movement of hands, the way someone walks, the way a woman holds her cigarette, the way a man scratches his head. Make a list of ten more movements a person might make.

2. Ask a friend to button a button or tie a shoe or slice a loaf of bread. Is she left-handed or right-handed? Ask her to do it again and this time do not watch her hands. Watch her face. Are her lips pursed? Eyebrows furrowed? Write a paragraph that conveys the expression on the face of someone performing a task.

3. Actions rarely have beginnings and ends. They flow from one to another and that is how Fitzgerald portrays Daisy, in a series of actions observed by the storyteller, each of which has an effect on the storyteller. A given scene can contain action and response. Some examples: He was crying and I started crying too. John tossed his keys and John Jr. snatched them out of the air. She leaned toward me and I leaned away. When I first saw him he was up to his waist in the stream and I thought how cold that water must be.

Choose one of these, or make up one of your own, and use it as part of a brief scene between two characters.

CREATING A CHARACTER BY ACTIVITY

READING

He started by building a miniature log cabin from notched Popsicle sticks. He varnished it and placed it on the TV set, where it remains. It reminds him of a rustic Nativity scene. Then he tried string art (sailing ships on black velvet), a macramé owl kit, a snap-together B-17 Flying Fortress, and a lamp made out of a model truck, with a light fixture screwed in the top of the cab. At first the kits were diversions, something to kill time, but now he is thinking about building a full-scale log house from a kit.

FROM THE STORY "SHILOH," BY BOBBIE ANN MASON

LESSON

You might find your character in need of activity, something to fill time or the head or hands. Maybe your character is laid up with a cold, a broken leg, or something drastic or consuming in his thoughts. What he chooses to do is a function of the person within. Just like life, our actions define us.

In Mason's passage, the building of the miniature log cabin from Popsicle sticks grows in his mind to thoughts of building a full-scale log house. In between are efforts at string art, macramé, a model airplane and a lamp. He is a person who gradually comes to big ideas. The action progresses as a straight chronology with a summary sentence to close the paragraph. *He started . . . Then he tried . . . At first . . .*

but now. It is told in the present tense, allowing for the simple past tense to tell previous time. Simultaneously, Mason places each move in the character's mind: *It reminds him . . . the kits were diversions . . . now he is thinking.*

WRITING POSSIBILITIES

1. Mason shows how an idea can develop in a character's mind. List five activities, such as building the miniature cabin, that can begin on a small scale and grow to a larger one. A few examples: a windowsill seedling to plans for a Japanese garden; a morning walk to full-blown triathalon training.

2. Select one activity and allow that to shape your character in a paragraph. Use Mason's simple chronology for the actions and remember also to chart the thoughts that accompany them. For example: She started by sinking a zinnia seed in some leftover potting soil and a Styrofoam cup. She set the cup on her kitchen windowsill and watched it become a full flower, quicker than she ever imagined. At first, the seedlings were just something to watch happen, but now she is sketching for a rock garden, complete with Japanese maple and ball juniper, a reflection pond and goldfish.

3. In Mason's passage, simple diversions become large plans. To what other ends can actions reveal our characters? Try reversing Mason's idea so that your character's large plans become simpler. This shift could create a completely different character. Rewrite the example from exercise two. Have her start out with her grand design and reduce it by increments.

CHARACTERS WHO REVEAL THEMSELVES

READING

It is impossible to say how first the idea entered my brain; but once conceived, it haunted me day and night. Object there was none. Passion there was none. I loved the old man. He had never wronged me. He had never given me insult. For his gold I had no desire. I think it was his eye! yes, it was this! He had the eye of a vulture—a pale blue eye, with a film over it. Whenever it fell upon me, my blood ran cold; and so by degrees—very gradually—I made up my mind to take the life of the old man, and thus rid myself of the eye forever.

FROM THE STORY "THE TELL-TALE HEART," BY EDGAR ALLAN POE

LESSON

All characters come to us with the potential of whole lives. Our focus is as wide or slender as we decide. Sometimes our characters have good intentions and mean well, but sometimes we imagine a character who intends to commit a terrible act. That character comes to us as a voice afflicted and bent on telling what he is going to do. Why does one commit a terrible act? Such actions are beyond reason, so rather than logic, we depend upon a voice that sounds reasonable and compelling.

Poe begins with *It is impossible to say how the idea first entered my brain.* This sounds reasonable, but think about it. It is impossible to say how almost any idea enters our brains. And so it begins, the disorienting spin of possible reasons for acting in ways we do not understand until the teller settles on the eye. It becomes a good reason because it is declared to be so. The teller makes up his mind *by degrees*—very gradually. This is the action of a rational, sane person. As readers, we follow him into his afflicted mind and insane acts with a certain sense of belief, of trust.

WRITING POSSIBILITIES

1. Think of a first-person character who has evil intentions. List five such intentions and their targets. Two examples: I want to kill my boss. I want to pour sugar into the gas tank of my ex-girlfriend's car.

2. Begin this character's story with a sentence that brings us into his mind. For example: I got the idea from television. I don't know where the thought came from, but. . . .

3. Follow your first sentence with a few sentences describing a small obsession. For example: I got the idea from television. I watched it day and night, soap operas, talk shows, cartoons, movies made for screen and those made for TV. I never left my sofa.

4. Finish your paragraph by inserting evil and its object and then rebuild a sense of sanity. For example: I got the idea from television. I watched it day and night, soap operas, talk shows, cartoons, movies made for screen and those made for TV. I never left my sofa. I came to despise all talk show hosts and so began my campaign of mailing death threats. It must have come from TV. Yes, the television. It is so very violent all the time and those were the people most apparently enjoying it in a manner of speaking.

5. Of course intentions need not always be of evil. Rewrite the quote for an opposite intention. Begin: It's hard to say how I first got the idea; but once it came to me, it *delighted* me day and night. . . . (Continue.)

CHARACTERS WHO ARE CRAZY

READING

The yard boy was a spiritual materialist. He lived in the Now. He was free from the karmic chain. Being enlightened wasn't easy. It was very hard work. It was manual labor actually.

The enlightened being is free. He feels the sorrows and sadness of those around him but does not necessarily feel his own. The yard boy felt that he had been enlightened for about two months, at the most.

FROM THE STORY "THE YARD BOY," BY JOY WILLIAMS

LESSON

In this passage, Williams begins to take the yard boy down the road to madness. This isn't easy to do. Too often, such characters are rendered as cartoons or stereotypes—the crazy aunt, the daffy neighbor, the demon child. As true writers, we can't turn away from the mysterious interiors of the afflicted.

Williams tells this story in the third person and the past tense. She does move to the present tense to define the yard boy's beliefs, to declare his feelings, and then moves back to the past tense to pick up the story again. This is a good strategy because we can't always ask characters to show themselves through their actions. This way she is not asking the yard boy to perform. By telling his story this way, she enriches and makes significant his condition. The verbs Williams chooses function for the most part as simple equal signs. There is no action. She is defining the yard boy, breaking the cliché of show, don't tell. Williams has sympathetic fun with the yard boy's ideas of himself. She uses phrases at the ends of some sentences like punch lines: *actually, at the most.* The yard boy becomes caught up in the fanciness of ideas, eventually falling in love with a plant.

WRITING POSSIBILITIES

1. Create five characters using a title instead of a proper name, the way Williams does with the *yard boy*. For example: deliveryman, butcher, auto mechanic.

2. Now pick one character and use the verb *was* to define him in one sentence as simply as possible. Let that definition be quirky, something that might give rise to conflict within the character. Two examples: The auto mechanic was a Buddhist monk. The English professor was a closet pyromaniac.

3. Now add five aspects, one sentence for each, to explain this character's understanding of self. Go back to the passage and see how

Williams does it. For example: (1) The English professor was a closet pyromaniac. (2) He lived for fire. (3) Burning things freed him from all his cares. (4) But being a firebug had its downside. (5) (Continue.)

4. By the conclusion of exercise three, you've written a paragraph. Continue with a three-sentence paragraph like Williams', moving into the interior of your character. (a) Make a general statement, some way to see the world, present tense. (b) Make a second statement describing an emotion the character has or an idea he thinks about, present tense. (c) Start this last sentence with your character, what he or she felt or thought, past tense.

CHARACTERS IN A CROWD

READING

Back in the dining alcove, the Barley twins were talking with Michael. They had flipped up their clip-on shades which stuck out above their glasses like the perky antennas of some sharp-faced, cute little creatures from outer space, and they were nodding earnestly, in unison. Jo Ann and Sugar were discussing mixed marriages—the consuming interest of Jo Ann's life for years before her wedding to Nat and evidently afterward as well. "But tell me the truth," Sugar was saying. "Doesn't it sometimes seem to you like *every* marriage is mixed?" And Serena's two little grandsons were surreptitiously bombarding each other with bits of cake. It looked good: angel food. Maggie thought about trying a slice but then she remembered her diet. She had a virtuous, empty feeling in the center of her rib cage. She traveled around the table surveying what was offered, resisting even the bowl of Fritos. "The dump salad is mine," Serena's neighbor said at her elbow.

"Dump salad?"

FROM THE NOVEL *BREATHING LESSONS*, BY ANNE TYLER

LESSON

Gatherings of people can be difficult to manage, but you may want to write a scene in which people have come together for a party or celebration or, as in this case, a funeral. In this excerpt, think of dialogue not so much as dialogue, but as another form of action taking place in the swim of the scene. There are eleven characters referenced in these few lines: the Barley twins, Michael, Jo Ann, Sugar, Nat, Serena's two grandsons, Maggie and Serena's neighbor.

The action is written as being simultaneous: *were talking, were discussing, were bombarding.* At the end of the paragraph, Tyler moves to Maggie's thoughts. Think of the dialogue in earlier lines as Tyler using spoken words to make characters, the same way the Barley twins are signified by their clip-ons flipped up. Characters are made memorable as much for what they say as for what they do or how they appear. Furthermore, this scene depends upon Maggie to guide us through. What we come to know and experience is what she knows and experiences.

WRITING POSSIBILITIES

1. List five occasions for which people come together. For each, create a cast of characters, one of whom will be like Maggie, a guide. Once you have finished, decide on one occasion to keep through the following sequence of exercises.

2. Tyler follows a pattern in which she first introduces the characters by name, three of them, and then distinguishes them by action and appearance. Begin like this for your own occasion.

3. Tyler introduces Jo Ann and Sugar by name, interest and dialogue. Use these lines to model your next ones.

4. Continue until you have accounted for all those present, concluding with the interior of your main character. Maybe he has a dialogue with another character or simply wanders away from the crowd.

CHARACTERS WHO PART

READING

After he left, her mood always varied; sometimes she was lightheaded, other times more somber, even teary. Every year she swam. Last summer there'd been a host of Medusa jellyfish sending off green light. The year before she'd stroked straight out, so far that when she turned, the shore looked like a mirage. Once she tried to stand on a sandbank. Barnacles, like white teeth, cut the fleshy part of her foot and blood dribbled into the sand.

FROM THE NOVEL *UP THROUGH THE WATER*, BY DARCY STEINKE

LESSON

The construct of time seems even and regulated, but time itself is strange and vague. Time expands and collapses and we are left to mark it as we will. So, too, do our characters experience time. As we mark time with actions specific and memorable, our characters do likewise. The parting in this passage is anticipated. He comes to the island for a visit in the summer and then must return home while she stays behind. Time is designated in sweeps: *sometimes, every year, last summer, the year before, once*. These phrases are then followed by very precise and specific actions. The small significant actions in these grand sweeps of time become sad and poignant. The character is made small and even more alone for all the poignancy and precision.

WRITING POSSIBILITIES

1. Think of a regular and anticipated parting—such as leaving for work—that might occur between two characters. For example: Christmas time; off to school. Then rewrite Steinke's first sentence using one of these situations. For example: Each time she left, he felt different; sometimes calm and patient and other times like the apartment was coming unhinged from the earth.

2. Now mark the previous times when the same parting has taken place, following each with a significant action. For example: Last time she left, he went through his closets and took almost half of his clothes to the Salvation Army.

3. Use these same constructs to evoke an anticipated arrival. Now the character is preparing for the event.

CHARACTERS WHO MEET

READING

"I would surely appreciate it if you'd call off them dogs," says Frank, as if those puppies weren't wagging their tails and jumping up to be patted.

He can see I am shivering and soaked. And I am mad. If I had a gun, I might shoot him.

"You ought to be ashamed . . . a man like you."

"Frank Bowman," he says, grinning and holding out his large thick hand. "From Bowman Corners." Bowman Corners is just down the road.

"What happened to you?" he grins. "Take a shower in your boots?"

How can you stay mad at that man?

FROM THE STORY "IT'S COME TO THIS," BY ANNICK SMITH

LESSON

We take for granted something so simple as two people meeting. It seems like such a commonplace event, but think again. When was the last time you came to know a stranger without being introduced by someone else? It is rare for strangers to meet, yet such an encounter may be needed in your story. In this passage, the meeting is told in first person, present tense. Notice how we learn the man's name before he introduces himself. Both characters are brought here for reasons other than to meet. They have reason to meet, yes, but it is not for the sake of each other. This event is told to us as something remembered. Its natural awkwardness is not recounted. In telling us how they met, Smith has winnowed it down to its finest details.

WRITING POSSIBILITIES

1. Remember three special meetings from your past, times when people came into your life unexpectedly and a friendship ensued. For each, write down names, place, season and time of day.

2. There was an occasion for these meetings. Maybe someone came onto your property or entered your place of work. Write down the conditions of each special meeting.

3. So far, we have some words doodled on the page. Now we need some spirit. The character Frank comes into her life with a style all his own. Write your own spirited beginning. For example: "Now I was wondering if you were the kind of person who might like some help or not," Dorie says to me, as if I didn't have my necktie fed into the fax machine about up to my chin.

4. Now combine the real elements from above, make up two names, and write a passage of your own modeled after the quote where two characters are brought together.

A CHARACTER'S FIRST WORDS

READING

. . . My father and I used to enjoy big cars, with tops that came down. We were both tall and we wanted what he called "stretch room." My father had been dead for fourteen years, but I resented my mother's buying a car in which he would not have fitted.

"Now what's wrong? Are you coming?" my mother said.

"Nothing's wrong except that my shoes are opening around the soles," I said. "I just paid a lot of money for them."

FROM THE STORY "PRETTY ICE," BY MARY ROBISON

LESSON

Be aware of when and how a character first speaks. The storyteller in this passage is waiting for her mother to pick her up and so, too, the reader is anticipating her arrival. We wait and wait and when we finally meet her, we hear her say: *Now what's wrong? Are you coming?* We make conclusions about this woman, especially since her daughter has been telling of her own resentment. The mother appears to be a mind reader, because the narrator does not mention the resentment—and don't miss the word *now*, the sense that something being wrong is common. We wonder if the mother is always suspicious, or if she has learned that when it comes to her daughter, there is usually a problem. Then we hear the storyteller speak. Are her first words true?

WRITING POSSIBILITIES

1. Create a set of three characters. Robison gives us a daughter, mother and father. Make up five sets. Like the father in the passage, maybe one in each set is dead.

2. Create a situation in which one set comes together. Robison has the daughter's memory evoke the father's presence. Instead of a car ride, perhaps the situation is a meal, or cleaning out the attic. List five more possibilities.

3. List five versions of the mother's question. Some examples: Now what are you looking at? Now what's on your mind?

4. Pick one from each of your lists and combine them for a movement. It may go like this:

My brother and I used to enjoy _____. We were both _____ and we wanted what he called _____. My brother had been dead for _____ and I had resented my sister's _____.

"Now what is it?" my sister said.

CHARACTERS WHO TALK TO THEMSELVES

READING

Bo felt this to be the royal time of his day—these sparse, solitary moments when the rest of the world was either going to bed or not up yet. He was alone, knew the power in singularity, yet was afraid of it. Insecurity crawfished through his blood, leaving him powerless again. Soon he began a conversation to make the light seem closer to the road.

"Coffee, Bo," he said to himself.

"Yeah, and Lucy, toosie," he answered.

FROM THE STORY "FOX HUNTERS," BY BREECE D'J PANCAKE

LESSON

We often talk to ourselves internally, and sometimes, when we are alone, we talk out loud. This is a small natural feature we might give to a character. In this passage, Pancake has Bo on a road in the early morning. He feels the power of the breaking daylight and enjoys his aloneness, and then is overwhelmed by these feelings. He begins a conversation with himself much as someone might whistle past a grave-yard. This is to say, Pancake gives him a reason to talk to himself: the buildup of fear and insecurity. The tension is made fun of but still maintained at the fore of the moment. Then we return to narrative.

WRITING POSSIBILITIES

1. We are most apt to talk to ourselves when we are alone. List five occasions that allow a character to be alone. Name a character for each. For example: It was late in the day, and the office was empty, but Sharon was working overtime.

2. Imbue each of the five occasions you have listed with a feeling of silence, an invitation to talk to oneself. For example: The game was over and the field was empty. It was the absence of noise that made for the most profound silence John could remember.

3. Choose one of your movements and continue, making a turn similar to the one Pancake made: *He was alone, knew the power in singularity, yet was afraid of it*. The feeling could be reversed though, pleasure instead of fear. For example: He was alone, knew how rare such an event was, and was thrilled.

4. Now move into dialogue, but first prepare for it by finishing your narrative with a phrase such as *soon he began a conversation*. For example:

He couldn't help but discuss this with himself.

"Chance to put the old feet up on the desk," he said to himself.

"Yeah. Maybe kick the shoes off," he added.

Now move back into narrative and continue writing. You may have the beginning of a good story.

CHARACTERS BY THEIR OBSESSIONS

READING

Miss Lonelyhearts found himself developing an almost insane sensi-tiveness to order. Everything had to form a pattern: the shoes under the bed, the ties in the holder, the pencils on the table. When he looked out of a window, he composed the skyline by balancing one building against another. If a bird flew across this arrangement, he closed his eyes angrily until it was gone.

FROM THE NOVEL *MISS LONELYHEARTS*, BY NATHANAEL WEST

LESSON

We all have habits, and sometimes they take hold of us in unkind ways. They seem to have lives of their own. Focusing on a habit in a character is like opening a small door on his personality. Miss Lonelyhearts is a man writing a column for the lovelorn. He receives letters and responds in the newspaper. In this passage, Miss Lonelyhearts develops a sensitivity to order, a desire to see the world and keep the world in a special way. This is larger than a habit, but it shows itself in small, habitual ways. Note the lack of the conjunction *and* in the second sentence about patterns. Without the *and*, the list feels partial, as if it will continue.

West gives a certain grace and artfulness to Miss Lonelyhearts' habits. He composes, balances and arranges. West could have provided a psychological label for Miss Lonelyhearts, something from the vocabulary of therapists. But that wouldn't be writing. That would be labeling and analyzing, fixing the character in a place and time where therapy is common practice. As writers, labels make our characters easily explained, instead of complex and interesting.

WRITING POSSIBILITIES

1. What might someone develop a sensitivity to? List ten of these large concerns. Remember, this is the obsession that shows itself in the smaller habits. For example: a heightened sense of smell; a need to number and compute; not wanting to be touched.

2. Select one from your list and try a first sentence. For example: Mr. Jones found himself developing an obsession with sets of numbers.

3. Continue by giving at least five examples of the small ways this large concern affects your character. Leave out the word *and* in your list to give West's feeling of unlimited possible habits. For example: Mr. Jones found himself developing an obsession with sets of numbers. He'd compute the sum of every phone number he came across, add up the prices on a menu, figuring what it would cost him if he ordered everything.

4. West closes his paragraph by naming the emotion that Miss Lonelyhearts' habits inspire with the word *angrily*. Find an emotion that reveals your character's attitude toward himself. For example: Mr. Jones found himself developing an obsession with sets of numbers. He'd compute the sum of every phone number he came across, add up the prices on a menu, figuring what it would cost him if he ordered everything. If he came across a grocery receipt, he gladly covered the printed total and tallied it up himself.

CHARACTERS WITH A PAST

READING

There had been better days: when she was up on the high wire, and her body was a flash of motion as she swung, hanging by her heels, across the top of the tent, the faces below like rows of lightbulbs, her body light as a firefly in her blue body suit. All alone up there, no nets below, with the tight thrill that was the joy bred of danger. The tingle in the blood. God, how she loved it! It was the years that had brought her down to earth. She'd nearly killed herself once in a fall. She'd lost her timing, her body had gotten heavy despite all her efforts. The pull of gravity, the reluctance of the flesh. And all the while Dusty trying to put together his misbegotten scheme.

FROM THE NOVEL *CARNIVAL FOR THE GODS,* BY GLADYS SWAN

LESSON

We may want to write a story with a character telling about an interesting past. We'd want to recount that telling in an artful way. How do we do it? This character is an aerialist past her prime. Her name is Alta; her scheming husband is named Dusty. She is remembering a better time, when her body was capable of extraordinary performance.

This passage comes near the beginning of the novel. It begins with the phrase *there had been better days,* peaks with the sentence *God, how she loved it!* and eases back into the present by recounting the toll the years have taken on her body. The better days are made real through images, through a kind of electricity: *the high wire, the flash, light bulbs, firefly, thrill, tingle.* The second part of the passage markedly lacks this kind of poetry, rather holding within itself loss and heaviness and reluctance. Moving from intense, detailed memories to feelings of loss is one way of showing your character's past.

WRITING POSSIBILITIES

1. Let's stay close to this model. Imagine a character who performs before an audience. Make a list of five characters who are past their prime and are looking back. For example: a retired jockey; an ex-baseball player who is now a coach.

2. Writer about one of your five characters. Your first sentence will begin: *There had been better days:* Continue this sentence with six images that vividly evoke the character's performing experience. For example: There had been better days: when he was on horseback and his body was weightless and tight . . .

3. Swan writes *The tingle in the blood. God, how she loved it!* Build your next movement to such excitement. First, internalize the feeling

CHARACTER

51

and then give comment. For example: The hair standing on end. How it amazed him!

4. Allow reality to set in. Your character becomes more somber with thought. His memory, having been re-experienced, now feels so distant. Finish your paragraph with a movement that begins: *It was the years that brought. . . .*

5. What other past pursuits might a character want to recount that have nothing to do with performance? Pasts can be something longed for or regretted. Make a list of ten possibilities. Some examples: an E.R. nurse who now works in a clinic; a mountain climber who used to be a computer consultant.

CHARACTERS IN A FIGHT

READING

The referee's call had a high joyous lilt: "Let'm roll!"

The handlers slipped the leashes and the dogs met in the center of the pit. The impact as they came together had the sound of an ax in wood, a deep solid joining. It was impossible to follow what was happening as they rolled in the dirt, but when at last they stopped, Tuffy had been cut along the back and across the top of the skull. But it was Devil who was caught. Tuffy had managed to close on the side of his neck, not far enough under to get the jugular, but it was a mean, wearing hold. He closed his eyes and rode the other dog down. Devil was strong enough to regain his feet at times and lift Tuffy nearly clear of the ground but he couldn't shake him and eventually they were in the dirt again.

FROM THE NOVEL *A FEAST OF SNAKES*, BY HARRY CREWS

LESSON

This fight comes late in the novel, but throughout we are led to anticipate it. Crews does not give us a blow-by-blow account. Rather, he says *it was impossible to follow what was happening.* The violence of the fight is poised; it's action withheld. The verbs go like this: *they came together, they rolled in the dirt, at last they stopped.* The results of the violence are told in the past tense, but not the gore and blood itself. There is distance between the action and the telling. Crews is not showing us, but is telling us what is happening. While the events are to the death, the storyteller does not lose sight of his characters. Notice that what is fast and furious does not consume the two characters the way a cloud of dust might consume a fight in a cartoon.

WRITING POSSIBILITIES

1. Imagine that rare encounter in which two people might come to blows. Who would it be? Brothers? A father and a son? A husband and wife? List five such pairs and write down several reasons why they might be violently inclined toward each other.

2. The challenge in this exercise is to lengthen your sentence. Make it read more slowly than the action it conveys, so as not to lose your characters. For example:

It was impossible to say how it got started or even when it started, but Joe felt himself to be nudged and thought it might even have been a push, so to be safe, he pushed back. Roddy, being the sort of guy he was, couldn't just turn the other cheek, so he wound up, paused a heartbeat or two and whaled Joe a good one right in the stomach.

Note the commas and conjunctions, the qualifying of each and every action to slow the pace. Now pick one of your five combinations from exercise one and write a paragraph.

3. Imagine another kind of encounter marked by physical confrontation: a pitcher and a batter in baseball; two volleyball players. List five more. The writing strategies used in the fight scene can also be used in less violent encounters such as these.

CHARACTERS IN A RELATIONSHIP

READING

He rearranged his body in the lawn chair and blinked, trying to look alert. He was a graying man of fifty-three, handsome in a ruddy, solid, ex-athlete's way, with strikingly pale blue eyes. He owned a chain of hardware stores. A safe man, Ilse thought each evening when he returned from work. And decent, competent, sexy: mornings, watching him dress—the ritual bending, reaching, zipping, and buttoning—she felt a reflexive pleasure, compounded with satisfaction, like the interest on capital, at how durable this pleasure had proved. If that was love, then she loved him well enough.

FROM THE STORY "KILLING THE BEES," BY LYNNE SHARON SCHWARTZ

LESSON

Ilse's husband is first evoked by his movements as he rearranges, blinks, tries. He comes into focus as if through a camera lens. Then Schwartz uses more opinioned description, which is placed in Ilse's head with the phrase *a safe man, Ilse thought,* and there it remains for the rest of this passage. What Schwartz tells us and what Ilse thinks are both rendered like sketches, almost complete. This development of character happens like a mind at work, delivering what comes quickest and surest and first. Schwartz creates the feeling they are creatures of habit; the words *safe, ritual, reflexive, durable* reveal a love that lives at the front of the mind. Ilse loves him *well enough.* Relationships are complicated in life and should be so on the page. How do you get two people in love, and is that love always giddy, always true? Think about the love Schwartz describes. Couldn't two people dislike each other for the same reasons? Maybe you have characters like that in mind.

WRITING POSSIBILITIES

1. Name ten places where one character might observe a significant other. For example: an unmade bed, an overstuffed chair, a red picnic table.

2. Select a place and sketch the character being observed as follows: first sentence, position and gestures; second sentence, physical description; third sentence, occupation.

3. Follow the sentences in exercise two with a sentence that moves into a second character's mind. For example: A good enough friend, as far as friends go, Abe decided.

4. Continue the paragraph. Give more attributes. Speed up the sentence the way Schwartz does by beginning with *And,* and list features of your character.

5. Now think of the relationship you've given to these characters, based on how they live in the character's mind. Describe this love, or lack of love, in a precise sentence, the way Schwartz does. Begin with the words: *If that was love.*

MOVING INTO DIALOGUE

READING
. . . Her voice was sandstone harsh.
   "Casey just might be tired of you." . . .
   Beth yanked his shirt.
   "Beth," he said.

FROM THE STORY "AUNT GRANNY LITH," BY CHRIS OFFUTT

LESSON
Sometimes we are vexed by the simplest of transitions. One such small and necessary transition is moving from narrative into dialogue. In doing so, we move from one voice to another. We move from the voice

of the narrator to the voice of another character. Is it simply a matter of stopping narrative because it's time for dialogue? Sometimes it appears to be that simple. In both examples above, Offutt makes a bridge to carry us into dialogue. In the first example, the voice is described by the narrator as a feature of the character, and then she speaks. In the second example, the narrator tells us that Beth yanked his shirt, and it's as if she were calling forth his words.

WRITING POSSIBILITIES

1. List five sentences that could describe a voice speaking and follow each with a line of dialogue. Two examples:

Her words were rocket-fast.

"Okay, okay, I get the picture already."

And:

His voice was something like the sound honey would make if it did such a thing.

"You can leave out the door, or you can leave out the window. Don't matter, you're gonna leave one way or another."

2. List five actions that call on a character to speak and follow each with a line of dialogue. Two examples:

Rosie took him by the shoulders and shook him.

"Rosie," he said. "I'll never do it again."

And:

He cupped his little boy's face in his hand and looked into the child's eyes.

"Daddy, it really was a snake, I swear."

MOVING OUT OF DIALOGUE

READING

"We'll see if you like the winters, too. You've never seen any snow, have you?"

"No, but I hear it's cold and white."

"That about sums it up. You've been doing some research, I see."

I don't remember when we started this kind of conversation, but we've had a lot of them. The general theme is that I'm barely able to keep from drooling on my collar, and require full-time professional help so I won't injure myself through stupidity. Dad blames it all on his family, who he claims have set records for Scandinavian incompetence since the days of Leif Ericson.

FROM THE NOVEL *RED SKY AT MORNING*, BY RICHARD BRADFORD

LESSON

The ambition when moving from dialogue into narrative is, as with all moves, to make it smooth and seamless. This passage is written in the first person, the narrator being a participant in the conversation. The last speaker brings the dialogue to closure by actually saying *That about sums it up*. The storyteller continues into narrative by referencing the conversation, by designating it as an ongoing event. The second sentence of the narrative moves us further from the dialogue by thematicizing it (*The general theme is . . .*), and the third sentence leaves the dialogue even further behind, moving into the father's attitudes. Still, words like *blames* and *claims* describe speech acts, so dialogue is not so much left behind as it is eased away from.

WRITING POSSIBILITIES

1. List five sets of characters, relatives or friends who might have a conversation similar to the one Bradford has written. As you make your list, include for each a reason and an issue for the conversation. For example: mother/daughter—moving to another town—daughter doesn't want to go; brothers—on the building of a barn—finances.

2. Pick one from your list of five and begin in dialogue. For example:

"You'll like it there. I promise. There's a lot of parks, nature. That kind of stuff."

"Mother, I don't care all that much for nature."

"Well that about does it. You don't care for nature."

3. Continue. Move into narrative the way Bradford does, gradually. Start with: We've been having these conversations pretty regular now. . . .

UNQUOTED DIALOGUE

READING

Why not, boys. Mrs. Hegel-Shtein smiled and invited them. Look it in the face: old age! Here it comes, ready or not. The boys looked, then moved close together, their elbows touching.

Faith tried to turn back to the children, but her father held her hand hard. Faithy, pay no attention. Let Mama take care. She'll make it a joke. She has presents for them. Come! We'll find a nice tree next to a bench. One thing this place got is trees and benches. Also, every bench is not just a bench—it's a dedicated bench. It has a name.

FROM THE STORY "DREAMER IN A DEAD LANGUAGE," BY GRACE PALEY

LESSON

Dialogue need not always be quoted and paragraphed. Paley uses combinations of spoken words and narrative, and the effect is that all her characters are conversing with each other. Whatever the reason, at no time should the writer risk confusion. Paley relies upon the way narrative and dialogue each have a distinct sound, making clear the difference between what is spoken and what is told. In narrative, she begins each sentence with a subject: *Mrs. Hegel-Shtein smiled and invited them. The boys looked, then moved close together, their elbows touching. Faith tried to turn back to the children, but her father held her hand hard.* There is a simple pattern here, easily recognized: mention of characters followed by what they are doing. The lines the characters speak in this passage are designated in several ways. Faith becomes Faithy. Contractions are used. Exclamation marks are used. One-word sentences are employed as commands and directives. Remember, the writer has an obligation to create structures the reader can depend upon.

WRITING POSSIBILITIES

1. Alternate between what is spoken and what is narrated. Try five of these yourself. Begin by completing this paragraph: What's the matter, girls. Mrs. Liebman grinned and held out her hand. Take it. It's so delicious! . . . Follow this with a sentence of narrative and then move back to words said aloud.

2. A second way of using unquoted dialogue is to paragraph your dialogue as usual and simply leave out the quotation marks. At some point it will be safe to no longer indicate who is speaking. The stream of conversation, the distinct quality of each voice, and the narrative that precedes unquoted dialogue between two people establish who the speakers are. Continue the following:

Mrs. Liebman grinned and held out her hand. She opened it slowly and offered up to the girl what she held.

What's the matter, girl, she said. Take it! It's so delicious.

I don't care for raisins, the girl said.

Why not?

3. Imagine that Betty is waiting for Jake and alongside her is Christine, their companion. Then let each character speak four times. Begin with: I wish you'd get a move on, Betty yelled from the high rocks.

4. As you complete each of these exercises, ask someone to read them to see if they are clear. Remember, readers have come to depend on quotation marks to separate dialogue and narrative. If you take license here, you must be vigilant not to confuse.

INDIRECT DIALOGUE

READING

. . . Stick said he wasn't going if they had to pick up anything. Rainy said no, there wasn't any product in the deal; all they had to do was drop a bag. Stick said, "And the guy's giving you five grand?"

"It makes him feel important," Rainy said, "it's how it's done. Listen, this's the big time, man, I'm taking you uptown."

Rainy told Stick he didn't even have to say a word unless the guy Chucky asked him something. Which he probably would, Chucky liked to talk. He was a you-all, he talked real nice and easy, real slooow, slower than you, Rainy said. Stick said he could hardly wait to meet the guy, thinking: Rainy and Chucky . . . like they were hanging around the playground.

FROM THE NOVEL *STICK*, BY ELMORE LEONARD

LESSON

Elmore Leonard is a writer of tough, hard-boiled novels. It's a safe bet that some of these people are up to no good. Safe to assume that your life could depend upon saying the right words and withholding the wrong words. In this passage, Leonard has made decisions about what is said, what is told, and what is asked. What is said is in dialogue. What is asked and told is in narrative. He has made decisions about what to quote and what not to quote. These decisions are important to writers. Talking and how to talk are important in creating characters. Leonard uses the mannerisms of a speaking voice to distinguish between characters. It is how they know each other and how we come to know them. Some words Leonard wants spoken and others he wants heard. Some words are more important for the information and are told rather than quoted to get out the information in the quickest and most efficient way possible.

WRITING POSSIBILITIES

1. Use unquoted dialogue as if it were narrative as Leonard does in his first paragraph. Conclude your paragraph with something said aloud. For example: Woody said there was no way he was going to stick his neck into that noose. Raylene said no, there wasn't any need to; everything had pretty much blown over. Woody said, "And they're still living together?"

2. Continue with what you've started, or feel free to continue the example above. The next move is to answer Woody's question. Now you have begun a narrative and a conversation at the same time. Keep writing.

3. Permeating Leonard's quote is the feeling that talk is artistry to these characters. Write about four characters who are signified by their manner of speaking. Two examples: (a) Marvin loved to gab. He was a run-off-at-the-mouth kind of guy, he talked from morning 'til night, probably talked in his sleep, Rudy said. (b) Elliot was creepy silent. You'd ask him a question and wait all day for an answer, a breath, a creaking in his jaw, nothing, Dickie said.

CHARACTERS WHO IMAGINE

READING
But I began to imagine bank shots with my car. I began to figure out at exactly what angle I would have to hit a telephone pole in order to bank the car across the street and into the pole on the other side. Then I began to do it with buildings—double banks into doorways, caroms off two fireplugs and into a brick wall, a massé around a parked car and into the plate glass of the corner drugstore. By the time I parked at my apartment, the knuckles of my hands were pale on the wheel.

FROM THE STORY "MASSÉ," BY LEIGH ALLISON WILSON

LESSON
Characters have interiors. Like everybody else, they have tastes, imaginations. A natural way inside a character is to reveal his or her imaginings. In this passage, the order of this character's life is beginning to unravel. She likes to shoot pool, and so for this activity to possess her while she is driving is terribly disconcerting. It begins in a simple way, one thought leading to another and building in intensity, until finally it seems to have taken over her mind. By the last sentence of the passage she has become a threat to her own safety. Wilson follows this passage with a line break, as if to further punctuate the condition of her character. When the story resumes, the moment has passed.

WRITING POSSIBILITIES
1. Wilson's character is imagining bank shots with her car. List ten consuming pastimes, such as shooting pool, that could stimulate imagination. For example: fly-fishing; bowling.

2. Wilson's character is driving. List ten places or activities that could free a character's mind to imagine. For example: dozing in the shade; jogging.

3. Now look at your two lists. Find a connection that interests you. Maybe it's thinking about basketball while doing laundry. Pick one

pairing and write a paragraph in which you open up your character's imagination. Use the first person for simplicity. Refer to the quote for cues as you need them. Begin this way: I imagined shooting baskets while I was doing laundry. I began to _____. Then I began to _____.

4. Allow your character's imaginings to build to a crescendo and then allow your character to find a way to stop what she is doing. Use the following frame to finish the small dramatic movement you have begun: By the time I _____ at my _____, the (hair on my head?) was _____ . . .

CHARACTERS WHO EXAGGERATE

READING

Ever since I could pronounce the word *Mycostatin*, I've wanted to be a philandering pharmaceutical sales rep tooling around the countryside in a 280Z in search of medical-arts buildings and uninhibited reception-ists. The idea of pulling physicians out of critical procedures or poignant consultations ("Yes, Mr. Haber, I'd try to do the Oaxaca ballooning trip within the next two months if I were you") in order to hawk product, the idea of making commodities out of anticoagulants, was just the most romantic and exciting thing in the world to me.

FROM THE ESSAY "TAKE MY THIRD COUSIN, PLEASE," BY MARK LEYNER

LESSON

This essay opens with the writer putting forth his exaggerated imagina-tion for all to see. He makes fun of his own desires in preparation for something even more outrageous. This is the writer-as-character. He has an idea he wants to pass on to us, a thought that is pretty strange, but to prepare us for it, he softens us up with humor. The ideas now arrive in a context, in the words of someone prone to performance, prone to posing on the page. The ideas are not his own; he is merely someone capable of harboring extraordinary thinking. The paragraph leads us into the world where he learns from an older salesman what he is about to tell us. Just for your information, it has more to do with philandering than with pharmaceuticals.

WRITING POSSIBILITIES

1. *A philandering pharmaceutical sales rep.* That's funny. Can you come up with five more? Choose jobs you have had in the past. For example: a crafty cockeyed computer programmer; a licentious librarian.

2. Imagine such a character in fiction. Imagine the quote is the opening to a story or novel. Begin again and this time make up the information you need. For example: Ever since I could say *cordon bleu*, I've wanted to be a dramatic and dangerous cruise-ship chef tooling through the dining room in search of heavy eaters and non-eaters, those who pick and those who gorge themselves, those with taste and those with no taste at all. The idea of . . . (Continue.)

3. The quote is two sentences. Let's gain even more distance from it than in the previous exercise. Let's pare it down to its most basic parts. Write on any subject, first or third person, fiction or non-fiction. Begin: Ever since I _____, I've wanted to be _____. The idea of _____, the idea of _____ . . .

CHARACTERS WHO ARE DESPERATE

READING

The sight of the dog put a wild idea into his head. He remembered the tale of the man, caught in a blizzard, who killed a steer and crawled inside the carcass, and so was saved. He would kill the dog and bury his hands in the warm body until the numbness went out of them. Then he could build another fire. He spoke to the dog, calling it to him; but in his voice was a strange note of fear that frightened the animal, who had never known the man to speak in such way before. . . .

A certain fear of death, dull and oppressive, came to him. This fear quickly became poignant as he realized that it was no longer a mere matter of freezing his fingers and toes, or of losing his hands and feet, but that it was a matter of life and death with the chances against him.

FROM THE STORY "TO BUILD A FIRE," BY JACK LONDON

LESSON

Sometimes a story dictates that we take our characters to their limits. To do this successfully, we must know those limits. Know the capacity of our character's mind and spirit. This passage shows us a way to access a character's core. Here is someone who is alone in a desperate situation. Follow the workings of the character's mind: He sees the dog and it gives him an idea. The idea leads to a memory. The memory informs him. The information returns his attention to the dog. He makes a decision based on that process. He acts and he fails. The second part of the quote shows that his wits will not be enough to save him. There is no easy way to see your only choice when it is a desperate one.

WRITING POSSIBILITIES

1. List five situations in which, if you do not act, you will die. Designate a character other than yourself for each one. For example: a fisherman whose boat capsizes; a logger who cuts his leg.

2. Select one from your list. Give your character an idea the way London does, but have him survive. For example: The sight of the steel-bladed ax next to the fire made it clear what he must do. He remembered his father telling him of one time being injured in the woods and searing the wound with a red-hot knife. After tightening the tourniquet on his leg, he crawled to the edge of the fire ring and eased the ax into the coals. . . .

3. Select another situation from your list. This time the fates will not be so kind to your character. Begin as you did in exercise two, but in this story the attempt is futile. Look to the London quote for a way to do this. For example: A fear that he would not make it, would not survive the cold water began to descend on him. . . . This fear became overwhelming. . . .

CHARACTERS WHO ARE MYSTERIOUS

READING

. . . Within a tin bowl beside her are soft cotton balls soaking up peroxide. She gets one and squeezes it and roughly abrades the dried blood from Mariette's palm until she's sure she's seen the healing of weeks in just one day. She tries to read Mariette's face, and then she says, "I'll have to see your foot."

"Which?"

The infirmarian looks for a trick and tries, "Your left."

Mariette unties the dressings and Sister Aimée kneels to find the healing there, too. She pauses and asks, "What are you up to?"

"Up to?"

Sister Aimée's sleepless eyelids open and shut like dull scissors. "You were supposed to stay put but you sneaked out this morning. Why?"

"Simply for Mass and Holy Communion."

Sister Aimée stares at her with honest interest and then she stands. "You truly amaze me."

"I have work to do," Mariette says.

She tries to smile at the postulant as she asks, "Then why are you still here?"

FROM THE NOVEL *MARIETTE IN ECSTASY*, BY RON HANSEN

LESSON

Are Mariette's wounds self-inflicted or are they visited upon her by God? That is the question that drives the entire novel. Mariette is an elusive character. She is the one to be figured out, and Sister Aimée has been charged with this responsibility. Yet Hansen does not make this easy in the least because, by all appearances, Mariette seems the more forthright of the two. Notice how Sister Aimée's dialogue is preceded by interior, by intention, by action, while Mariette's dialogue stands alone. Consider something as simple as the line *Sister Aimée stares at her with honest interest and then she stands.* It's as if the act of standing cancels out the honest interest. It's often said that dialogue isn't what we say to each other, it's what we do to each other. Dialogue is a feature of character. The actions that surround our words are as likely to betray them as support them. By using gestures to contradict what a character says, you can make your dialogue richer, more interesting and complex.

WRITING POSSIBILITIES

Rather than work toward recreating a dialogue as complex and embedded in context as this one, try beginning with one small move that Hansen makes. Consider the following:

Sister Aimée stares at her with honest interest and then she stands.
"You truly amaze me."

"I have work to do," Mariette says.

1. These characters are not responding to each other. Try three of these simple exchanges yourself. For example:

"I don't get you," he said.

"It's time for me to go," she told him.

2. Remember, what characters say is a function of who they are. In the example above, which character is being elusive, he or she? Decide this for your own exchanges. Now work backward and give your more straightforward character some intention, some action, like Hansen does for Sister Aimée. For example:

He smiled at her with true affection. "I don't get you," he said.

"It's time for me to go," she told him.

3. With this small dialogue, characters in a relationship have been established. Now you have something to explain them. Continue your scene with a paragraph of narrative. For example:

He smiled at her with true affection. "I don't get you," he said.

"It's time for me to go," she told him.

He tried to keep smiling at her because he truly did not understand her, but wanted to. . . . (Continue.)

CHARACTER

63

CHARACTERS WHO DREAM

READING

Danner sinks deep, completely, finally, into a dream she will know all her life; the loneliness of her mother's voice, *Oh, it's hot*, rises in the dream like vapor. In the cloudy air, winged animals struggle and stand up; they are limbed and long-necked, their flanks and backs powerful; their equine eyes are lucent and their hooves cut the air, slicing the mist to pieces. The horses are dark like blood and gleam with a black sheen; the animals swim hard in the air to get higher and Danner aches to stay with them. She touches herself because that is where the pain is; she holds on, rigid, not breathing, and in the dream it is the horse pressed against her, the rhythmic pumping of the forelegs as the animal climbs, the lather and the smell; the smell that comes in waves and pounds inside her like a pulse.

FROM THE NOVEL *MACHINE DREAMS*, BY JAYNE ANNE PHILLIPS

LESSON

Think about the last time you recounted one of your dreams to someone else, how hard it was to get the facts straight, make sense to someone who didn't experience it. Think, too, about the many dream interpretation books and how dry they can be. In this passage, Phillips depends on the familiarity of the horse dream, something many young girls experience, but she doesn't stop there. She makes this dream enter her character's body: *Danner aches . . . she touches herself . . . she holds on. . . .* But as powerful as this dream is to Danner, it's still a dream. As you think about your characters and their dream worlds, keep in mind that writing a dream requires the same level of attention and intention as any other element. Think of a dream as a story out of sleep. It is only as important as you make it.

WRITING POSSIBILITIES

1. What are some of your most familiar dreams? Okay, now that you've remembered the one where you are in a public place without your clothes, think of five more, good and bad, and describe each dream in a single sentence.

2. Which of these five dreams are yours alone, and which do you think you share with other people? Take one of these more universal dreams and give it to a character. Write one paragraph in which you enter this dream as Phillips does, with the sound of a voice. This gives the dream a solid base.

3. Now, following Phillips, move into the fractured language we use to tell about our dreams. Notice how, in her first descriptive sentence,

Phillips doesn't mention horses, but *animals*, as if these were completely new creatures to Danner's mind. Familiar things often become unfamiliar in dreams. In her next sentence, she calls them horses, for clarity, but the mood has been set. Write five phrases that sketch in your dream images. Note here that the words *fractured* and *sketch* do not mean incomplete or vague. Phillips is precise in her image making.

4. Danner's dream carries out of sleep and affects her body. List five ways dreams can take hold of us. For example: tossing, turning, mumbling, talking.

CHILDREN

READING

Juniper breathes a cloud across her window and writes "ADAM." Jade, after glancing over her shoulder, fogs her window and writes "ADAM LOVES JADE." Juniper makes tongue prints; Jade draws a dozen deft Xs, for kisses. Caught between them, awed by the twins' cold second-grade glamour, Fanny feels herself whittled down to a ragged scarecrow—a scarecrow with a note, weighing like lead in her pocket, that her kindergarten teacher asked her to take home.

FROM THE STORY "BLACK HOLES," BY ELIZABETH TALLENT

LESSON

Using children as characters is one of the easiest things to do poorly. An eight-year-old, for example, is trying on language and idea, almost dressing up in it. One minute he acts like a five-year-old and the next he seems closer to eleven. They can be tough subjects. We must be careful not to patronize or condescend, not to make them too cute, or too pitiful, or too much the smart aleck. They have personalities as apparent and as secret as any adult. Juniper and Jade are doing what children do, and we are told so in a precise way. They are breathing on cold windows and writing words. Fanny is caught between them. She is carrying a note from her teacher. For a child, this is the equivalent of being fired from work. The writer comes as near to Fanny's interior as she can without presuming to move inside her. It is safe to say that Fanny feels less than herself and safe to assume she is very aware of the note she carries.

WRITING POSSIBILITIES

1. Choose a small, contained, precise action that children do to entertain themselves, such as clouding up a window. Then write a sentence in which a child character performs the action, and follow this sentence

with one in which a second child character imitates the first. For example: Eartha twirls on the lawn until she falls down dizzy. Beauty, after watching from a distance, begins to spin herself, her arms outstretched, until she falls down dizzy too.

2. Think of something that weighs on a child like a note from a teacher. List five things. For example: being picked last; the prospect of spinach for supper.

3. Turn one of these concerns into a sentence. For example: Inside, Thor feels his stomach rolling like a coaster at the prospect of spinach for supper again.

REAL-LIFE CHARACTERS

READING
For a toddler, the nanny followed a printed menu of activities that Sera had prescribed to stimulate visual, motor, and auditory progress: finger painting, crayoning, stencils, Colorforms, Legos, Bristle Blocks, puzzles, tools, Mr. Potato Head, alphabet tapes, farm toys that made animal sounds. Television was out of the question. ("TV is just like sex. The more you have it, the more you want it. And you don't need it. There are better things to do.")

FROM THE ARTICLE "MOM OVERBOARD!" BY MARK SINGER

LESSON
Our writing of successful nonfiction is so very dependent upon having a good true story to tell. At first we tend to think in terms of the big story, the fascinating person, the exotic place, but here we have a story about a rather everyday concern, one so common we could easily overlook it. The issue is child care. Simple enough, but the writer has come across an interesting story that has the capacity to renew the reader's interest, to make the issue as powerful as it deserves to be. Sera is a mother and an architect. She has children, and wanting to be as significant as possible in their upbringing, she mapped out on spreadsheets highly detailed instructions for the nanny. There are three characters in the passage—the nanny, the mother, the toddler. We feel they are players in a highly organized pageant, which of course they are. Sera's comments come in parentheses, as if to reinforce the fact of her job removing her from the activities she is prescribing. The important point is that a good story can be taking place right under your nose.

WRITING POSSIBILITIES

1. At the heart of "Mom Overboard!" is the story of a family living in the modern world. Think of some other situations where families have to adjust to being apart. List five. Two examples: father or mother in the military; child in boarding school.

2. Let's focus on how the writer brings Sera to the stage. It's really quite simple and can be used in fiction as well as nonfiction. Try five movements similar to the last five sentences of the quote. Two examples: Sweets were out of the question. ("Candy is a drug. Once you get a taste for it, there's no stopping. It's better to have never even tasted it.") Hard work was the one thing my father loved. ("If a man works hard in this life . . .") Finish this and then try your own.

3. The passage includes a mother, a toddler and a nanny. What are other combinations of three? Always keep in mind that fiction writing can rise from nonfiction. List five more combinations where people share a strong connection. For example: father/son/nanny; architect/builder/owner.

4. *For a toddler, the nanny followed a printed menu of activities. . . .* What other documents or means of communication can exist between people? List ten. A few examples: letters, blueprints.

5. Let's try a rewrite of the paragraph. Begin: For the north garden, the landscaper followed a plan that _____ had drawn up calling for _____. _____ was out of the question. ("_____.") (Continue with this example and then do one of your own.)

OLD PEOPLE

READING

"Put cotton in your ears and pebbles in your shoes," says a gerontologist, a member of that new profession dedicated to alleviating all maladies of old people except the passage of years. "Pull on rubber gloves. Smear Vaseline over your glasses, and there you have it: instant aging." Not quite. His formula omits the messages from the social world, which are louder, in most cases, than those from within. We start by growing old in other people's eyes, then slowly we come to share their judgment.

FROM THE ESSAY "THE VIEW FROM 80," BY MALCOLM COWLEY

LESSON

Did you ever think of actually turning yourself into one of your characters as a way of understanding their intricacies? The ambition of Cowley's essay is to convey as fully as possible what it is like to be eighty years old. As a writer, he depends upon every means possible to render all aspects of being an octogenarian. He uses statistics. He ranges from the first to third person. He remembers his own life and provides anecdote. This passage is preceded by a list of occasions upon which one receives the message he is old.

Cowley's essay is a good example of how a writer places inside our imaginations the experiences of another. It gives us a glimpse into what it's like to be old, it teaches us something about our own characters who might be old, and it shows how a writer might employ the words of another in illustrating his intentions.

WRITING POSSIBILITIES

1. Think about a piece of fiction. You have an old woman who wants to tell her son what it's like to be old. Rewrite the quote. For example: "Put your fingers in your ears and Grapenuts in your stockings," she said, really getting all cranked up. "Pull on mittens, lose your glasses and go try to pick up a dime. You want to know how I am? That's how I am."

2. Think about a piece of nonfiction, a travel piece. Often we enter environments with the intention of writing about them or their inhabitants—the jungle or the factory, the desert or a gymnasium at championship time. Use the methods of Cowley's quote as a way to convey place. For example: We entered the abattoir with hard hats and glasses and ear protection. But still, put yourself ankle-deep in fluid like honey, look down and see it's blood. Put cotton in your ears and still imagine the sound to be deafening. (Continue.)

CHARACTERS IN THE NEWS

READING

. . . the stories that show folk tell about themselves have the shorthand sense of being scenes from a screenplay, with dialogue, set decoration, and camera movements. In such circumstances, truth is an acceptable casualty, the narrative all.

In the biographical narrative Simpson provided, he was the son of stern Baptist parents, and characterized his churchgoing Alaska childhood as "a more sedate form of the wacko from Waco." The stories about him were legion, and were rarely denied; he carried a flight bag holding a split of champagne, a stash of cocaine, and a loaded handgun.

FROM THE ARTICLE "BULLY BOY," BY JOHN GREGORY DUNNE

LESSON

There is some truth to the theory that we all get fifteen minutes of fame in our lifetimes. Some of us get a lot more, and these people become revered or even legendary. Often we know details of these famous people's lives because of that time they spend in the spotlight, but almost everyone holds in their pasts a brush with renown. Maybe your great-aunt went to Hollywood in the thirties to become a starlet. She may have come straight back home in two weeks' time, but the story she would tell has the makings of a legend. So clearly, the first step in an article like Dunne's is finding a person to write about.

The subject of a profile does not have to be someone still alive. Those who have recently passed away might be all the more newsworthy. Maybe you never met the subject of your profile. Maybe you knew the person, but not intimately. In any case, you are obliged to piece a person's life together by what he or she has left behind. People sometimes leave behind their own version of their story. They also leave behind others who know them, and those people have their own details to add. In the passage above, Dunne gives a sentence to the story movie producer Don Simpson told about himself, but he follows this by telling one of the stories told about Simpson.

WRITING POSSIBILITIES

1. The writer informs us that *the stories that show folk tell about themselves have the shorthand sense of being scenes from a screenplay.* Let's imagine several other occupations for which the same might be true, even if it may not always be the case. Write five of these. Two examples: The stories that soldiers tell about themselves have the shorthand sense of being scenes from a war. The stories that baseball players tell about themselves have the shorthand sense of being highlights from a ball game.

2. Select one of your examples and follow it with a prepositional phrase such as *with dialogue, set decoration and camera movements.* For example: The stories that baseball players tell about themselves have the shorthand sense of being highlights from a ball game, with innings, double plays and athletic prowess.

3. Now settle into your real life or fictional character. Dunne does this with the phrase *In the biographical narrative Simpson provided.* He then goes on to let Simpson tell his own version of the story. Complete a sentence like this for your own character.

4. Continue with exercise three, filling in the real or made-up data for this life. Use the following frame: The stories about him were many, and were (rarely, always?) denied; he _____.

PART III
SETTING

SETTING BY WHAT YOU SEE

READING

And the ground never dries. The yard is rich mud with no definition between it and the riverbank. Tiny fish swim in the marks our feet make. The trees are tall and always look wet as though they'd been dipped in grease. Many of them are magnolias and oaks. Pods, nuts and Spanish moss hang in wide festoons. The river is the perfect representation of a southern river, thin and blond, swampy, sloppy and warm. It is in everyone's geography book. I was not shocked at all when I saw it. I was not pleased, although it is quite pretty.

FROM THE NOVEL *STATE OF GRACE*, BY JOY WILLIAMS

LESSON

This setting relies on what can be seen. To create a setting this way, you need to have a sharp storyteller like Williams does, with an eye for her surroundings and a discerning language for her particular vision. It seems as though this woman's world is oozing and shimmering. The movement here suggests a person's gaze crossing a landscape, moving from the ground, to the trees, to the river.

Williams begins each tight descriptive sentence the same way: *The yard is . . . , The trees are . . . , The river is . . .* These are simple verbs. The storyteller relates simply what she sees, what it is. Description like this names and defines. We are told these trees are magnolias and oaks. We are told *pods, nuts and Spanish moss hang in wide festoons.* These names are precise, and the adverbs are superlative: the ground *never* dries, the trees *always* look wet. This storyteller has confidence in how she perceives this land. It will forever have these qualities for her. And notice, too, at the end of the passage, she does not say how she felt, but how she didn't feel: *I was not shocked . . . I was not pleased. . . .*

WRITING POSSIBILITIES

1. Choose a setting that you know well, be it your yard at home, a favorite hiking trail, or a particular stretch of water or highway. Describe this scene piece by piece in a paragraph. Isolate the parts and move in a direction: bottom to top, right to left, inside to outside.

2. Naming something gives authority to your narrative. It is a bold move to say what something is, to say *I know this, and it is this way.* Try such description with ten phrases of your own. For example: The ice is sheer and glassy . . . ; The trees here are short and leafy . . . ; The green is groomed and flawless. . . .

3. Now give your descriptions a push with a metaphor. Developing precise language for your storyteller is vital if we are to trust what she

sees, feels and tells. For example: The ice is sheer and glassy and seems like something unable to hold the weight of the skaters and the fishermen and ice boaters. . . .

This is very different from: The ice is sheer and glassy and seems like something that stretches forever beneath us, the earth frozen clear and to its core. . . .

The ice is given qualities of sheerness and glassiness, but these words also have to do with delicacy and clarity. Try this with your examples from exercise two.

4. Sometimes if you cannot say what something is, it is just as ambitious to say what it is not. It seems like Williams is showing quite a bit. But look at how she uses the words *never*, *not* and *no*. Things are being described for what they aren't. Sometimes we cannot say how a character feels, but we can eliminate other feelings. This is another way of being specific. Try five reversals like this yourself: When I received the news, I was not sad or disappointed . . . ; The river was not a slow river . . . ; The trees were not tall. . . .

SETTING BY WHAT YOU HEAR

READING

It was a child, screaming in nightmare, which awoke me. As I rose from the depths of my sleep, sluggishly, like a diver surfacing from the seabed, the corridors of the hotel echoed with those pealing, terrified cries. They poured over the balcony beyond my room and filled the courtyard beneath; they streamed out into the town which was cooling itself, ankle-deep in sand under a new moon, and they were lost, plaintively, among the low dunes scattered to the south and to the east. I reached consciousness to the dimmer sound of a father's voice gentling the infant terrors away, and the night became stealthy with silence again.

FROM THE BOOK *THE FEARFUL VOID*, BY GEOFFREY MOORHOUSE

LESSON

This is the opening to Moorhouse's book about his travels across the Sahara desert. It's a dramatic beginning. In a sense, he, too, is like the child, waking in darkness. He has come to this place that is strange and exotic, and we are entering the experience with him. He wants us to know who he is and what it is like for him at this moment of embarkation. He is in darkness and nervous about what lies ahead. Notice how the sound of the child can be thought of as being like darkness, or like sand or heat. It *poured, filled, streamed, was cooling, ankle-deep, scattered.* And, too, we associate these with water, not so unlikely given where he is.

A setting can be crafted by sounds, even by those not particular to the place being described. For instance, waking to the sound of barnyard animals when visiting a farm is expected and may not advance the writing as quickly as you would like. It may add texture but not a new level of texture. The child's cry serves more purpose than the simple sound of setting. It carries with it the innocence of the child and the innocence of the narrator to his setting. The sound conveyed in the last few words of the passage is perhaps the most common one of the desert, the *silence again,* but even here, it is turned a degree. The whole phrase is *and the night became stealthy with silence again,* as if to say even the silence has a human attribute, the ability to move like a thief.

WRITING POSSIBILITIES

1. The quote begins a story of highly personal travel. The traveler is as much a subject of his own writing as the desert. The sensibilities of the adventurer are as important as the adventure. How far do you have to go to unmoor yourself? Perhaps you don't have to go the Sahara. Begin a list of where you might go: Another state? Mexico or Canada? How far across such borders?

2. As you wake in an unfamiliar place, what other sounds might there be? Might the sound be delivered by your own sleep, by the sound in a dream? For example: It was a child, screaming in my nightmare, that awoke me. I came to abruptly, as if pulled on a rope. . . . (Continue.)

3. What about using such an opening in your fiction? Perhaps your character has returned to a setting from her youth. For example: It was a car engine, backfiring in the silent deserted street, that awoke me. As I awoke _____, (adverb), (simile), the outside of the motel echoed with those rumbling, gunshot-like sounds. The car backfired again and the sound. . . . (Continue.)

SETTING THE LARGE AND SMALL

READING

One night during my first week in South America some new friends took me to a rocky crest high up on the east side of Quito, the capital of Ecuador. To our east rose the fullest of moons, so frighteningly near and brilliant that we could almost have reached it with a stepladder. Below us glittered the city of 900,000 stretched out over the base of Pichincha, the 15,400 foot mountain that dominates the city from the west. Many miles away the snow-covered peaks along the "Avenue of Volcanoes," as the German naturalist Alexander von Humboldt called it, appeared gin clear. My friends swept their hands along an east-west arc to the north, indicating the approximate path of 0 degrees latitude, the equator. At a slight angle to the equator they pointed out the eastward route followed by sixteenth-century conquistador Francisco de Orellana, who led the first recorded expedition from the Andes down into the Amazon jungle and out to the Atlantic Ocean.

Turning south my hosts showed me where the pipeline carrying oil from the eastern jungle crosses the mountains on its way to the Pacific Coast. . . .

FROM THE BOOK *THE PANAMA HAT TRAIL*, BY TOM MILLER

LESSON

Miller's book is about the making of the Panama hat. As a subject of nonfiction, the travels of a small object can be the thread that brings together lands and cultures and histories. The writer's ambition here is to give us a simultaneous sense of the large and the small, a sense of size, of distance, of the past and present. The Panama hat seems like a small, particular subject, but in Miller's mind it tells a much bigger story. Miller is in a single place, a *rocky crest*. From here, he can see *To our east, Below us, from the west, Many miles away, along an east-west arc to the north, At a slight angle, Turning south*. Each of these directions is a setting from which he can recount history or geography or science. The directions become prompts. They work as a method of organization. The *new friends* are not so much characters as guides to setting. They are his compass.

As you think about writing and your own subject matter, do not allow yourself to be limited by the obvious. A tiny object does not necessarily translate into tiny writing. Its interest is latent, potential. Interest resides within, and when you give full rein to your imagination, you will begin to see what is behind and above and below.

WRITING POSSIBILITIES

1. The writer is on top of a mountain. He subtly organizes the paragraph by using points on the compass. You can do this too, but what other methods of organization can you use? Consider even the most simple as a way to help you through. List ten to start, but make it a list you keep adding to. For example: top to bottom; bottom to top; right to left; left to right; latitude and longitude; degree of angle.

2. Begin another list, one you keep expanding, of subjects like the Panama hat that might make for a fascinating read. For example: what are the stories behind the Louisville Slugger, the Cuban cigar?

3. Where can you go to begin your writing? Perhaps a place like Miller has found to begin his story of the Panama hat? Let's pretend we have found such a place. We are in a place where X comes from. Begin: On my first night in Canada some old friends took me to the top of a church steeple high up above the town of Bear Tail, the only town for miles. To our east was the sliver of a moon, so slender and delicate that we could almost have reached out and tipped it with a finger. Below us was the darkened town of 300 stretching to the banks of the Scalawag River, the 3,000-mile-long stream that winds sinuously through the prairie. . . . (Continue with this passage. Keep in mind that we are only at play, experiencing another writer's work from the inside out. Try one of your own.)

SETTING BY SOUND

READING

The Iban laughed. The river grew louder in the darkness. Something hooted. Something screamed in earnest further off. Something shuffled and snuffled around the discarded rice and fish bits flung in a bush from our plates. A porcupine? A civet? A ground squirrel? A long-tailed giant rat? Why not a Clouded Leopard? Or, the only really dangerous mammal in Borneo, the long-clawed, short-tempered Sun Bear?

I switched off the torch and tried to sleep. But it was no good. The decibel-level was way over the limit allowed in discotheques.

FROM THE BOOK *INTO THE HEART OF BORNEO*, BY REDMOND O'HANLON

LESSON

Sometimes the writer, particularly in nonfiction, must transport his readers to a place they have never been before. The writer must find familiar points of reference to make what he sees and experiences clear to those of us at home. O'Hanlon accomplishes this with sound. This passage describes his first night sleeping in the jungles of southeast Asia, his first experiences with the darkness and heat and insects and strange night noise. He hears his Iban guide and the river, which he can identify, then a series of hoots and screams and snuffles that he can't name. The list of possibilities reveals more about the place he is sleeping than if we'd been told exactly what was making that noise. And how is a ground squirrel different from a gray squirrel? How long-tailed and giant are these rats? O'Hanlon achieves quite a bit of suspense with a simple list of native fauna.

WRITING POSSIBILITIES

1. O'Hanlon creates his jungle through sound. Think about the familiar sounds you hear lying in bed at night. You can tell who is awake in your house and who is asleep, what rooms they inhabit. You can hear the wind outside in the shutters or the clanking of the furnace in the basement. Take your notebook to bed with you and record at least ten of these small noises. Use them in a paragraph where your character is soothed and comforted by what he or she hears.

2. Now use the same noises and imagine you did not know what was making them. How might the creaking in the attic be frightening? The clanking in the basement might seem like doors opening or footsteps on the stairs. As O'Hanlon does, describe your sound with one clear verb (he uses *hooted, screamed, shuffled* and *snuffled*). List your possible sources in the form of questions, and let them grow progressively more ominous.

3. Assume you've never been to the jungles of Borneo. Think about how O'Hanlon's setting makes you feel as you reread it. Do you find yourself reaching for your own backpack and sleeping bag, anxious for a night under the stars? Write a paragraph in which you give these feelings to a character as he reads a passage for himself about the jungle.

SETTING BY WEATHER

READING

The sky had gone black at sunset, and the storm had churned inland from the Gulf and drenched New Iberia and littered East Main with leaves and tree branches from the long canopy of oaks that covered the street from the old brick post office to the drawbridge over Bayou Teche at the edge of town. The air was cool now, laced with light rain, heavy with the fecund smell of wet humus, night blooming jasmine, roses, and new bamboo.

FROM THE NOVEL *IN THE ELECTRIC MIST WITH THE CONFEDERATE DEAD*, JAMES LEE BURKE

LESSON

Any kind of weather can give texture to your story. Thunderstorms, blizzards, hurricanes, extreme heat or cold can strengthen your setting. We live in weather every day. We devote TV and radio time to it, and if there is one concern that has endured throughout human existence, it's probably the weather. Burke's passage evokes the quiet after a storm, the lingering poised silence on the heels of wind-driven rain. Quite simply, by employing the natural touch of the weather, he gives us place and features of place: *the Gulf, New Iberia, East Main, post office, drawbridge, Bayou Teche.* But beware of the "dark and stormy night." Weather and mood can certainly travel together, but try to link them subtly.

WRITING POSSIBILITIES

1. Make a list of thirty words that can describe or evoke weather. Burke's passage gives a good beginning: *churned, drenched, littered, cool, laced, light, heavy, fecund, wet, blooming.* Weather reports on television or radio offer words for the taking.

2. Rewrite Burke's passage for where your characters might live: The sky had gone black at sunset, and the storm had churned _____ and drenched _____ and littered _____ with leaves and tree branches from the long canopy of _____ that covered the street from _____ to the _____ at the edge of town. The air was cool now, laced with light rain, heavy with the _____ smell of wet _____, _____, _____, and new _____.

3. A weather event is a small drama with beginning and end. You decide where to enter it. Rewrite the passage, but this time, have the storm in progress and foretell the calm weather to come. Begin: The sky is black at sunset as the storm churns. . . . The air will soon be cool. . . .

SETTING BY GEOLOGY

READING

The floor of the Salinas Valley, between the ranges and below the foothills, is level because this valley used to be the bottom of a hundred-mile inlet from the sea. The river mouth at Moss Landing was centuries ago the entrance to this long inland water. Once, fifty miles down the valley, my father bored a well. The drill came up first with topsoil and then with gravel and then with white sea sand full of shells and even pieces of whalebone. There were twenty feet of sand and then black earth again, and even a piece of redwood, that imperishable wood that does not rot. Before the inland sea the valley must have been a forest. And those things had happened right under our feet. And it seemed to me sometimes at night that I could feel both the sea and the redwood forest before it.

FROM THE NOVEL *EAST OF EDEN*, BY JOHN STEINBECK

LESSON

Sometimes you must go deeper for your setting than what you can sense around you, or even what you can find on a map—straight through to the formation of the land itself. The history of how a place comes to have its features can bring texture and weight to a story. There is a belief in geological study that you can tell a lot about what is going to happen by knowing what has happened. This translates well into fiction writing. The Salinas Valley of California holds a vital place in Steinbeck's novel. His characters rise and fall by this land, so it is only fitting that, as he reveals the histories of his characters and how they came to be, he also reveals the same about the place they live. Notice the way he presents these details about the forming of the land inside an anecdote, the storyteller and his father digging a well through the strata of soil. The information about what lies beneath the storyteller's feet comes to him in a personal way. He makes his own inferences and deductions about how the valley might have looked years ago, knowing this affects the way he thinks about himself in the world: *And it seemed to me sometimes at night that I could feel both the sea and the redwood forest before it.* There is a language for the earth's details: Steinbeck includes *ranges, foothills, inlet, river mouth, valley, topsoil* and *inland sea.*

WRITING POSSIBILITIES

1. To write about the geology of a place, you need to know it. Go to the library and find a topographical map of your home state. These maps give a lot of information. You can, for example, see where the mountains are. This tells you where a character might go hang-gliding, or run into a bear, or catch a chill in the summertime. Find three more features on your topographical map and write down three story possibilities they suggest.

2. Choose one of the features on your map and find out how it was formed. Now, how to present this information? Reveal the lay of the land with anecdote, the way Steinbeck does. Maybe your character is in the mountains in the summertime and catches a chill. This allows her to tell how long these mountaintops have been chilly, and maybe what they were before they were mountains, such as lava flows or magma or part of the ocean floor. Pick a scenario from your topographical map exercise and bring some geology into your story.

3. Steinbeck uses exact geological terminology and proper names. Use precise words for your setting. Complete this frame as a way to begin: The _____ of the (river, range, lake? A proper name), between the _____ and below the _____, is (level, split, rocky?) because this _____ used to be _____ . . . (Continue.)

SETTING THROUGH CHARACTER

READING

O'Hanlon composes his books in an upstairs study that is even more impossibly cluttered than the rooms below. He takes me there very late in our evening together, clutching a bottle of port in case of emergency. You don't so much walk into O'Hanlon's study as wade in, clearing a path through books, manuscripts, charts, maps, and other assorted detritus. He works with monumental slowness, writing longhand in a neat, almost Victorian script, which he then passes on to a typist.

FROM THE ESSAY "HE IS CRAZY AND HE IS FEARLESS," BY BILL BRYSON

LESSON

Setting is just as important in writing a profile as it is in fiction or travel writing. The worlds we create around ourselves help tell our story. Redmond O'Hanlon is an adventurer who writes of his travels: Borneo, the Amazon, central Africa. The last two sentences in this passage illustrate how the place makes the person, makes the process. Bryson tells how O'Hanlon's study is cluttered, and he follows this observation by saying that O'Hanlon is a slow worker. The clutter of his study seems to fit with his writing habits. It is interesting that Bryson uses the word *composes* instead of *writes,* contributing to the sense that O'Hanlon is constantly on the move. Wading in and clearing a path is what O'Hanlon does when he is off on his exotic travels. This setting and Bryson's delivery of this setting are consistent with the spirit of O'Hanlon himself.

WRITING POSSIBILITIES

1. Become aware of the connection between subject and setting. List ten such connections. For example: an actor and the stage; an artisan and his studio; a surgeon and the operating room.

2. Imagine we have a sculptor who carves ice. Begin: O'Grady creates her sculptures inside a walk-in freezer even more impossibly cold than the winter outside her door. She takes me there very early late in our morning together, clutching a thermos of coffee to ward off the cold. You don't so much walk into O'Grady's studio as you skate in. . . . (Finish this one and try to make up one of your own.)

3. How does Bryson know O'Hanlon *works with monumental slowness*? It isn't likely that he has witnessed O'Hanlon at work. No doubt he asked him about his work habits and chose this moment to recount what he learned from the conversation. He also learned of O'Hanlon *writing longhand in a neat, almost Victorian script, which he then passes on to a typist.* With the example of our ice sculptor, we could

see her at work maybe, but not everyone is open to such possibility. Take, for instance, a thinker, a philosopher. What do they do that we can see? Not a whole lot. How do we get this information? List several questions that might give us access to what we cannot see. For example: (a) Where do you work best? Is there a time of day that is best for you? (b) We're always reading about baseball players having their habits and superstitions. What are some of yours, even ones that are not very important? (c) When you reach for something to record your thoughts, what is it likely to be? Yellow legal pad? Ballpoint pen? (d) As you are working on the block of ice, can you actually picture the sculpture you want to make? (e) How is place important to you, to your work?

MOUNTAINS

READING
On the afternoon of May 15, when the blizzard finally abated, I returned to the southeast face and climbed to the top of the slender ridge that abuts the upper peak like a flying buttress on a Gothic cathedral. I decided to spend the night there, on the narrow crest, sixteen hundred feet below the summit. The evening sky was cold and cloudless. I could see all the way to tidewater and beyond. At dusk I watched, transfixed, as the lights of Petersburg blinked on in the west. The closest thing I'd had to human contact since the airdrop, the distant lights triggered a flood of emotion that caught me off guard. I imagined people watching baseball on television, eating fried chicken in brightly lit kitchens, drinking beer, making love. When I lay down to sleep, I was overcome by a wrenching loneliness. I'd never felt so alone, ever.

FROM THE BOOK *INTO THE WILD*, BY JON KRAKAUER

LESSON
Into the Wild is about Chris McCandless, a young man who goes to Alaska to survive by living off the land and ends up dying there. In trying to make sense of this man whom others thought so impetuous and foolhardy, Krakauer tells us about one of his own adventures. In doing so, he makes this book his own story also. The author, in an attempt to fully reveal his subject, must also reveal himself. As he looks for answers to explain the actions of Chris McCandless, he turns to his own life. This setting becomes more than just a setting. It must carry the importance of the story the writer is trying to tell, the story of being young and bold, of coming up against the hardness of the natural world.

In a sense, the story in this passage is also about McCandless, a way to imagine how he must have felt in his own isolation in a different part of Alaska, one in which he could not survive. Setting is never so simple or antiseptic as the "descriptive paragraphs" we were assigned to write in school. Setting is inextricably wed to story and character. Krakauer's need to tell us of this place, the story of this place, illustrates that intimate union.

WRITING POSSIBILITIES

1. From the passage we learn of mountains, but also we see that our own experience can shed light on the experiences of another. List ten situations in which you inject your own experience into writing about someone else. It can be something as simple as, when writing about a bulldozer operator, describing your attempt to drive a bulldozer. Or it can be as extraordinary as, when writing about a ship gone down, telling of the time you were lost at sea.

2. Select one from your list. Krakauer explains why he's telling us of this setting earlier in the book, so let's accomplish that too. For example: I, too, have been lost at sea. On the evening of August 15, when the storm finally let up, I found myself going down. . . . (Continue with this made-up situation and then try one of your own.)

3. The inner workings of the quote are for the most part simple first-person subject and verbs, and these are dressed with the setting. Maintain Krakauer's order and finish these sentences in a single paragraph for a different setting: I returned to . . . I decided to . . . The evening sky was . . . I could see . . . I watched . . . The closest thing I'd had to . . . I imagined . . . When I lay down to sleep, I was . . . I'd never felt . . .

RIVERS

READING

. . . The moment I felt I was getting a little more distance I ran for a fresh hole to make a fresh start in life.

It was a beautiful stretch of water, either to a fisherman or a photographer, although each would have focused his equipment on a different point. It was a barely submerged waterfall. The reef of rock was about two feet under the water, so the whole river rose into one wave, shook itself into spray, then fell back on itself and turned blue. After it recovered from the shock, it came back to see how it had fallen.

FROM THE STORY "A RIVER RUNS THROUGH IT," BY NORMAN MACLEAN

LESSON

Often you hear setting, description and character development spoken of as if they are independent of each other. But this is never the case. In setting, there is always a human presence—at the very least, the eye of the beholder. In this passage there is the river as the source of life for the narrator, the river as companion. The storyteller places his very hopes for life into this setting. He acknowledges his presence at the river. He acknowledges other possible points of view, fisherman or photographer. And in the last two sentences, he gives to the river a spirit that is not unlike his own. Study the behavior of this water. It *rose, shook, fell, turned, recovered, came back to see, had fallen.* The river is animate, like something that lives and breathes and has a consciousness. This is not mere personification. It is a description full and heartfelt and of the storyteller.

WRITING POSSIBILITIES

1. List five forces in nature that are like a trout stream, that have motion. Imagine a character with a passion for each. Examples might be the surf or the wind and a sailor. Now list five natural features that do not move but can be described as having motion. Examples might be a ski run or a jogging trail.

2. Choose a natural feature from one of your lists and describe it in a paragraph by breaking it down into its elements, its discrete parts. For instance, how might the surf perform? What are the parts of a wave?

3. Maclean's character is a fly-fisherman, a man with untold passion for his avocation. We want to capture this spirit. Rewrite the passage. Begin with a man who, for some reason, on a night is moved to take out the toboggan he bought for his children.

OCEAN

READING

None of them knew the color of the sky. Their eyes glanced level and were fastened upon the waves that swept toward them. These waves were the hue of slate, save for the tops, which were of foaming white, and all the men knew the colors of the sea. The horizon narrowed and widened, and dipped and rose, and at all times its edge was jagged with waves that seemed thrust up in points like rocks.

FROM THE STORY "THE OPEN BOAT," BY STEPHEN CRANE

LESSON

Setting can be the force to be reckoned with, the hard fast thing our characters come up against. In Crane's story, the difficulty of the characters' surroundings tells quite a bit about the situation they are in, the kind of people they are. These men are shipwrecked sailors drifting at sea. The ocean is what they know; it is how they see the world. They do not notice the sky, do not know what it could tell them, but *all the men knew the colors of the sea.* Sometimes a good way to get a firm hold on the place of your story is to narrow the perspective. The focus of Crane's characters is pinpoint specific. Their eyes are *level* and *fastened* on their reference of the horizon. This is a serious way to approach your setting, with a cool measured stare, and fitting for a setting of consequence like Crane's. His description of the sea lies in opposition—the waves are like rocks, the waves are like slate, but they are made of water. This turn of words echoes the severity of the characters' situation. If this were a pleasure cruise, maybe the waves would be soft as cotton.

WRITING POSSIBILITIES

1. Describe a big, broad setting like the ocean, and narrow what your character notices. Your character would need a particular reason for doing this, a vocation that directs his eye, a fear, a love. Crane tells us what his sailors see in the ocean, but you could use a different sense. Write a paragraph with one of your combinations. For example: a woman who can't swim and is in a sailboat, what she feels in the waves beneath her; a fisherman on the shore before sunrise, what he hears out to sea.

2. In Crane's passage, the sailors focus on the empty horizon. What would change in the story if they focus on a sliver of land, or the smoke from the engine of another boat? Take your paragraph from exercise one and change the character's focus on his surroundings. Write a new paragraph in which the woman in the sailboat feels the strength of the sun on her skin and almost forgets she can't swim. Which paragraph has more weight?

3. Remember that in a writer's hands, surroundings are malleable. When you are describing something, use a hard image for something soft or a soft image for something hard. This can give your setting the texture and feel you want. If your character is in danger, even a sparkle off the water can seem glaringly ominous, and if your character is not in danger, then something dangerous could be just a lark. Come up with five descriptions in this kind of opposing style. For example: the table had a milky finish; her hair was ice blue in the dark light.

FOOD

READING

. . . They had lunched, as was their wont, on sugar, starches, oils, and butter-fats. Usually they ate sandwiches of spongy new white bread greased with butter and mayonnaise; they ate thick wedges of cake lying wet beneath ice cream and whipped cream and melted chocolate gritty with nuts. As alternates, they ate patties, sweating beads of inferior oil, containing bits of bland meat bogged in pale, stiffening sauce; they ate pastries, limber under rigid icing, filled with an indeterminate yellow sweet stuff, not still solid, not yet liquid, like salve that has been left in the sun. They chose no other sort of food, nor did they consider it.

FROM THE STORY "THE STANDARD OF LIVING," BY DOROTHY PARKER

LESSON

Sometimes setting is what we set for ourselves. In this case, it's lunch, but of course it could be breakfast or dinner. Food is one of those great things that everyone needs and knows about and responds to. In this passage, Parker writes more about the nature of the foods consumed than the foods themselves. She gives texture to this scene, and it's fatty and greasy and gritty and wet. The passage is in the third person, and it's the coming together over this food in shared delight that also joins these characters. But realize that it's the food itself, the setting made by food, that rises up as almost a third character.

WRITING POSSIBILITIES

1. These characters are eating lunch, and it seems to be something they do together on a regular basis. List ten occasions on which characters might regularly come together over food. Let's get beyond breakfast, lunch and dinner. For example: a coffee break at work; an annual tailgate picnic; Sunday brunch at the country club.

2. Select one occasion from your list and dream up a spread. Write about it based on color. Maybe all the food is one color: Scandinavian meals tend to be all white. Or maybe the food is of boundless variety and you have to go to your thesaurus for the exact shade of the tomatoes, the correct sheen of the pale soufflé. This is a way to talk about food, too, a variation on Parker's texture words. This description relies on appearance, as opposed to feel.

3. Think about how ethnic foods can set a scene. Write a paragraph in which your characters eat Chinese, Italian, Spanish or Indian, or maybe something uncommon like Indonesian or Swedish. You're probably going to have to research this one. Go to your phone book and find a restaurant that specializes in the food you'll be writing about.

Drive by and pick up a menu, or better yet, take a friend out to eat and record what you order, the spices, the smells, the strange items on the menu like fish cheeks or frog legs. The paragraph you create almost gives a flavor to your story.

4. Another way to use food in a story is to cook it. If you don't have much fun in the kitchen, you must know someone who does. Ask him to make a favorite dish, and watch with your pen in hand. For example, there are nearly a dozen steps to making lasagna. What happens first? Which part is the hardest to get right? What's a secret ingredient? Record which pans and pots are used, what gets chopped up, sprinkled in, or beaten with a fork. Shape these details into a paragraph and use it to open a story that takes place in a home or a restaurant, somewhere cooking is a common activity.

WEDDINGS

READING

Truthfully, Cora Mae had not been the bride he expected. The best part was seeing her in that white dress. It had been a hot day and he was sweating something fierce in his CCC dress uniform, but she looked cool as a cucumber when she walked out of that front bedroom and into the living room. The preacher, a fat man with big pink hands, dropped the Bible, and when Leon bent down to pick it up for him, the man touched him on the shoulder and said, Bless you, boy.

FROM THE STORY "THE BRIDE OF HIS LIFE," BY ROBERT LOVE TAYLOR

LESSON

As life's celebrations go, a wedding is usually a big one. But even the most memorable occasion depends on the smallest events that occur within it for a good story. This passage is an example of a wedding as a setting, but this isn't any old wedding. This wedding is remembered from the perspective of the bride's funeral, just a few months later. The reason for remembering the wedding at all might be the fact that she is wearing her wedding dress in her casket.

Often we remember big events for their small, incongruous details, rather than recalling the whole of the pageant. Our minds rarely record life in play-by-play. Notice how Taylor uses the phrase *the best part was*. No matter how auspicious this wedding was, it could still not escape things like heat, sweat, pink hands, a mistake or a clumsy moment, the odd thing said. A good rule of thumb, then, is to think small, even when you are conveying something big to your readers.

WRITING POSSIBILITIES

1. Let's start where Taylor starts, with a confession. The first word of this passage is *truthfully*. Why might this be a good place to start? Perhaps because the storyteller isn't giving us happiness and light, isn't giving us a stereotypical (thus not very real) description of his wedding. Come up with five opening confessions. Two examples: To be honest, Kathy didn't usually go to weddings. Actually, Elliot hated cake and, above all, birthday cakes.

2. Taylor's next sentence begins with *The best part was* and goes on to present a small concise detail about the wedding. This fixes the event in our minds. There was nothing better on that day than Cora Mae in her white dress. You could just as easily talk about the worst part. Follow each of your confessions from exercise one with a best or worst small detail.

3. One of the harder aspects of big events is just that fact—they are big events and there are lots of people present. Taylor has chosen the preacher to deliver the strange, memorable slip-up of this wedding, but it could have been any member of the cast. As an exercise, describe a quirky misstep by five different characters at your wedding that your main character can witness. For example: The maid of honor, who was hardly ever out of jeans and cowboy boots, took a canapé from the buffet table and left two of her brand new fingernails behind.

When you come up with five of these, think about how they fit together. Can you string them one after the other? Or perhaps spread them throughout your story?

EERINESS

READING

They came down the steps into the windowless room, the dim glow of candles illuminating a carefully arranged tableau: Two department-store-mannequin heads, one wearing a blue bandanna, the other a Raiders cap bumped to the right, pointed toy pistols from their disembodied hands. Blue bandannas were hung everywhere, and gang graffiti decorated the bedspread and the headboard. A black leather couch faced the TV and stereo; scattered around were a scale, a blue bong and a glass case holding a pair of pet pythons.

FROM THE ARTICLE "GANG MURDER IN THE HEARTLAND," BY ADAM MILLER

LESSON

This is the bedroom of a seventeen-year-old Wisconsin boy. The writer uses straightforward reportage, taking note of amounts and arrangements as if preparing the report of a crime scene. But consider this sentence: *Two department-store-mannequin heads, one wearing a blue bandanna, the other a Raiders cap bumped to the right, pointed toy pistols from their disembodied hands.* Now it could be imagined that a teenage boy would have a mannequin in his bedroom. But the mannequin isn't really wearing a bandanna in the way that a person would wear one; the mannequins' hands aren't disembodied because mannequins don't actually have bodies, not in a whole and inviolate sense. The mannequin is described as if it were human. Even a simple word like *headboard* begins to take on strange meaning. This is a crafty piece of writing.

Miller holds the detail of the pet pythons until the end of his description, and this, too, has design and intention. Was the cage of pythons actually the last thing the writer noticed, and therefore the last observation recounted, or was the fact withheld for the sake of creating a small drama? Holding such a piece of information until the end of this paragraph gives the reader something to linger over, a mood to take into the rest of the article.

WRITING POSSIBILITIES

1. Let's crawl around inside the passage and list the words that help create eeriness. Start with *windowless room* and *dim glow.*

2. As a way of organizing and emphasizing, the writer uses the color blue three times: *blue bandanna, blue bandannas, blue bong.* The writer implies blue two other times. Can you find these? What about the color black? We have the *black leather couch* and the Raiders cap. The colors in here are black and blue, darkness and pain. Strange how at first it all seems so colorless. What are the colors of the graffiti? Try rewriting the passage for an opposite effect, one where the setting is lighted and vibrant, colorful, not eerie but pleasant.

3. Let's use this nonfiction quote for purposes of fiction. Maybe you've always wanted to try your hand at true crime or hard-boiled detective writing. Let's rewrite the paragraph to create a crime scene. For example: I went down the steps into the windowless, basement room, the flickering of candles illuminating a precisely arranged setting: Two life-size cardboard cutouts, one with a painted red heart and the other with a black smile-face, were hung from the ceiling, dagger in the heart, ice picks in the eyes. . . . (Continue. What's in your glass case? Make sure you save it for last.)

FUNERALS

READING

Under Mr. Pitts' awning Laurel could smell the fieriness of flowers restored to the open air and the rawness of the clay in the opened grave. Their chairs were set on the odorless, pistachio-green of Mr. Pitts' portable grass. It could still respond, everything must respond, to some vibration underfoot: this new part of the cemetery was the very shore of the new interstate highway.

Dr. Bolt assumed position and pronounced the words. Again Laurel failed to hear what came from his lips. She might not even have heard the high school band. Sounds from the highway rolled in upon her with the rise and fall of eternal ocean waves. They were as deafening as grief. Windshields flashed into her eyes like lights through tears. Beside her, then, Fay's black hand slid from her cheek to pat her hair into place—it was over.

FROM THE NOVEL *THE OPTIMIST'S DAUGHTER*, BY EUDORA WELTY

LESSON

Everyone has attended a funeral, so the challenge is in making such a familiar event new again. Since the most emotional events in our lives are often subsumed by the rituals that surround them, the tendency is to recount this ritual at the expense of the writing. Welty doesn't give us what Laurel is experiencing, but she gives us a description of the place where she experiences it—the cemetery on the edge of the interstate.

We come to this funeral through its setting, not through the interior of the character who is experiencing it. She might not have even heard the minister or the band that played. We are not overwhelmed by Laurel's grief but by the presence of the highway. This is because we can't know Laurel's grief, but we can know what it's like to stand on the edge of a highway. Welty suggests Laurel's emotional state in these images: the sounds from the interstate as deafening as grief, the windshields in her eyes like tears. We find ourselves at this most solemn of occasions, and while there seems to be nothing sacred about it, we are nevertheless overpowered by the setting. We experience a feeling like vertigo or too much heat.

WRITING POSSIBILITIES

1. Welty has placed this funeral next to an interstate. What other events could be placed next to an interstate, or train tracks or an airport? Make a list of ten pairings. Begin with a playground beside an interstate, a wedding in an airport chapel, a trout stream beside a factory.

2. Choose one of your pairings and instead of entering that place through the senses of your character, let the place surround your character. Try the following sentences: _____ assumed position and called out to the children. Again _____ failed to hear what came from his lips. She might not even have heard _____ . . .

3. Laurel is in grief, a commonly extraordinary emotion. The world looks different. To that end, Welty mixes sensory images: *Laurel could smell the fieriness of flowers* and *they were as deafening as grief.* Try your hand at five more of these. For example: He could taste the airiness of the small closed cellar and the rawness of _____. They were as silent as love.

4. The final sentence of the passage is gemlike in how it brings to closure the swirl of what has been in and out of Laurel's consciousness. This is a structure you can learn and perhaps use to close out a dramatically intense event. Rewrite the sentence. Two examples: Beside her, then, _____ hand slid from her _____ to pat her _____ —it was over. And: One step down, _____ turned and smiled—it was over.

CITY IN NONFICTION

READING

All cities begin as a point of activity, usually a harbor, and settlement concentrically grows around this point in increasingly wider rings. Manhattan is unique in its shape and circumstances and in its growth, which resembled (to add to an already crowded roster of metaphors) a thermometer. The speed of this growth—its rising temperature—is best conveyed by a well-known fact: when the present City Hall was built, between 1803 and 1812, its front and sides were made of marble, but its rear was thought to be so far north that no one would ever see it, so it was built of much cheaper red sandstone. Needless to say, this back face was already surrounded by buildings before it was finished.

FROM THE BOOK *LOW LIFE: LURES AND SNARES OF OLD NEW YORK*, BY LUC SANTE

LESSON

In but a few hundred years, writers have explored every nook and cranny on the face of the earth. Or so it seems. So why write about something as documented as Manhattan? Because time affords us new ways of seeing what we have been seeing all along. Sante writes about Manhattan because he has the vision of a new eye, insight, to settle on its history. No matter how picked over the settings of the world may seem, a talented writer can always find a new way to talk about them.

The quote begins simply enough with a commonsense statement about the beginnings of cities. The next sentence then moves to one city, Manhattan, and one building, City Hall. This is followed by a sentence about the speed of growth and concludes with a fourth sentence, quick and sharp, that ices the movement.

WRITING POSSIBILITIES

1. Think of this paragraph as a movement, like in music or dance. Try rewriting this paragraph sentence by sentence. Pick another place and begin your paragraph with a general statement about it. This is nonfiction, so you have to begin with an intelligent observation, something you think up yourself that seems smart and worth writing. For example: All roads begin as . . . All universities begin as . . .

2. The next sentence settles us into one university or onto one road, or something better from your list. As your first sentence needed to be smart, this one needs to tell the reader what is special: _____ is unique in its _____ and _____ and in its _____, which resembles . . .

3. To complete a paragraph like Sante's, you need to have a collection of facts at your disposal. But how might you adapt his nonfiction style to fiction? You could create a fictitious town or city and thereby be licensed to completely invent its features and history. Try this for one of your stories, using the starting sentences in exercises one and two for your fictitious place. Keep going.

CROWDS

READING

Here they come, marching into American sunlight. They are grouped in twos, eternal boy-girl, stepping out of the runway beyond the fence in left-center field. The music draws them across the grass, dozens, hundreds, already too many to count. They assemble themselves so tightly, crossing the vast arc of the outfield, that the effect is one of transformation. From a series of linked couples they become one continuous wave, larger all the time, covering the open spaces in navy and white.

Karen's daddy, watching from the grandstand, can't help thinking this is the point. They're one body now, an undifferentiated mass, and this makes him uneasy.

FROM THE NOVEL *MAO II*, BY DON DELILLO

LESSON

This crowd is assembled for a mass marriage, an instance where setting and event become one. The people on the field are observed by the crowd in the stands. It's as if the stadium were an ark and the couples are arriving two by two to fill its hold. The unions are arranged and assigned. The passage begins with the narrator saying *here they come,* as if he were sitting beside us. Building this crowd beyond numbers, transforming it into a singular body and putting it in motion is accomplished by counting up: *twos . . . dozens, hundreds, already too many to count . . . linked couples . . . one continuous wave . . . one body now, an undifferentiated mass . . .* The language is that of size and mass, beginning with the entrance. They enter not the stadium but the American sunlight itself. The effect is hypnotic, their movement something without effort or consciousness. The music is what draws them, much like the children mesmerized by the Pied Piper. Then, as if to echo that feeling of not thinking, strangely enough it is Karen's daddy who *can't help thinking,* a construction of words that makes him sound helpless in his own thinking.

WRITING POSSIBILITIES

1. At first thought, it seems there could be nothing like mass marriages in our world. But not so. We have many occasions to witness the assembling of people, not all so strange and eerie as this. List ten similar events. Start with: a cotillion, a prom, part of a parade.

2. Write a paragraph to open a story with the approach of a crowd. Begin: Here they come, _____ into _____. They are in twos, stepping out of the . . .

3. Now write a second paragraph in which you make the transition into one character. Begin: _____'s daddy, watching from the (bleachers?), can't help thinking . . .

HOUSES

READING

The house was built on the highest part of the narrow tongue of land between the harbor and the open sea. It had lasted through three hurricanes and it was built solid as a ship. It was shaded by tall coconut palms that were bent by the trade wind and on the ocean side you could walk out of the door and down the bluff across the white sand and into the Gulf Stream. The water of the Stream was usually dark blue when you looked out at it when there was no wind. But when you walked out into it there was just the green light of the water over that floury white sand and you could see the shadow of any big fish a long time before he could ever come in close to the beach.

It was a safe and fine place to bathe in the day but it was no place to swim at night. At night the sharks came in close to the beach, hunting in the edge of the Stream and from the upper porch of the house on quiet nights you could hear the splashing of the fish they hunted and if you went down to the beach you could see the phosphorescent wakes they made in the water.

FROM THE NOVEL *ISLAND IN THE STREAM*, BY ERNEST HEMINGWAY

LESSON

The main purpose of a house is to keep us out of the elements, safe and warm and dry. This house is as *solid as a ship*, subject to hurricanes and trade winds, in view of the white sand and the Gulf Stream. It is an ocean house, almost an extension of the land and water it rests on, and most people will tell you it is not such a smart thing to build a house next to the ocean, where it is subject to storms and eroding sand. But look at what a spectacular viewpoint this house provides: From the ocean side you could step out into the Gulf Stream by day, and from the upper porch you could hear the sharks hunting by night. Rarely are we afforded such closeness to our surroundings from a house, and notice Hemingway doesn't dwell on its interior, doesn't give the layout of the bedrooms. He talks about the places in this house that lend themselves to a view on his world. In this way, the setting becomes the place from which to experience other settings.

WRITING POSSIBILITIES

1. What are some not-so-smart places to build a house besides the beach? A mountainside, in a ditch, on top of some old ghosty cemetery land? List ten.

2. What parts of a house connect with the out-of-doors? Windows, porches, balconies, patios. What about sleeping porches or widow's walks? Leaf through a book of house plans or an architectural magazine. List the names for these unusual features.

3. Now begin as Hemingway does, replacing his words and phrases with new ones of equal length. Keep in mind the passage is long for a reason. Hemingway wants to convey the size and sprawl of place being open to larger setting. Begin: The house was built _____. It had lasted through _____ and it was built _____. It was shaded by tall _____ that were bent by the _____ wind and on the _____ side you could walk out of the door and down the _____ across the _____ and into the _____ . . .

SPECIAL PLACES

READING

To those who understand the slightness of an American's traditions, the place of sports in his life, and New York City's need to make do with what it has (the stadium, for instance, is a nearly impossible place to watch football), the Yankee Stadium can be a heart-stopping, an awesomely imposing place, and never more so than on a temperate and brilliant afternoon in late November. The vivid reds and oranges, the plaids and tans, the golds and greens of autumn clothing flicker incessantly across the way where the stadium, rising as sheer as a cliff, is one quivering mass of color out of which there comes continually, like music from a monstrous kaleidoscope, the unending roar of the crowd.

FROM THE FICTIONAL MEMOIR *A FAN'S NOTES*, BY FREDERICK EXLEY

LESSON

A memoir is a narrative composed from personal experience. It depends upon memory, which itself is someplace between the truth and how a writer sees the truth. Setting in a memoir, therefore, is also intensely personal and often emotional. Exley's Yankee Stadium is a prime example. He takes a fall day from somewhere in his memory and evokes a stadium that is *heart-stopping* and *awesomely imposing,* a structure that moves and vibrates and seems to have veins and breath of its own. Such an image is only possible if you understand what Exley understands—that Yankee Stadium is and does something extraordinary in the city of New York. It is *rising* and *quivering* and contains *the unending roar of the crowd.* The colors that Exley lists are colors of the season—red, orange, gold and green—but in his sentence they describe the clothing of the masses in route to see the game. Most of us have seen Yankee Stadium, some of us have even been in that crowd, but it is through Exley's memory that such a crowd is held together.

WRITING POSSIBILITIES

1. List five places where you have gone with a mass of strangers to witness an event. The places need not be so grand as Yankee Stadium, but grand to your experience. For example: the annual hot air balloon race in ＿＿＿; the block party you've attended since you were a kid.

2. Select from your list and begin making an Exley-like setting. For example: To those who understand the parsimony of New Hampshire traditions, the place of Old Home Day in the life, and New Hampshire's need to make do with what it has (the state, for instance, is a nearly impossible place to live), the town common can be a . . .

3. Exley, in his mischievous way, plays with the standard threadbare description of autumn leaves. See how at the last moment he turns them into clothes: *The vivid reds and oranges, the plaids and tans, the golds and greens of autumn clothing flicker incessantly.* . . . Try this with another event and write a sentence of your own that makes this move. For example, imagine it is the Fourth of July at the town square: The bursting flames and sparks, the glittering gold, the strange pure light of children's faces flicker excitedly across the way where the show is just beginning. . . .

PESTILENCE

READING

And now from out the sky gushed down with cruel force a living, pulsating stream, striking the backs of the helpless folk like pebbles thrown by an unseen hand; but that which fell out of the heavens was not pebbles, nor raindrops, nor hail, for then it would have lain inanimate where it fell; this substance had no sooner fallen than it popped up again, crackling, and snapping—rose up and disappeared in the twinkling of an eye; it flared and flittered around them like light gone mad; it chirped and buzzed through the air; it snapped and hopped along the ground; the whole place was a weltering turmoil of raging little demons; if one looked for a moment into the wind, one saw nothing but glittering, lightninglike flashes—flashes that came and went, in the heart of a cloud made up of innumerable dark-brown clicking bodies! All the while the roaring sound continued.

FROM THE NOVEL *GIANTS IN THE EARTH*, BY O.E. RÖLVAAG

LESSON

This style of writing may have enjoyed better days, but anyone can appreciate what is conveyed as the locusts descend and pop to life. Pestilence is a horror of Biblical proportions, and Rölvaag begins the passage with such language. *From out the sky, cruel force, helpless folk, unseen hand, out of the heavens.* Locusts have descended upon the cropland, but Rölvaag doesn't give us a specific name for the plague. Rather he tells us of its activity in a single grand sentence. He tells us the pestilence is not pebbles or raindrops or hail and why it is not and this leads into telling what it is. It is known by what it does. It is a mass of destruction made up of tiny insects. In its separate parts, it is not significant, but as a unit it takes on a whole new capacity. The parts moving together is what is so horrifying.

WRITING POSSIBILITIES

1. Maybe you've endured a pestilence of your own. Name ten possibilities with settings. For example: roaches in a rundown apartment; slugs in the garden.

2. Know your species. Research three forms of pestilence from your list above. Take notes, paying special attention to their habits. Create a catalogue of verbs that tell what the insects do, how they behave, how they perform.

3. Rölvaag's pestilence is noted for its mass and speed. Select a plague from your list that has different characteristics. Maybe your plague seethes or bubbles or creeps. Maybe it is not biblical, not catastrophic, maybe just irritating. Rewrite the passage. Begin: And now from _____ gushed a _____, striking the _____ like _____; this substance had no sooner fallen than it _____ and disappeared in the twinkling of an eye; it _____; if one looked for a moment _____, one saw nothing but _____. All the while the _____ continued.

ROOMS

READING

Matthias's apartment had the same amount of space as my mother's studio, but it was divided into three cramped rooms. Most of his living room was taken up by his piano, which he played for me, his long fingers gliding through Mozart's piano concertos and Schumann's etudes. He collected books of photographs from countries all over the world. In his apartment I saw the fjords of Norway, the great wall of China, the beaches of Bermuda, and the glaciers of the Italian Alps. On his walls he had Japanese charcoal drawings of birds and flowers. He talked about wanting to take a train south through Austria and into Italy, about flying to Japan or Africa.

"I can't imagine staying in Burgdorf forever," he said and ran his hands across the globe he'd set on top of the piano.

FROM THE NOVEL FLOATING IN MY MOTHER'S PALM, BY URSULA HEGI

LESSON

In Hegi's novel, the main character's parents rent rooms in their house to boarders. Matthias has just recently moved in. Hegi tells us his three rooms are cramped and taken up by his piano. But see how she also opens the walls wide: Matthias plays classical piano, collects books of photographs and charcoal drawings, wishes to travel. In just three sentences, Hegi mentions Norway, China, Bermuda, Italy, Japan,

Austria and Africa. She makes these three rooms large enough to contain most corners of the earth. The main character says *in his apartment I saw the fjords of Norway.* Hegi emphasizes her point with Matthias' casual touching of the globe on his piano. The details of this room are so fine and particular—no lists of furniture or wall coverings or colors of draperies. Everything counts in the opening up of this setting.

WRITING POSSIBILITIES

1. Imagine a small setting for a character that also might contain as much evoked space as Hegi's setting. What might these settings be? A carriage house? A basement apartment? A sleeping room? List five more.

2. Matthias' apartment contains music, literature, photography and drawings. What other arts could open up a setting so small? Videos of foreign films? Pottery? Sculpture? Tapestries? List five more.

3. Now select a setting from exercise one and imagine a character in that setting. Name this character and fill up his space with big things of art from your list in exercise two. Find your frame in the Hegi passage. For example: Most of _____'s living room was taken up by her drum set, which she played for me, her fast hands . . .

Or start again with:

He collected books of _____ from all over the world. In his _____ I saw _____, _____, _____, and _____. On his walls he had _____ drawings of _____. He talked about wanting to _____, about _____.

"_____," he said and ran his hands across the cover of the worn atlas on top of the coffee table.

BARS

READING

When I finally caught up with Abraham Trahearne, he was drinking beer with an alcoholic bulldog named Fireball Roberts in a ramshackle joint just outside of Sonoma, California, drinking the heart right out of a fine spring afternoon.

Trahearne had been on this wandering binge for nearly three weeks, and the big man, dressed in rumpled khakis, looked like an old solider after a long campaign, sipping slow beers to wash the taste of death out of his mouth. The dog slumped on the stool beside him like a tired little buddy, only raising his head occasionally for a taste of beer from a dirty ashtray set on the bar.

FROM THE NOVEL *THE LAST GOOD KISS*, BY JAMES CRUMLEY

LESSON

Sometimes our characters find themselves in a bar. The impulse is to describe the bar, but how many beer signs, liquor bottles and Boston ferns can literature sustain? In all likelihood, we have been to your bar. Crumley simply tells us it's a *ramshackle joint*, that there's a stool, a dirty ashtray and a bar outside of Sonoma, California. Enough said. The setting is evoked. The bar is a stage for character and action. No doubt the most wonderful thing about your bar is actually you, and in this setting, the most wonderful aspects are Trahearne and the bulldog, their actions and appearances. The characters and what they do are the significant decor of a bar. The rest can be bought off the shelf. The rest is standard fare in one version or another.

WRITING POSSIBILITIES

1. For the sake of being contrary, can we describe a bar we've never been to? This is to say, renew a bar setting with a few fine details? What would they be? Keep in mind that a single detail can say most everything about your bar. List a dozen such details. Begin with: a gallon jar of pickled eggs; a pair of boxing gloves; leopard skin on the stools.

2. Crumley writes hard-boiled detective novels that have an outsized, gritty feel to them. Rewrite Crumley's first paragraph. You can go for the same tone he evokes or for something less animated: When I finally caught up with _____, he was drinking beer with _____ in a rundown gin-mill just outside of _____, drinking (if you can, try to beat Crumley's phrase, *the heart right out of a fine spring afternoon*).

3. Rewrite the second paragraph, continuing to make a setting that reveals as much of place as it does of character: _____ had been on this _____ for _____, and the big man, dressed in _____, looked like _____. The _____ slumped on the stool beside him like a . . .

DEATH

READING

Even when it started to snow she did not lose her sense of direction. Her feet grew numb, but she did not worry about the distance. The heavy winds couldn't blow her off course. She continued. Even when her heart clenched and her skin turned crackling cold it didn't matter, because the pure and naked part of her went on.

The snow fell deeper that Easter than it had in forty years, but June walked over it like water and came home.

FROM THE NOVEL LOVE MEDICINE, BY LOUISE ERDRICH

LESSON

We all know how brutal severe weather can be. Yet no one knows the increments of drowning or freezing to death or dying of thirst except those who experience it, and they are never left to tell the story. Since we lack any first-hand experience or accounts of such events, this is a challenge and yet an exciting opportunity for the writer. In both regards, grave demands are placed on imagination and artfulness. To be successful, we must be willing and ready to meet these demands.

Erdrich places the elements of her character's fate within each line: snow and numbness and wind establish a cause. She then follows with effect. June does not lose direction, does not worry, does not lose course. June's body experiences this setting and her mind explains it. At the point where June is at her most essential self, pure and naked, Erdrich ends the paragraph. She begins the next paragraph with a larger perspective, giving us a nugget of information that encompasses forty years only to turn that sentence back onto June. Consistent with the sensibility of this movement, June's death becomes a homecoming.

WRITING POSSIBILITIES

1. Think of three types of deaths and the settings they occur in, such as drowning in a river or heat stroke at a Fourth of July picnic or heart failure while shoveling snow on a cold winter day. Research the documented incremental steps that attend such deaths. Stay away from anecdote and narrative. Go to the medical texts that can give you accurate and detailed information about the type of death you've chosen. Learn exactly what happens to the mind and body as best we know. List these steps in an outline.

2. Write a paragraph about a death you researched. Decide how you want your paragraph to sound. It may be artful and accurate like Erdrich's or could take on a more scientific tone. Arrange your sentences as Erdrich does, with the setting as cause and thought as effect: *Her feet grew numb, but she did not worry about the distance* and *Even when her heart clenched and her skin turned crackling cold it didn't matter, because the pure and naked part of her went on.* For example: Her lungs ached, but she did not worry about breathing. Even when his heart tightened and his skin _____ it didn't matter, because _____.

3. Use your paragraph as the opening to a story. As this character is dying, imagine another character waiting for her arrival. Write at least two paragraphs from this second character's point of view, describing the thoughts and actions of waiting. If you want, continue to use Erdrich's cause-and-effect approach. To do so, place your waiting character in an interesting setting.

TRAVEL BY SAILBOAT

READING

. . . Somewhere he had read that waves were always about three fifths the size they appeared.

On deck, the icy rain fell from every direction. Hunched up and partly blinded, he pulled on his canvas gloves and tightened the stay with the hydraulic jack. Then he winched up the halyard, trimmed the mainsheet and cleated it in the cockpit. He wore oilskins over his wool-lined foul-weather gear.

By evening the wind was still increasing. The sea was gathering itself up in towering masses that rolled from the horizon, trailing ghostly wands of foam. The sight of these enormous rollers and their fragile, attendant spindrift hypnotized Browne. He had never been out in such a sea before and never heard such wind. The boat felt as though she were gliding, airborne. The sky overhead was prison gray. He understood that he was about to experience the true dimensions of the situation in which he had placed himself.

FROM THE NOVEL *OUTERBRIDGE REACH*, BY ROBERT STONE

LESSON

To evoke a setting, precise words and exact names can be used. This setting, the sailboat on the ocean, is made real by Stone's vocabulary—the nuts-and-bolts language you would only need to know and use on a sailboat: tightening the stay, winching the halyard, trimming and cleating the mainsheet. The writer knows the language and in turn earns the respect of the reader, who will be willing to suspend disbelief, confident he is reading the words of an authority.

WRITING POSSIBILITIES

1. As Stone does, use a fact from your reading to start you off in a place. Begin: Somewhere (he/she) had read that . . .

And what might it be? Perhaps: Somewhere he read that the troposphere loses one-thirtieth of its density with every nine hundred feet of altitude gained. This begins a story about mountain climbing or hiking. In a small way, it says your character is someone who reads and has a mind for facts. Maybe your character is an anthropologist conducting a field study.

2. Let's consider how Stone wrote the second paragraph. *On deck, . . . Hunched up and partly blinded, . . . Then he . . . He wore . . .* Use these to continue with our mountaineering opening: On the limestone outcrop, the cold rain . . . Hunched up and partly blinded, he pulled on his wool . . . Then he . . . He wore . . .

3. Look at the last few lines. Even experts find themselves in settings unkind to their activity. This is the risk, the test they confront. Do not forget this about your character and his relationship to the setting. The two sentences are not the drama of panic, but the drama of a mind confronting its setting. It is consistent with the impulse that put him in this setting in the first place. Use the following words to do this for your own character and setting: He had never been _____ before and never heard such a _____. The (dangerous aspects of your setting). He understood that _____.

TRAVEL BY FOOT

READING
The boy and his father hiked along a level path into another canyon, this one vast at the mouth and narrowing between high ridges of bare rock. They crossed and recrossed the shepherd's creek, which in this canyon was a tumbling free-stone brook. Following five yards behind his father, watching the cold, unapproachable rage that shaped the line of the man's shoulders, the boy was miserably uneasy because his father had grown so distant and quiet. They climbed over deadfalls blocking the trail, skirted one boulder large as a cabin, and blundered into a garden of nettles. . . .

FROM THE STORY "WALKING OUT," BY DAVID QUAMMEN

LESSON
The boy and his father have gone into the woods to camp and hunt. The boy is young and has been away from his father, living in the city. The writer melds setting and character. The landscape is anonymous and malevolent, much like the father. The boy is unsettled by both. The writer withholds proper nouns, character and place names and the specific names we give to the features of the natural world. He weaves the natural and the human worlds. To have used names would designate arbitrary distinctions. He wants these worlds to blend.

In the third sentence of the passage the landscape turns into the man. If we follow the sentence, we could say the word *rage* does the job. But not necessarily. Rage could be personifying the brook they cross. The sentence is a turning point and we feel it turning, but it isn't until we read *the man's shoulders* that we know where the writer has turned us. The man and boy are together at the comma. The sentence concludes with the reason for the boy's misery and then the writer returns us to the trek.

WRITING POSSIBILITIES

1. What verbs attend the act of hiking? Quammen uses *hiked, crossed, recrossed, climbed, skirted, blundered.* List twenty more: wade, walk, traverse, ascend, and so on.

2. Create a passage similar to Quammen's in which the natural world melts into the human world. Imagine two hikers. Who are they and what is their relationship? If two people are out hiking, it is likely they are more than acquaintances. One is following behind, observing the other. Perhaps your setting is not malevolent. Begin this way: The _____ and _____ hiked. . . . (Now finish with a trail and a meadow and what surrounds it.) They waded and waded again the (stream, creek, brook, deep wet grass?). Following ten yards behind _____ . . . (Here you must turn the sentence.) They climbed over . . . (Go to writing possibility number three.)

3. Notice how Quammen uses the words *mouth* and *bare* in his first sentence, words generally reserved for human beings. Notice in the last sentence that, however remote the setting, the creek is the shepherd's creek, the rock is large as a cabin and the patch of nettles is called a garden of nettles. This is intended. Partly it's the way the boy would think and partly it is Quammen at play with the ideas in his story, which have to do with fathers and sons and home. Complete your paragraph from exercise two. Maybe you have a garden of wildflowers, a blanket of late spring snow or a patchwork vista.

TRAVEL BY TRAIN

READING

Riding down to Port Warwick from Richmond, the train begins to pick up speed on the outskirts of the city, past the tobacco factories with their ever-present haze of acrid, sweetish dust and past the rows of uniformly brown clapboard houses which stretch down the hilly streets for miles, it seems, the hundreds of rooftops all reflecting the pale light of dawn; past the suburban roads still sluggish and sleepy with early morning traffic, and rattling swiftly now over the bridge which separates the last two hills where in the valley below you can see the James River winding beneath its acid-green crust of scum out beside the chemical plants and more rows of clapboard houses and into the woods beyond.

FROM THE NOVEL *LIE DOWN IN DARKNESS,* BY WILLIAM STYRON

LESSON

In America today, a train ride is most often a commute, but there was a time when trains took us east and west, north and south, for holidays and vacation, business and pleasure. The train carried grain and coal, immigrants and soldiers. The train and the train station were standard settings of the big screen. Think of it this way: A train carries us through a setting. It takes us across the land. It is also a setting unto itself. Out the window is the world as seen from the tracks. We sit and look out, maybe wander down to the club car, or more recently a snack bar, all the while approaching our destination, traveling the thin steel tracks through land where only the great tons of the train can travel. Styron's passage is simple enough. There is the weight of the train at ever-increasing speed evoked in the first line, and the rest is the landscape that sweeps past our window. The images come to us rapidly and clearly because we are moving so quickly and because our eye focuses through the window as if it were the lens of a camera.

WRITING POSSIBILITIES

1. The quote is but one sentence. It mirrors the action of the train, moving over the page the same way the train moves over the land. What the sentence says and does are the same. Give it a different reading. Imagine it's a small airplane. Now it reads: Flying low from Richmond to Port Warwick, the plane begins to pick up speed (passing over?) the tobacco factories. . . . Finish this sentence, making the necessary changes as you read. What other words must change? Can we use *sweetish dust*?

2. Re-ordering and unstitching prose is not easy. Styron has written this scene as a departure from Richmond. Rewrite this passage as an arrival in Richmond. You must reverse the trip: Riding to Richmond, the train begins to slow as it . . . (now you must go to the end of the passage for your cues), as it leaves the woods behind, past the rows of clapboard houses. . . . (Now finish this revision.)

3. Let's look at how Styron accomplishes the interior of this single sentence passage: ". . . tobacco factories *with* their ever-present haze of acrid, sweetish dust *and* past the rows of uniformly brown clapboard houses *which* stretch down the hilly streets for miles, *it seems*, the hundreds of rooftops *all* reflecting the pale light of dawn; past the suburban roads *still* sluggish and sleepy *with* early morning traffic, *and* rattling swiftly now over the bridge *which* separates the last two hills *where* in the valley below you can see the James River winding beneath its acid-green crust of scum out beside the chemical plants *and* more rows of clapboard houses *and* into the woods beyond." The words in

italics are simple, but they make this sentence work. They are as important to master as the clever turn of phrase. They are like gristle or cartilage. They are the stuff between joints and bones that smooths the action. Without them, the setting goes flat. Try this yourself. Fit the words of your own train ride between the words in italics.

TRAVEL BY BUS

READING

Jamie sat by the window looking out and smoking a Kool. People still crowded at the bus's door, people she hoped never to meet—struggling with mutilated luggage and paper sacks that might have contained, the way they handled them, the reasons for their every regretted act and the justification for their wounds. A black man in a tweed suit and straw hat held up a sign for his departing relatives: "THE SUN SHALL BE TURNED INTO DARKNESS AND THE MOON INTO BLOOD" (JOEL 2:31). Under the circumstances, Jamie felt close to this stranger.

Around three in the morning Jamie's eyes came open. Headlights on an entrance ramp cut across their flight and swept through the bus, and momentarily in her exhaustion she thought it was the flaming head of a man whipping like a comet through the sleeping darkness of these travellers, hers alone to witness. Suddenly Miranda was awake, jabbering in her ear, excited to be up past bedtime.

FROM THE NOVEL *ANGELS*, BY DENIS JOHNSON

LESSON

A bus ride is not like one on a train or plane, because the course of travel is known to us. The roads are like those we travel every day. On a bus we are not so apt to look out the window at what passes by. Out there is what we see from the windows of an automobile. Consequently, this setting turns us in the direction of ourselves, turns us inward. On this bus, Jamie is leaving a bad past behind her. The writer surrounds her with opportunities to reflect on pain and danger, transgression and consequence.

WRITING POSSIBILITIES

1. When was the last time you rode a bus? Take time to remember. Sitting and remembering is one of the jobs a writer does. Who rides the bus? What is the smell of diesel? Could the smell of diesel be described as sweet? What does the air taste like on a bus?

2. It's time to begin a story. Imagine you have a character like Jamie who is on the run. His name is James. It's okay to not yet know what he is running from, but we know he's on the run and with him is his son, Michael. Begin as Johnson does. Notice the small differences: James sat next to the window looking out and sipping a coffee. (You do the second sentence.) A man in blue jeans and a windbreaker held up a sign for someone on the inside: (use a different quote from the Bible). After what he'd done, James felt (your word would be what?) to the stranger.

3. You shouldn't miss the move Johnson makes between these two paragraphs. Think of all that has taken place that he has chosen not to tell us. The passengers settle in, the bus pulls out. . . . You get the picture. This action would be tedious and attenuated. Besides, on a bus time becomes a different sort of thing. What you don't write is just as important as what you do write. Let's make this move: Sometime around midnight James woke up. (Look at Johnson's next sentence and notice the way it was created. The world delivers up a common enough thing. The writer's imagination latches onto it. Talent kicks in and, bingo, there you have it and the writer hands it over to his character so she might use it to reveal herself to us. Try one yourself. Be relieved to know it isn't easy, and in your third sentence, go ahead and wake up Michael so now we know James has his son with him as he flees his past.)

TRAVEL BY HIGHWAY

READING

Bob drives, and Elaine, seated beside him, holds the road map in her lap, and the two of them keep their eyes away from the horizons and close to the road ahead and the buildings and land abutting the road. They avert their gaze from the flat monotony of the central Florida landscape, the palmettos and citrus groves and truck farms. They ignore, they do not even notice, the absence of what Bob would call "real trees." They look right through, as if it were invisible, the glut of McDonald's and Burger Kings, Kentucky Fried Chickens and Pizza Huts, a long straight tunnel of franchises broken intermittently by storefront loan companies and paved lots crammed with glistening Corvettes, T-Birds, Camaros and Trans Ams, and beyond the car dealers, surrounded by chain-link fences, automobile graveyards, vast and disordered, dreary, colorless and indestructible.

FROM THE NOVEL *CONTINENTAL DRIFT*, BY RUSSELL BANKS

LESSON

Setting is as much about character as it is about place. Bob and Elaine are on their way south, and Banks confronts them with something they do not want to see. Banks presents the landscape as he sees it, a dull and predictable collection of fast-food franchises, car dealerships, monotonous farmland. Bob and Elaine are shown to be uncomfortable travelers.

Sometimes we are like that. We are in a place we dislike. Elaine holds the map as if it will deliver them from the boring and often ugly landscape. We are told what they see in the context of their not seeing it. They *keep their eyes away* and *They avert their gaze* and *They ignore, they do not even notice* and *They look right through*. The writer shows us so very much with two characters intent on not seeing anything at all. In this passage of seemingly perfunctory description, we learn of a crucial aspect of these characters, one that will play a vital role in their future lives.

WRITING POSSIBILITIES

1. Rewrite this setting in a better light. As the saying goes, beauty is in the eye of the beholder. In this case, it may not necessarily become beautiful but certainly can be seen in a less judgmental way. This approach would, of course, make for two completely different characters. So begin with two new names, maybe Rusty and Joyce—two people who are intent on making the best of a bad situation. You must convert the following words: *keep their eyes away, avert, monotony, ignore, look right through, glut, crammed* and *dreary*.

2. Now change the setting to one that is groomed and manicured, one that is stately and by most accounts a thing of beauty and grandeur. Maybe it's Saratoga, New York, or Newport, Rhode Island, or Princeton, New Jersey, or Asheville, North Carolina. Think about it. How do Bob and Elaine see such a place? How would Rusty and Joyce see such a place? As you write, keep in mind that the rendering of setting in this example is about character.

3. Bob and Elaine are from a place where there are "real trees." They are in Florida. What else makes this Florida? Palmettos and citrus groves? Remove the words *Florida, palmettos, citrus groves*. Substitute another state, another tree and another crop. How far can you travel with this paragraph?

4. This time substitute for the following: *horizons, flat monotony of the central Florida landscape, the palmettos and citrus groves and truck farms, "real trees."* Now, how much further can you travel with this paragraph?

TRAVEL BY HIGHWAY

READING

What is that feeling when you're driving away from people and they recede on the plain till you see their specks dispersing?—it's the too-huge world vaulting us, and it's good-by. But we lean forward to the next crazy venture beneath the skies.

We wheeled through the sultry old light of Algiers, back on the ferry, back toward the mud-splashed, crabbed old ships across the river, back on Canal, and out; on a two-lane highway to Baton Rouge in purple darkness; swung west there, crossed the Mississippi at a place called Port Allen. Port Allen—where the river's all rain and roses in a misty pinpoint darkness and where we swung around a circular drive in yellow foglight and suddenly saw the great black body below a bridge and crossed eternity again.

FROM THE NOVEL *ON THE ROAD*, BY JACK KEROUAC

LESSON

Again, the landscape is of our own invention. It is the spirit we bring to place, no matter how blank and shabby. *On the Road* is about the romance of travel. It isn't important how or where we travel, but that we are traveling, that we are witnessing as much landscape as quickly as possible. In this spirit, the setting is not something we leave behind, but something that travels with us for a time until we take on a new swath of the world.

Kerouac begins with a complex question. He isn't asking about the physics of what you see, but the feeling that attends such a sight. He then answers his question with more spirit than logic and comes close to confessing as much before the second paragraph. The *but* functions mainly as *who cares*, or *what the heck, we're on our way.* It undercuts the very process we have been asked to engage in. The second paragraph leaves behind the thinking. We are on the road. It's two sentences. The information is real. The actions and images could be the stuff of reportage, but they are set down by design and with intention, and just like that we are crossing eternity.

WRITING POSSIBILITIES

1. What is your passion? How does it manifest itself? Is it flying? Is it motorcycles? Is it not borne of speed? Or is it on the road? Indulge yourself in a page's worth of phrases and thoughts and solid lines about this thing you love to do, and draw from this for the remaining exercises.

2. Kerouac asks a question he could give the appearance of answering. It is a question asked while on the move. Sometimes we drive

to be alone and think, to question ourselves and ponder the answers. What's your question and answer? It doesn't have to make sense, just seem that way. As Kerouac does, write down your question and answer and write another sentence that undercuts the process. For example: What is that sensation when you ascend a mountain and pause and let off the brake and the land below rises up to . . . (Continue.)

3. Now you are thinking. In your next paragraph, make the swift bold move into setting. Let's stay on the road for this example. Change the setting from Louisiana to where it's cold and there is forest instead of city. Begin with: We wheeled through the (cold new light, frozen blue darkness?) of _____. Continue, using the italicized words from Kerouac as you can to keep you up to speed: ". . . *back on* the ferry, *back toward* the mud-splashed, crabbed old ships across the river, *back on* Canal, *and out*; on a two-lane highway *to* Baton Rouge in purple darkness; *swung* west there, *crossed* the Mississippi at a place called Port Allen. Port Allen—*where* the river's all rain *and* roses in a misty pinpoint darkness *and where we swung* around a circular drive in yellow foglight *and* suddenly saw the great black body below a bridge *and crossed* eternity again."

PART IV
TIME

OPENINGS IN TIME

READING

"Once upon a time . . ."

"In the beginning . . ."

LESSON

These are two of the greatest openings ever written. They are as precise as if a day, a month and a year were given. Both share a singleness of moment. They mark time. In the first quote is the word *once*, and in the second quote is *the beginning*. These are both specific moments in time. It's as if you've taken a long unfurling rope and driven a spike into one spot, pinned it down. This is your *once*. This is your *beginning*. A story makes an opening in time. It has a time when it begins and a time when it ends. These openings have a sense of timelessness. They have endured for thousands of years. They give a story the feel of a fairy tale or a fable or an epic adventure. They have a history.

WRITING POSSIBILITIES

1. Listen to a good storyteller, someone who is telling you a story, however simple, maybe even of how her day went. How did she begin? What phrase did she use? Use that phrase to begin a story of your own. Write a paragraph after your opening phrase.

2. Collect these spoken phrases and think of them as ways to open in time. A few examples: There was this one time when . . . ; In the morning . . . ; It all started when . . . Now come up with one of your own and use it to start a story.

3. You began to love storytelling, began to love the sound of words, by reading children's books. Read the openings of several such books now. Choose the beginning you like most and use it to open a story of your own, even if it's not a children's story.

OPENINGS IN TIME, NONFICTION

READING

Toward evening of a late-winter day, late in a dark decade in the fortunes of American city life, I rented a car at a small airport in western Kentucky and started driving on a two-lane highway toward Illinois.

I was headed for a town—a violent and sorrowful little town that lay wedged between two rivers at the southern tip of the state, a place of cruel secrets and gothic ruin, which bore the tragically hopeful name of Cairo.

FROM THE BOOK *FAR FROM HOME*, BY RON POWERS

LESSON

This book opens in time—*evening, late-winter day, late, dark decade, gothic ruin.* It is about two American towns, one in Illinois and one in Connecticut, and their histories, how they were once one way and now they are another way. Knowing this, the writer is acutely aware of time and its passing. He goes out of his way to establish himself in time, but the time he fixes on is fluid and recurring. He must fix himself in time the way a fiction writer would, because the story he is going to tell us has more to do with these towns and their secrets, as if the towns were characters and not places. His story is not reporting, though he does report and adheres to accuracy when he does. His story is not about numbers and facts, it's about people and families and where they live and how those places change.

WRITING POSSIBILITIES

1. Have you ever considered writing the story of a place and its existence over time as Powers does in *Far From Home*? Create a list of places important to you and also important in a broader sense. Designate the time period you think to be important. For example: the South in the last twenty years; the U.S.-Mexican border in the last five years; _____ since (a man-made disaster?); your hometown since you grew up and went away.

2. Go through the Powers quote and collect the small moments of beautiful writing. Notice the repetitions that he uses to give rhetorical power to his description of arriving in Cairo. Make a list and then rewrite the phrases for your own use. For example: *late-winter day, late in a dark decade*—might become *early-summer day, early in a dark year. A town—a violent and sorrowful little town* becomes *a house—a rundown and sad house.*

3. Rewrite the quote not for time and place, but for time and character. Begin: Toward morning of a late-summer day, late in a dark year in the workings of my life . . . (Continue.) I was leaving a relationship behind, an association—a _____ and _____ little affair that . . . (Continue.)

4. Rewrite the quote in present tense. Change *rented, started, headed, lay* and *bore.* Does it work? Yes. Is it as effective? Your call. If you feel it's not as effective, ask yourself what is missing.

5. Phrases such as "late in the dark decade in the fortunes of American city life" create a tone of grandeur and importance, which is complicated and undercut by the humble subject—a small Midwestern town that has seen better days. Try this technique yourself. Pick a small subject—your first car, a childhood friendship, etc.—and write about it in a paragraph full of grand language.

CONCRETE TIME

READING

Lars had gone back to the carcass, flaying off its blubber and setting the pink slabs aside. With the animal on its back, he opened the abdominal cavity, revealing the entrails in their well of dark blood. Cutting off the heart, he split it in half and patted it in the snow, propping it open to drain. Then he pulled out the small intestine, looping it like a lariat over his left hand and slicing each loop with one-inch cuts. As he pulled the intestine through his clenched fist, the contents jumped from the incisions. He laid the intestine by the heart and washed his hands with snow. Next, he cut away the liver and placed it in the center of one of the flanks of blubber. Kneeling by the slab of fat, he sliced off a thin piece of liver, popped it in his mouth, and chased it with some blubber.

"*Mamaq!*" he exclaimed, tasty, and offered me some, his round face beaming.

FROM THE BOOK *BLOODTIES*, BY TED KERASOTE

LESSON

Time on the page is never complete. A story does not exist as an absolute record of a day's or year's or lifetime's events. There is no way to accomplish this word for word, action by action, but this is often our ambition when we are writing nonfiction. We want to record and pass on all of what we see, because in nonfiction we are accurately relaying the facts of an event. Kerasote's book *Bloodties* explores the act of hunting as a way of life, as opposed to a pastime or sport, and in the telling of this he is interested in the beauty of technique, the clarity of action. In this passage he has found a way to chronicle time so that it appears almost complete; as readers we seem to see the whole process. The telling of time resides within the verbs and adverbs. The words *then, as, and, next* mark time step by step with their simple judicious placement. Notice how Kerasote uses dialogue to move from this process.

WRITING POSSIBILITIES

1. The writer tells us the story of an animal being dressed in the field. List ten processes that have beginnings and ends and that may be contained in a piece of writing you are working on. For example: the installation of a flagpole; making chicken enchiladas.

2. Lars is engaged in a process. He flays, sets, opens, reveals, cuts, etc. What else does Lars do that we are not told about? How did the animal get on its back? Kerasote doesn't tell us. How would you write that sentence?

3. Rewrite each sentence of Kerasote's quote in the simple past tense. Begin with: *Lars went back to the carcass. He flayed off its blubber and set the pink slabs aside. . . .* Which is better?

4. Look at the sentence: *Cutting off the heart, he split it in half and patted it in the snow, propping it open to drain.* Rewrite this sentence swapping the simple past tense for the -ing verb forms to read: *He cut off the heart, splitting it in half, patting it in the snow and then propped it open to drain.* Now fit your rewrite into the quote. Does it work? Maybe it does if you do not begin the next sentence with the word *then* as Kerasote does. Try doing this with the last sentence of the paragraph before the dialogue. Perhaps this one goes a little easier.

TIME AND MYTH

READING

Here's the thing about Diana the Huntress: misunderstand her and bad things can happen swiftly. Take Actaeon, for instance. Just one peep at Di's high-energy water aerobics, and before he knew it he sprouted antlers and turned into lunch for the hounds. Treat her badly and she'll treat you to a quiverful of arrows, for all that she looks so demure, so white, so chaste.

Who knew? There she was in St. Paul's Cathedral, hymned by a thousand choristers, her doe eyes shyly cast down, her voice throaty with nerves. . . .

FROM THE ESSAY "ROYAL FLESH," BY SIMON SCHAMA

LESSON

We often recount stories from myth or the Bible to make comparison and analogies, to point out consistencies and ironies, to illuminate and edify and sometimes just for fun. In this piece about Princess Diana, the writer plays off the name *Diana*, attempting to make a comparison between the Princess and the Huntress. Diana the Huntress becomes Di, her bathing becomes *high-energy water aerobics.* It becomes not so much going back into mythology, but bringing mythology forward into the modern world. With only the most oblique of transitions, *Who knew?*, the piece moves to St. Paul's Cathedral and the wedding of Lady Di and Prince Charles. This move doesn't wait around for anyone. Most often we are tempted to provide context, to add phrases such as *in Greek mythology* or *from the ancients.* Schama bothers with none of this and maybe we should learn something from that.

WRITING POSSIBILITIES

1. The opening to the piece is *Here's the thing about* . . . List ten similar openings. Two examples: Here's the angle on . . . ; This is what you should know about . . .

2. The transition the writer uses is *Who knew?* Simple enough. List ten of these. Some examples: Who'd have imagined such a thing? Such is life. So it goes.

3. The writer is using the ancient story as if it were contemporary. The story is unhinged from time. What are some stories out of mythology or folklore you can match with people you know? List ten. For example: my cousin Paul and Paul Bunyan; my neighbor's pit bull and Cerberus, the three-headed dog of Greek myth guarding the entrance to the underworld.

4. Complete the following fictional frame. Then select items from your lists in exercises one, two and three and do one of your own:

This is what you should know about Paul Bunyan the lumberjack: . . . (Continue.) Take _____, for instance. Just one . . . (Continue.) Treat . . . (Continue.)

So it goes. There he was at the family cookout, clapped on the back by aunts and uncles alike. . . . (Continue.)

TIME'S REACH

READING

I ran up the hill toward home as our voyageur ancestors had run through the original wilderness, frantically, fleeing time. For some reason I felt that I had to be in the dooryard by sunset. Fleetingly I thought of other, earlier voyagers. Of Odysseus, to whom Cordelia had compared my father, yearning homeward toward his wife and son. Of Aeneas, carrying his old father away from their home on his back. Of Daedalus, watching helplessly as his son soared into the sunlight.

I ran faster, inhaling the redolence of smoke and tobacco, thinking again of my father, no longer sure whether I was carrying my father or my son. I came over the crest of the hill into the freshly planted garden and thrust Henry into my wife's arms just as the sun went behind the mountains. My head was spinning. The garden and hilltop were spinning. Time was spinning backward on its axis, and once again I was fleeing through the swamp with my father in my arms, his jacket pressed close against my face and Carcajou howling close behind us.

FROM THE NOVEL *DISAPPEARANCES*, BY HOWARD FRANK MOSHER

LESSON

It might be safe to say that no other art form can travel in time like the written word. If we were to see the action of Mosher's passage on a film we'd see a man running up a hill, carrying a baby. At the top of the hill, we'd see him thrust the baby into a woman's arms. The best actor could draw so much from those simple actions, but in that brief moment, could he evoke Odysseus, Aeneas or Daedalus? Mosher makes this move inside the mind of his character. His storyteller has this experience of running uphill with his son in his arms and his mind reeling.

In essence, however, the experience is twofold. Our storyteller experiences these events and feelings yet again, in the act of telling them. While the character is running the length of the hill, his mind is traveling back thousands of years in a few sentences. Notice the progression in the last three sentences: inside the storyteller's head is spinning, then he sees the garden and hilltop spinning, and the next sentence spins time itself. Mosher's layered use of this one verb allows him to mix the past and present, the interior and the exterior of his characters at will.

WRITING POSSIBILITIES

1. How do you tell of the recent past and the distant past simultaneously? Mosher does this with a very simple construction: *I ran* _____ *as* _____ *had run* _____. Do five of these. For example: I drove the interstates as my father had driven the highways before them, fast and in a ragtop sports car. I baked poorly as my mother had baked Christmases ago, blackened cookies, cakes weighted like lead or cement block, the inedible sweets covering the counter tops.

2. Mosher makes the move back in time using two sentences: *For some reason I felt that I had to be in the dooryard by sunset. Fleetingly I thought of other, earlier voyagers.* Select a sentence of yours from exercise one and make the same move. For example: I drove the interstates as my father had driven the highways before them, fast and in a ragtop sports car. For some reason, I felt I had to be down the road faster than anybody. Fleetingly, I thought of the quick and the swift. Of Mercury, _____. Of Secretariat, _____. Of Richard Petty, _____.

3. In the second paragraph, Mosher makes the move again using three sentences: *My head was spinning. The garden and hilltop were spinning. Time was spinning backward. . . .* Write three sentences like these. Remember, the first move was to the classics, and this second move is in the direction of personal history.

4. Try a two-paragraph movement like Mosher's, using the elements from exercises one through three. Notice how the first paragraph begins *I ran*, and the second paragraph begins *I ran faster*.

TIME AND TIMELESSNESS

READING

Southern Peru, late August 1985. Beneath a rust-colored winter sky an old GMC flatbed bounced slowly through the high Andean badlands known as the *puna*. It is a lunar landscape, flat, treeless, ringed with bald dun hills and sharp gray peaks, bone-dry nine months of the year, beaten by frigid, dust-coated winds.

FROM THE BOOK *RUNNING THE AMAZON*, BY JOE KANE

LESSON

It's as if this opening were simultaneously ruled by time and timelessness. The fact that it is 1985 quickly seems so insignificant, so inconsequential. Time gets the briefest of mentions, not even a sentence. This mention is followed by the landscape and what time has done to it. The GMC is old and moves slowly. The landscape is *lunar* and *bone-dry nine months of the year.*

As the writer crafts the opening scene of his adventure, he is stepping out of time, the same way he must have felt when it was happening to him. The quote opens in the past tense but moves to the present tense in the third sentence. What came before is the past, the date, the truck, our presence—all are in the past. What came before are names and dates, all man-made. What is present is what will always be. It exists even as this is being written. The smallest, most intricate move, such as from past tense to present tense, can have a subtle and haunting effect. Following this second sentence, the writer returns to the past tense. The landscape is in present tense; the movement of men is past tense.

WRITING POSSIBILITIES

1. Reverse the tenses. Make the first sentence present tense and the second sentence past tense. *Southern Peru, late August 1985. Beneath a rust-colored winter sky an old GMC flatbed bounces slowly through the high Andean badlands known as the* puna. *It was . . .* Does it seem as if there is a shifting of weight? Show both versions to someone else, perhaps a nonwriter, and ask for an opinion.

2. Let's move away from the natural world and into the world of abstractions, thoughts of love and hate. How does this shift work here? For example: Southern Mississippi, late August 1985. I sat in the shade, nursing a beer and my young broken heart, watched an old truck as it jounced over the road, passing through the zephyrs of heat that rose from the hard red clay. It is only love in the end, no matter what else has been put on the table. It is love that endures and nags and won't

go away to let you rest. . . . (Try one of these yourself. Maybe hate or envy or civility is what's on your mind. Also try a reverse as in exercise one. See how that works.)

3. Let's return to the natural world. In your life there are no doubt landscapes that have an enduring quality for you. Use the following frame to craft your own setting in timeless time: (Place), late (date). Beneath a _____ sky (a/an) _____ (verb) (adverb) (prepositional phrase). . . . It is a (adjective) landscape, (adjective) . . . (Continue.)

4. Perhaps you are a city dweller or creature of the suburbs. Start this way: (City), (date). Beneath a _____. . . . It is a _____ landscape. . . .

TIME BACKWARDS

READING
In black tie, Dean sleeps forever. He lounges in his marble vault, behind the bank in Westwood, draped in midnight attire, in the uniform, a crimson hankie peeking from his breast pocket. He was the beautiful one. Always did know how to dress. The Leader liked that. Sam was another story. He was the youngest, the wild card. Onstage, 1963: "What are you doing in that cockamamy street suit?" Frank admonished, emerging godlike from the wings of the Sands, Dean by his side. "And what is this, with the tie down and the collar open? Where the hell did you learn that?"

FROM THE ARTICLE "AND THEN THERE WAS ONE," BY BILL ZEHME

LESSON
This is the opening to Zehme's article, written shortly after Dean Martin's death. And that is precisely how the piece begins: present day, Martin *in his marble vault*, laid out in his tuxedo. There is a language to this piece that you have to know from the outset. You have to know who Dean and Sammy and the Leader were and what they were to each other. Knowing these things has to do with time.

If you were young in the days when they were young, you know precisely what is being said. Zehme toys with this, runs an inside game. His transitions are fluid, conversational. From inside Dean's vault, Zehme comments on his looks, his attire, the way Frank Sinatra felt about all such, his opinion important because he was *the Leader*. We then move from a dead man's grave to a live man's mind, and even better, the opinions of this man when he was younger and in the spotlight. Then we hear how Sammy fit none of these opinions, and thus another dead man's spirit is invoked. Not too surprisingly, the next sentence begins with *Onstage, 1963*. We have traveled back in time, thirty-odd years from the present. This quote shows us a way to transport ourselves in time.

WRITING POSSIBILITIES

1. Let's isolate and focus on the clutch of words that make the move in time. *He was the youngest, the wild card. Onstage, 1963: "What are you doing in that cockamamy street suit?"* Rewrite this brief passage six times. Think in terms of nonfiction, memoir and fiction. Try two of each. An example in fiction: She was the youngest, the baby in the family. Concord, 1954: "What are you doing staying out so late on a school night?"

2. Maybe you had a group of friends similar to the famed Rat Pack. Maybe it's time to begin looking back at them. Who is in this group and why was the group formed? The older you are, perhaps the more groups you have been a part of. Name several. Be precise. Here are two examples: 1964, my Little League Team—Alan, Bill, Terry, Brian, Jim . . . ; College, 1956-1960, a bunch of us lived together in a house— Joanie, Wendy . . .

3. Let's try a complete rewrite of the quote. A friend has passed away and we are reminiscing on the page. Begin: In _____, Deanie sleeps for eternity. She resides in her concrete vault, behind the church in _____, dressed in _____ attire, in that dress, a _____ peeking from her _____. She was the talented one. Always did know how to light up a room. The Queen Bee liked that. Nancy was different. She was the pretty one, the dangerous one. Florida, 1972: "_____?" _____ admonished, emerging queenlike from the waters of the ocean, Deanie by her side. "_____? _____?"

Now try one of your own. Try memoir, fiction or perhaps a nonfiction piece. This technique will give life where you need it.

BACKSTORY

READING

And when the knitting went on and on, she agreed to get help. I'm talking a psychiatrist. Our life was made better, but then she started sleeping with him. The three of us had it out. I went to jail.

FROM THE STORY "AN EASY THING TO REMEMBER," BY BLAIR OLIVER

LESSON

When we start a story, our beginning is always a point in time we have decided upon. Of course, we know that prior to that point in time there is everything that has gone before. There is history. Sometimes that history is necessary to reveal our characters, to shed light on a relationship, to give reason for an action, to explain what is happening before our very eyes. This is backstory.

In this example, notice how the first person narrator fills in backstory like a stone skipping across water. The past is given to us quickly, with only the most important events mentioned at all. The writer does not want to stray too far from the action at hand. The telling has a familiarity to it, as if this is the usual, something you can fill in for yourself, and no doubt we can. And also it is an attribute of his first person character to skim and skip the way he does. He is in conflict over the dissolution of this relationship, troubled by his own inability to handle it in a more intelligent and sympathetic way.

WRITING POSSIBILITIES

1. The quote is the sketching of backstory, the compression of time. It is a single paragraph written in the past tense. Write five separate sentences that might follow the quote. For example: Jail was okay, not so bad as you would think.

2. Imagine a first person narrator like the one in the Oliver quote, one who has bad news to tell on himself. He begins by setting it up through the actions of others. Try this yourself. Begin: And when the (bingo, gardening, listening to C.B. radio?) went on and on, she agreed to _____. I'm talking _____. Our life was made _____, but then she started _____. The three of us _____. I _____.

3. Focus on the sequence of the last three events of the quote: . . . *but then she started sleeping with him. The three of us had it out. I went to jail.* List five such sequences. For example: . . . but then she started cutting his roses. He stopped by to consult. I bought new roses.

4. The sentence that actually follows the quote is: *I live in a studio in west Boulder, a place built for college students.* Did you think to move into the present tense as a possibility? Try five sentences in the present tense.

5. After *I live in a studio in west Boulder . . . ,* the story continues: *It's one mile from my old house and Carol expected me to head over and see what happened, so I went.* Notice the writer moving back into the past tense. The story is written in the present tense and the past tense. Try five such moves yourself. Make the move in a single sentence. Try at least one using Oliver's sentence as a frame.

FIXING TIME BY THE CLOCK

READING

I'll compromise by saying that I left home by eight and spent an hour traveling to a nine o'clock appointment. Twenty minutes later is nine-twenty.

Now let's jump ahead to the taxi ride. The trip from Newton to Belmont takes about half an hour. And I remember waiting fifteen minutes in the Administration Building to sign myself in. Add another fifteen minutes of bureaucracy before I reached the nurse who wrote that report. This totals up to an hour, which means I arrived at the hospital at half past twelve.

And there we are, between nine-twenty and twelve-thirty—a three-hour interview!

FROM THE MEMOIR *GIRL, INTERRUPTED*, BY SUSANNA KAYSEN

LESSON

Kaysen's memoir tells of when she was a teenager and checked herself into a mental institution. At this point in her story, there is a discrepancy over time. Her nine o'clock appointment is with her psychiatrist in Newton. It is rare when we can break down our days, moment by moment, and remember what we were doing; even more rare when we are as compelled as she is to do so. Perhaps we can when it is something important, like being witness to some event or crime, the day we got good news or bad. There are times when we need to, when we must. Think about trial testimony or police reports: It is very important to remember what you were doing and when. But are we truly capable of this? If we are otherwise occupied with something, it's unlikely we're also watching the clock. How completely can we trust someone who so closely accounts for her time? Kaysen seems to be playing with this idea too, as she is telling of a period in her life she needs to piece together for the sake of her mind.

WRITING POSSIBILITIES

1. It takes a particular kind of character or a particular happening in a character's life to bring about such attention to time. List five such conditions. For example: a dead, half-clothed male body is lying in the snow outside your apartment on New Year's day; an old woman goes to her husband's funeral and when she returns discovers the house has been robbed.

2. Remember, relying on clock time is tricky. Clocks run fast or slow sometimes, and they even stop on occasion. What would happen to the characters you listed in exercise one if their clocks were wrong, or if

they didn't wear a watch? How would they tell the time? By church bells? The sun? A factory whistle? List ten more.

3. There has been a chlorine gas leak in your town, causing an emergency. Who is your character? Begin writing with this echo of the Kaysen quote: I will split the difference and say that I left the house by six A.M. and spent a half hour traveling to . . .

FIXING TIME BY THE CALENDAR

READING

In the hotel dining room Sara heard the clock chime the half hour. She ate a crust of the quartered roll and searched the paper for other news. The dateline at the top of each page reminded her that eleven months of the projected span had already passed. Last July was the month of diagnosis. Six years, six active years.

FROM THE NOVEL *STONES FOR IBARRA*, BY HARRIET DOERR

LESSON

When you are working on a long piece, such as a novel or a book of nonfiction, your story often spreads. You need a large frame of time to work within—a year, a decade, even a lifetime. Natural frames like these are important to both big stories and small; they seem to give us a good place to begin and a logical place to end. The calendar is a valuable way for writers to talk about time in its vastness. After all, a calendar exists on paper too. In this passage, Sara's husband has been diagnosed with leukemia and given six years to live. It's easy to see how the calendar would then become important to this man and those around him. Doerr gives Sara a tally in her head; she knows so many months have passed, so many months remain. Such attention to dates adds tension to the story. These characters are racing time.

WRITING POSSIBILITIES

1. Doerr refers to the calendar when Sara comes across the dateline in the newspaper. What else might remind a character of the date? Think of times when you have to remember the date. Come up with a list of ten. For example: paying bills; an important appointment.

2. Doerr's character is in a special relationship with time because her husband has only so much of it left. What are some other reasons a character of yours might watch the date carefully? List five time-conscious characters. For example: a pregnant woman; a soldier on a tour of duty.

3. Doerr chose to write in the past tense. How would the mood of the passage change if you rewrote it in the present tense? Try it. Now consider tense for a character from exercise two. Do you want the urgency of present tense or the flexibility of past? Write a paragraph incorporating your character and a calendar reference from exercise one.

FIXING TIME BY THE SEASON

READING

It was early, but dark as a pit outside. When they happened to look out, turning from the oval wooden table near the bar, it seemed to them all, one way or another, a surprising and vaguely unnatural thing—though they'd seen it every year of their lives—that sudden contraction of daylight in October, the first deep-down convincing proof that locking time, and after that winter and deep snow and cold, were coming. Whether or not they cared for winter—some claimed they did, some claimed they didn't—every one of them felt a subdued excitement, a new aliveness that was more, in fact, than the seasonal change in their chemistry.

FROM THE NOVEL *OCTOBER LIGHT*, BY JOHN GARDNER

LESSON

It is always the writer's responsibility to be the master of time within the boundaries of a manuscript. Readers absolutely must know when one event occurs in relation to another. Otherwise, they will be confused and frustrated. Gardner lets us know the season is changing. Simple enough. It could have been done with a sentence, but no, the telling of time, the passage of time, the work of keeping the reader abreast of narrative time is also an opportunity to write something smart and beautiful. Gardner goes so far as to invent a time. He calls it *locking time.* The quote is but a taste of a long passage on autumn turning into winter, and this moment of turning he has invented. The locking time is when it seems as if we can know for fact one season has ended and another has begun. His characters witness this and all seem agreed in the feeling they have for it.

WRITING POSSIBILITIES

1. Time can be a bugaboo. By now you know how hard it is to keep a simple flow of events moving in the direction you want while the mind and memory can be so uncooperative. Take a moment to imagine a time between each season. Try to name it the way Gardner has.

2. Let's frame the quote and try out one of your times from exercise one. As we go along, more words will be your responsibility. Let this begin a story, or perhaps you have a story in progress where the season changed and you didn't use it as an opportunity: It was (early, late, midday?), but (dark, light?) as a _____ outside. When they happened to look out, turning from the (card game, quiet conversation?), it seemed to them all, one way or another, a (sad, surprising, comforting, strange?) and (oddly, vaguely, faintly?) _____ thing—though they'd seen it every year of their lives—that _____, the _____ that _____ time, and after that _____, were coming. Whether or not they _____ . . .

FIXING TIME BY TRADITION

READING
The holidays themselves were unexceptional enough. I do not recollect that the fire department got Santa and his sleigh and his reindeer onto the courthouse roof with any sort of remarkable velocity, and I do believe the Methodist Christmas pageant was fairly much of an unblemished success except for a brief interruption when one of the shepherds tending his flock by night got tangled up in the hem of his raiments and fell onto the crooked end of his staff which took his breath temporarily but did not cause any lasting injury. On Christmas morning I gave Momma a new sugar bowl and gave Daddy a hat and Daddy gave Momma a green skirt and a new book to read in February. . . .

FROM THE NOVEL *A SHORT HISTORY OF A SMALL PLACE*, BY T.R. PEARSON

LESSON
Traditions can work in time like signposts reminding readers that time is passing without calling unnecessary—and distracting—attention to such reminders. They are simple, and often anecdotal, markers. Pearson tells about a Christmas by mentioning the traditional happenings and how they went fairly smoothly. This passage occurs close to the end of his novel, and the fire department's decorating of the town, the Methodist Christmas pageant, and the exchange of gifts are all features of this holiday we've seen celebrated before. In effect, Pearson's storyteller is bringing to mind Christmases that passed earlier in the novel, as well as noting that another year has gone by.

It is important to remember that if your story ranges over a whole season, or several months or years, you might want to mention a tradition to keep your readers anchored in the world you are presenting to them, to avoid confusion. You can rely on the knowledge and experience you share with your reader. The small ways to do this are just as helpful as the big ones.

WRITING POSSIBILITIES

1. Think about your life over the course of an entire year. What do you do in celebration or remembrance of a particular person or event? Think about holidays, but go beyond just that type of tradition. Maybe there is something peculiar you do on the first day of each month or a feeling that comes over you every winter. Try to come up with five yearly traditions.

2. As writers, we can think about these traditions as whole frames in time or as parts of larger frames. For example, let's say that on the first day of every month you visit your grandmother in the nursing home. You can use this detail for a short story in which you work within the time frame of that one day. Or you could use it to help organize a longer piece, where you visit your grandmother three or four times. Make this decision for one of your traditions from exercise one.

3. Now we have to let your readers in on this tradition. Pearson has it easier, as we know by this point in his novel all about the fire department and the Christmas pageant, but look at his language: *The holidays themselves were unexceptional enough. I do not recollect that . . .* Begin your own paragraph this way. For example: April began without exception. I do not remember how long it took me to get to Sleepy Peace and Rest, but Grandma Lou was fit to be tied when I knocked on her door. . . . (Continue.)

QUICK SHIFTS IN TIME

READING

. . . For a few hours, as the memories circulated through the 50-room mansion that her father had built back in the most glorious days of the monarchy—America's monarchy—it seemed possible to still hear her.

"Are you having fun, darling? Are you having fun?"

The house, a Georgian brick completed in 1912—before the Great War and the income tax—was imposing enough, with its 13-foot ceilings and 38 family portraits and the diningroom table that could comfortably accommodate 32 for dinner.

FROM THE ARTICLE "MAIN LINE MADCAP," BY H.G. BISSINGER

LESSON

The occasion for this article is the death of socialite Hope Montgomery Scott, and in the first paragraph, the setting is her memorial service. This memorial service has the mood of a fine party. Bissinger begins his wrangling with time with the phrase *it seemed possible to still hear her.* He follows with a clip of dialogue he imagines to be in Hope's own voice. He says it is almost as if she is still alive, and then he brings her back to life. He does it quickly. This is quite a writerly feat, but it seems so seamless and smooth, you probably wouldn't notice it. From there, Bissinger can easily travel farther back in time to reveal the history of the mansion. Why is this easy? Because early on he establishes the mansion was important to Hope and her family, he opens his article with a description of the gathering, and he cinches it with his play on the elasticity of time to bring us Hope's voice. A deft move such as this dislodges us, prepares us for fast travel backward and forward through time.

WRITING POSSIBILITIES

1. Where to use this wonderful move? In the quote it's a mansion. What other places might someone call to you from the past? List ten people and ten places. For now, use people from your own life. For example: a grandfather who was a sailor—the ocean? a lake? the seashore?

2. The move the writer makes is quite gemlike, the sort of thing you get to do once or twice before it loses its capacity to delight and becomes tedious. Let's begin by rewriting the quote using a fictional setting. Complete the following example and then do one of your own:

For a few days, as the memories come back to me throughout the gentle hills that were my father's, the homestead that he built in the early days of first settling this rich land—it seemed possible to still hear him.

"We're having fun now! We surely are!"

The house . . .

3. Go back to your list in exercise one. For each, give a line of speech, the words you might hear from the past. The line in the quote is *"Are you having fun, darling? Are you having fun?"* It's a common line, one we could readily hear spoken. As you craft your ten lines be careful to make them particular, yet something we could have heard.

4. The setting is a mansion. The quote from the past is surrounded with numbers and, always, we honor the accuracy of numbers. There's just something about facts that we love: *50-room mansion, completed in 1912, 13-foot ceilings, 38 family portraits, 32 for dinner.* How could

we not believe this voice from the past, given the company of numbers it keeps? Try this in a fictional exercise. Use the following frame:

For _____ hours, as the memories circulated through the _____ that her _____ had built back in the _____ it seemed possible to still hear her.

"_____. _____."

The house, a _____ completed in _____ —before _____ and _____ —was . . . (Continue.)

SIMPLE PAST

READING
The year was in full swing now, days going by like a blurred landscape out the windows of a train. It was dark outside when she started her homework around seven o'clock, after washing the dishes and helping Billy put their children to bed. The beige carpeting in the dining room was soft under her stockinged feet. The wallpaper was of a calm pattern and cool colors, dark blue flowers against a white background. She sat at a round table made of blond oak, her grandmother's table. She remembered sliding around on her bottom under it, playing cowboys and Indians as a child.

FROM THE BOOK *AMONG SCHOOLCHILDREN*, BY TRACY KIDDER

LESSON
Simple past tense is traditionally used by storytellers. It has a certain elastic quality. It's roomy. The past tense positions the writer and the reader so they can observe an event from a comfortable distance. The past tense honors traditional notions of time's progression insofar as what happened in the past is written of as being in the past. Kidder has spent a stretch of time with this schoolteacher, and now he's telling us what he observed. The adverb *now* in the first line lends a touch of immediacy to the story time, but other than that, the passage resides in the past. We sense the action to be habitual, something she does most evenings, but it is not written as habit. The second sentence gives us the feeling not of a single night, but of many. The last two sentences are examples of the past tense stretching back a good number of years.

WRITING POSSIBILITIES
1. The past tense is perhaps the one we know best as writers. But we should not depend on it without scrutiny or for lack of intention. Rewrite the passage in the present tense.

2. Examine your rewrite from exercise one. Your new beginning should read: *The year is in full swing now.* Do *is* and *now* seem redundant? Try leaving out the word *now.* Is it necessary? It's not incorrect to write *The year is in full swing now,* but as a writer you may be uncomfortable. You may feel as if you are talking into a microphone.

3. Again, scrutinize your rewrite from exercise one. Your last two sentences should read: *She sits at a round table made of blond oak, her grandmother's table. She remembers sliding around on her bottom under it, playing cowboys and Indians as a child.* How is this different? The shift is subtle, but still it's there. Does the table seem like it is still her grandmother's? Does she seem to be sitting and remembering simultaneously? Is that the intent?

4. Now consider the intriguing rewrites of the middle sentences: *It is dark outside when she starts her homework around seven o'clock, after washing the dishes and helping Billy put their children to bed. The beige carpeting in the dining room is soft under her stockinged feet. The wallpaper is of a calm pattern and cool colors, dark blue flowers against a white background.* Changing tense adds drama, a certain element of suspense, but alas, probably not what the writer intended.

SIMPLE PRESENT

READING
A quarter-mile down the canyon road, Manuel brakes to a halt, gets out of the truck, ducks under some barbed wire, and walks to a tree from which the first of 29 traps on this route is suspended. He finds no bees. We take off again. He stops and looks again. No bees.

FROM THE ESSAY "THE BIG BUZZ," BY ED ZUCKERMAN

LESSON
The simple present tense is journalistic in style. It makes events seem immediate, near at hand, as if we are experiencing them as they happen, and there is no place to go except forward. But of course, time is always in the hands of the writer, and these events actually happened in the past. The writer sees, writes about what he sees, and some months later, we readers see it on paper. Zuckerman also arranges his words in short, simple phrases, and this accentuates the directness of the passage. Clarity is important in nonfiction and is just as much an asset in fiction. Telling stories in the present tense for immediacy and impact is a time-honored tradition and something that people do in conversation every day.

WRITING POSSIBILITIES

1. Listen closely for someone who naturally tells a story or recounts an event in the present tense. Maybe it's a joke. Joke-tellers often use the present tense. Tell yourself a joke. Begin: This guy goes into a bar and he has a monkey on his shoulder. . . .

2. Rewrite the quote in the past tense. Decide which tense you like best. Try this with a passage from your own writing. Sometimes such a change can open up new possibilities. A piece that has been resisting you may begin to flourish in a different tense.

3. Rewrite the quote in the future tense. This, of course, has a much different feel to it. Oddly enough, it may seem more dramatic. It may feel like a beginning or an ending, something to be used judiciously.

SIMPLE FUTURE

READING

In my early thirties, at a time when I am especially frightened of death, I will have a dream of my maternal grandfather; he will appear before me one night as a skeleton draped in a theatrically flowing grave shroud. When he sees me staring at him, he will greet me by bowing elegantly from the waist, one arm sweeping slowly before him. Nothing further will happen except that, after taking his bow, he will stand once again and gaze directly at me. The dream will take only a moment; it will be little more than an image seen through a briefly opened shutter.

FROM THE NOVEL *AN AMERICAN MEMORY*, BY ERIC LARSEN

LESSON

We use future tense every day. We say: "I will arrive tomorrow" or "It is going to rain." In a sense, we are making predictions. We are foretelling and we don't think twice about it. We will even have a character say such things. As writers, though, the future tense holds many more possibilities. We should not be shy about writing down our predictions or even about directly stating what will happen long before the dramatic moment occurs. This quote opens Larsen's novel. For this bold move, we already feel ourselves to be in the hands of someone who commands time. He seems to be foreseeing events. The future tense is bold because it tells what is to come instead of withholding such in an attempt to create drama. It sets out a future, and we will run headlong into it. We have a sense, like fate, of where we are going, yet for all of that, it is but the realness of a dream, which strangely enough can be as real as real gets.

WRITING POSSIBILITIES

1. Rewrite the quote in the simple past tense. Your rewrite will begin: *In my early thirties, at a time when I was especially frightened of death.* It just doesn't have the incantatory power of the future tense, does it?

2. Larsen begins with this passage. Can you imagine ending with it? Do you have a story in which the action has concluded and perhaps a gesture toward the future would be fitting?

3. Imagine you are concluding a chapter, or coming close to an anticipated line break in a story. Imagine it is the evening and your character has come to rest. He or she is settled in a motel room or in front of a fire. Your final paragraph of this scene might begin: In the morning, he will . . . Finish this paragraph. Make it at least fifty words long.

4. Now use the paragraph you wrote for exercise three as the beginning of a story. Begin your second paragraph with the words: But right now, he can't help but remember . . . Keep writing.

FLASHBACK—MOVING FROM PRESENT TO PAST

READING

How long ago? It was autumn then, and the ground was getting hard because the nights were cold and leaves from the maples around the stadium blew across the practice fields in gusts of wind, and the girls were beginning to put polo coats over their sweaters when they came to watch practice in the afternoons . . . Fifteen years. Darling walked slowly over the same ground in the spring twilight, in his neat shoes, a man of thirty-five dressed in a double breasted suit, ten pounds heavier in the fifteen years, but not fat, with the years between 1925 and 1940 showing in his face.

FROM THE STORY "THE EIGHTY-YARD RUN," BY IRWIN SHAW

LESSON

Memory is very important. We have faith that the past will deliver answers about our present condition, as if back there is the cause of the effect we are now experiencing. In this classic story, Darling has returned to the site of his glory days, more precisely, to that one special moment in his life where everything for some seconds was perfect. He comes to this place with the burden of a life coming undone. He has come for a reason, for an answer, for a bit of respite from what he faces. He cannot flee the time he is in, but he can remember another time, perhaps not even to find strength or answers, but memory for the sake of memory. This is the second paragraph of the story, a paragraph intended to transport Darling and the reader back in time, while remaining in the present; the character is not lost in backstory, but remains before the reader.

WRITING POSSIBILITIES

1. Such a simple way to begin the act of passing back through time— *How long ago?* List ten such questions. For this list, see if you can pluck them from the air, from the voice of someone else in the course of your day. Some examples: When was it? What year was it? How far back?

2. Let's rewrite the quote. Change the question. Change the time of year. Begin: _____? It was spring then, and the ground was softening because the days were . . . (Continue.)

3. Try rewriting the quote in the future tense. Imagine someone isn't remembering better days, but looking forward to them. Begin: How soon will it be? It will be autumn then, and the ground will be getting hard because the nights will be . . . (Continue.)

4. Our rewrite in exercise three is strange and provocative. Rewrite it again, letting it stray farther from the original quote. Perhaps it concludes a chapter or comes prior to a line break.

5. Imagine it is but a single day and the time passed is only a few hours. Perhaps someone is waiting on word from a loved one in surgery, a child missing . . . Begin: How long had it been? It was morning then, and the sky was getting blue in the east, but the sun had yet to show. . . . (Continue.)

CATCHING UP WITH TIME

READING

So where are we? We've got Earlene curled up asleep on a motel bed. We've got Billy Wayne, his head on George Binwaddie's bony shoulder, dreaming of the voice in the window. We'll get to him and to Dencil Currence, who, at the moment of Billy Wayne's nuptials, stood on the entrance ramp to I-75 in Alachua, Florida, hitching a ride to Monroe. . . .

FROM THE NOVEL *LOUISIANA POWER AND LIGHT*, BY JOHN DUFRESNE

LESSON

Probably the most important point to remember about time in writing is that it just doesn't matter what fancy tricks you know if your reader still gets lost. Time can become a distraction if it is treated haphazardly, can drive someone from your writing if it is confused or inconsistent. Dufresne has taken a very direct approach to make certain everyone is on his boat. Notice how he keeps his characters in suspension with the phrase *We've got* . . . This is really neither past nor present, but past time in continuum. The construction is called the past perfect and indicates action begun and completed in the past. More precisely, the writer uses the present tense of the past perfect.

The characters here are waiting for us. Dufresne also arranges events in time according to other events in the book. For example, earlier in the book when Billy Wayne was getting married, Dencil Currence was hitching a ride back home. This is different from being concerned with the actual day or month on the calendar. Your readers can keep straight with time because they know the order of events in the course of the story. Movement isn't so much related to the clock as to other movement within the novel.

WRITING POSSIBILITIES

1. Dufresne does in the quote what we so often do in life: He stops and takes stock of where everyone is. It is the voice of the novel and consistent with the writer's responsibility of keeping the reader informed. Let's rewrite the quote, imagining a sleepover and a Mom or Dad taking inventory. Begin: So what have we got? We've got _____ asleep on the sofa. . . . (Continue.)

2. Rewrite the quote as if it were a character taking stock of where his old friends are now living. Begin: So where is everyone these days? . . . (Continue.)

3. Now imagine a situation more consistent with the quote. You are working on a longish piece with many characters whose actions take them hither and yon. It's time in the writing to recount for the reader. Begin: So what's going on? We've got _____ sleeping on a couch in Denver. We've got _____, his arm slung across _____'s ample shoulder, singing a song about bad love. We'll get to him and to . . . (Continue.)

4. What other ways might you stop a piece of writing, stop time for the sake of recounting where your characters are? We can settle on a time of day or month. Here are two examples of how we might begin: It's evening now. John is . . . (Continue.) It was then September. Kit had returned to school in Houston. Billy was at Fort Drum and wouldn't be able to get away until Christmas. . . . (Continue.)

THE PASSING OF TIME

READING

Night after night, summer and winter, the torment of storms, the arrow-like stillness of fine weather, held their court without interference. Listening (had there been any one to listen) from the upper rooms of the empty house only gigantic chaos streaked with lightning could have been heard tumbling and tossing, as the winds and waves disported themselves like the amorphous bulks of leviathans whose brows are pierced by no light of reason, and mounted one on top of another, and lunged and plunged in the darkness or the daylight (for night and day, month and year ran shapelessly together) in idiot games, until it seemed as if the universe were battling and tumbling, in brute confusion and wanton lust aimlessly by itself.

In spring the garden urns, casually filled with wind-blown plants, were gay as ever. Violets came and daffodils. But the stillness and the brightness of the day were as strange as the chaos and tumult of night, with the trees standing there, and the flowers standing there, looking before them, looking up, yet beholding nothing, eyeless, and so terrible.

FROM THE NOVEL *TO THE LIGHTHOUSE*, BY VIRGINIA WOOLF

LESSON

This passage is between two longer, tightly chronological parts separated by years. Woolf manages great speed while clearly showing that time is passing. Notice her first sentence: *Night after night,* days are not mentioned; *summer and winter,* spring and fall disappear; and storms and fine weather mark the time, not characters. Woolf has emptied her setting of people. No one is there to listen to the storms, and consequently, to pass the time. If there is no one present to experience time, Woolf seems to say, how can we gauge its length and breadth?

Why might a writer choose to speed through time this way, to change her methods of handling time? It seems like an easy way to get through a chunk of un-event in your story, quickly and cleanly, and the change makes a point of time, each method drawing attention to itself. But how does this speed keep from seeming too easy, too convenient? By the quality of the writing. This is to say, the writing itself becomes the event. The author needs time to pass within the context of her novel. What better way to do it?

WRITING POSSIBILITIES

1. Perhaps you have a story in progress in which a character needs time with an issue or a person or a decision before your story can continue. In Woolf's case, the issue was war. Come up with three scenarios outside your story, yet important to its telling, that might

require more time than you want to spend on paper, time you must account for, while in the same moment, must eclipse.

2. Now look at Woolf's first sentence. Notice how time speeds up. Night after night becomes summer, becomes winter with autumn left behind. Try this. Do five sets. For example: Minute after minute, hours to days and months . . .

3. Rewrite the quote to account for less time, say a single day. A character is waiting for what? The return of a loved one? An important letter? A phone call? Maybe a house is waiting for its occupants to return, a summer house. Begin: Hour after hour, morning through noon, the white snowfall, the pause at nine o'clock, then coming down again without let-up. Waiting . . . (Continue.) By evening the porch furniture was a furl of whiteness. . . . (Continue.)

THE PASSING OF TIME

READING
Yes, she said, eyeing him doubtfully, you make half the man he was an you'll be goin some.

The fire ticked on in the little stove, cherrying softly the one side of it till the cracks in the old iron showed like thin spiders sprawled there.

Rocking quietly in her chair she had the appearance of one engaged in some grim and persevering endeavor in which hope was the only useful implement. Not even patience. As if perhaps in some indistinct future the chair itself would rise and bear her away to glory with her sitting fiercely sedate and her feet maybe tucked under the rung, her skirt gathered about her. She was humming something in her high nasal hum, faint evocation of summer bees. The coals chuckled, settled with easy sifting sounds. She rocked. That was how winter came that year.

FROM THE NOVEL *THE ORCHARD KEEPER*, BY CORMAC MCCARTHY

LESSON
This passage begins with a mother addressing her son. The dialogue anchors the scene in place and time: She said that, then. The narrator paints the scene vividly: the fire, the rocking, the woman's faint humming. We are thrust through time with the final sentence: *That was how winter came that year.* McCarthy has taken us from the fireside and simple conversation into the winter months of his story. The relentlessness of time is apparent at every step. The fire ticks like a clock. The rocking action is like a pendulum or metronome. She hums not so much

a tune, something modulated, but mechanically, like summer bees. The words, the phrases, the actions all suggest time passing, so when the last sentence is invoked, it is almost a relief. The scene builds up to this rush of time in all subtle and obvious ways.

WRITING POSSIBILITIES

1. Try to make time pass like McCarthy does. Find a story you are already working on or write a new dialogue between two characters in the past or present tense. Bring the dialogue to closure.

2. Now describe the scene. Follow your dialogue from exercise one with a paragraph in which you give one character a continuous motion like the mother's rocking. What other verbal nouns have this pent-up energy? Find two or three ways to use such words in your description. For example: tolling bells; tapping feet; dripping water.

3. End your paragraph with a version of McCarthy's final sentence to release your characters into the future. Use this frame: That was how _____ came that _____. Your blanks can be filled with seasons, months, times of day, weather, holidays, in short, any event in the future, no matter how near or far away.

MORNING

READING

. . . When the first rays of the sun strike the cliffs I fill a mug with steaming coffee and sit in the doorway facing the sunrise, hungry for the warmth.

Suddenly it comes, the flaming globe, blazing on the pinnacles and minarets and balanced rocks, on the canyon walls and through the windows in the sandstone fins. We greet each other, sun and I, across the black void of ninety-three million miles. The snow glitters between us, acres of diamonds almost painful to look at. Within an hour all the snow exposed to the sunlight will be gone and the rock will be damp and steaming. Within minutes, even as I watch, melting snow begins to drip from the branches of a juniper nearby; drops of water streak slowly down the side of the trailerhouse.

FROM THE BOOK *DESERT SOLITAIRE: A SEASON IN THE WILDERNESS*, BY EDWARD ABBEY

LESSON

This quote is about the passing of time, and simultaneously time is passing. The writing is in the present tense, the event unfolding before our eyes, event experienced alongside the writer. There is a small move into the future tense, predicting what will happen within the hour and in the very next sentence the words *Within minutes, even as I watch,* which serve to draw us back to the moment. Here the present tense also seems to sprawl backward and forward. It isn't just this morning, but so many mornings before and so many mornings to come when the writer has greeted the sun with his mug of steaming coffee. By recognizing time in such a way, by weaving it so deeply into our prose, as deeply as it is in our lives, we give the reader the comfort of knowing the time while giving form to our work.

WRITING POSSIBILITIES

1. Rewrite Abbey's quote in a way that simultaneously subdues the prose and transports it to another setting. Remain in the present tense. Begin: When the first rays of the sun strike the barn I fill a mug with coffee and sit in the doorway facing the sunrise, waiting for the warmth. . . . (Continue.)

2. Rewrite for an urban setting and move into the past tense. Begin:

When the first rays of the sun struck the _____ I filled a mug with coffee and sat in the doorway facing the sunrise, hungry for the warmth.

Suddenly it came. . . . (Continue.)

3. Rewrite the quote for whatever setting, but move into the future tense for the second paragraph. Begin:

When the first rays of the sun strike the _____ I . . .

When it comes, the flaming globe, will blaze on the . . . We will greet each other. . . .

4. Select one of your rewrites and rewrite again, letting the prose become more your own while maintaining the spirit of the Abbey quote.

AFTERNOON

READING

Sometime during the afternoon—the cartoons are on television, the turbines have spun all day, in the Town Hall they are counting money, the skiers are sunburned in their shining boats, and the fishermen are drunk—the water level drops back down to full pond and the alarm goes off.

FROM THE STORY "THE PROPHET FROM JUPITER," BY TONY EARLEY

LESSON

Earley seems to tell the time, to justify his statement about it being afternoon, with a list of five regular afternoon happenings in this town. He says we can know it is afternoon not because the clock says so, but because these things are taking place. The events he names all have a winding-down quality: the turbines had to start in the morning to have spun all day; they must have made money at the Town Hall to be counting it; the water skiers have been out a long time to be sunburned; and the fishermen had to start earlier to be drunk now. These images bring out the rosy-glow feeling of late afternoon, a time by which we have settled into our day after a morning's activities. Some clocks are biological this way, and you can evoke the time as a writer with feelings and sensations and images as well as exact dates and times.

WRITING POSSIBILITIES

1. There's a smoky smell to winter afternoons, a wavy glare to midday in the middle of August, the blaring horns of five o'clock traffic in a big city. Go through your senses and come up with five particular afternoon sights and smells and sounds for where you live.

2. Continue with exercise one. How precise can you be? Make a list of occurrences, as in the quote, that accompany the times of your day. Make the list chronological, by the hour or half-hour. Go back through your day and fill in wherever you have a time without an occurrence.

3. The quote signifies the afternoon, but surely we can use its frame for any time of day. Let's settle into the morning. Begin: Sometime during the morning—the _____, the _____, in the _____, the _____, and the _____ —the (story event).

4. Try another time of day. This is perhaps the beginning of a story.

NIGHT

READING

In the night, way into the middle of the night, when the night isn't divided like a sweet drink into little sips, when there is no just before midnight, midnight, or just after midnight, when the night is round in some places, flat in some places, and in some places like a deep hole, blue at the edge, black inside, the night-soil men come.

They come and go, walking on the damp ground in straw shoes. Their feet in straw shoes make a scratchy sound. They say nothing.

FROM THE STORY "IN THE NIGHT," BY JAMAICA KINCAID

LESSON

Read this passage out loud. Hear how rhythmic it is, how the word *night* rings like a high note. This is truly beautiful language. A time can be akin to setting: a place or thing to step our characters into.

Kincaid sinks us right into the night like it's thick water: We don't get an exact, nameable time, but rather a time of night recognizable because it is empty of all other time, not marked by clock, visible shape or available light. Time here is place and event and almost a character. Time is there, waiting for us to immerse ourselves. As the writer makes the plunge into time, she also seems to free herself of it. She abandons the idea of night as the other half of day, takes it from such a context and sets it free to be whole and other and exotic.

WRITING POSSIBILITIES

1. How do you talk about the dark? It's the time when most of us are asleep. Who is out and about? List ten jobs performed at night.

2. What are other ways to name the time of night besides by the clock? Make a running list. Feel free to invent ways, invent phrases. Two examples: the cave of night; the hour when night is halved.

3. The quote is the foundation of a beginning for one of your future stories. Try a rewrite replacing the word *night* with the words of day. For example: In the *day*, way into the middle of the *day*, when the *light* isn't divided like a sweet drink into little sips, when there is no just before *noon*, *noon*, or just after *noon*, when the light . . . (Continue.)

4. Go back into your own night and begin a story. Immerse yourself in the time you choose. Depend on the quote to get you started. For example: In the bath of night, down in the middle of darkness, when the darkness isn't the other half of day . . . (Continue. See where it takes you. Fill a page with such incantations until you get the half dozen you want. Imagine you are the musician listening for some elusive combination of sounds.)

MOVING FROM THE PRESENT TO THE FUTURE

READING
. . . he thanked him for the molasses and Lucas had answered exactly as his grandfather himself might, only the words, the grammar any different:

"They turned out good this year. When I was making um I remembered how a boy's always got a sweet tooth for good molasses:" and went on, saying over his shoulder: "Dont fall in no more creeks this winter:" and saw him twice more after that—the black suit, the hat, the watch-chain but the next time he didn't have the toothpick and this time Lucas looked straight at him, straight into his eyes from five feet away and passed him and he thought *He has forgotten me. He doesn't even remember me anymore* until almost the next year when his uncle told him that Molly, the old wife, had died a year ago. Nor did he bother, take time to wonder then how his uncle (obviously Edmonds had told him) happened to know about it because he was already counting rapidly backward; he said thought with a sense of vindication, easement, triumph almost: *She had just died then. That was why he didn't see me. That was why he didn't have the toothpick:* thinking with a kind of amazement: *He was grieving.*

FROM THE NOVEL INTRUDER IN THE DUST, BY WILLIAM FAULKNER

LESSON

Reading Faulkner can be a lot like watching someone put together a clock: seeing that jumble of works on the table, it seems a miracle, the tweezering into place of springs and gears to end up with something that tells time. Go slowly. Watch carefully. The leaps in time in this short passage are amazing. We start with Lucas telling a man about his molasses, and with the words *and saw him twice more after that,* we are shot through time to their next meeting on the street when Lucas thinks the man doesn't recognize him. Then it's a year later when Lucas' uncle explains to him the man's wife died and we are taken *backward* a year in Lucas's mind to their meeting. All in one sentence.

Why might you want to handle time this way? Notice we are inside Lucas' mind. Sometimes we hold complete thoughts about people or events that are made up of several separate occurrences in time. This is the luxury of memory, the ability to store things. Faulkner was trying to be true to that timepiece of memory.

WRITING POSSIBILITIES

1. Let's unstitch the prose in the quote. Begin with the nouns and grammar to make them more of your own experience. Begin:

He thanked him for the strawberries and John had answered exactly as his grandmother might have.

"They turned out good this year. When I was raising them I remembered how a body's always got a taste for strawberries. . . ." (Continue.)

2. This time, rewrite your rewrite, letting it stray further from Faulkner. Begin:

She said thank you for the apples and Mary replied the same way her widowed aunt would have replied.

"The apples turned out the best this year. When I was watching them get round and fat I remembered how a apple tastes on a cool autumn day. . . ." (Continue.)

MOVING FROM PAST TO PRESENT

READING

You're too hard on yourself.

Yes. I am. He blinked at the checked tablecloth, trying to get his eyes to focus on its pattern.

And I'm not hard enough. Bernie smiled. Such confessions.

They're necessary. Who else can absolve us of our sordid pasts?

Now the room has the contours and atmosphere of all rooms in which people stay awake talking. The fluorescent light is grainy, staring. The clutter on the kitchen table—ketchup bottle, sagging butter dish, tin of Nestle's Quik, the rowdy crudded ashtray—the world is narrowed into these. . . .

FROM THE STORY "APPLAUSE, APPLAUSE," BY JEAN THOMPSON

LESSON

Ted and Bernie are old friends. The quote comes toward the end of the story, a time of reckoning, of truth-telling. Bernie speaks first, says to Ted, *You're too hard on yourself.* The dialogue is not quoted in the story, making for that strange intermingling of what is said by the characters and what is said by the writer. This conversation between Ted and Bernie has been going on for the whole of the page and this quote is but the last few exchanges.

As the conversation is in the present tense, the break from narrative past tense and the shift to narrative present tense for the last paragraph do not seem abrupt or jarring or fanciful. The writer is taking command of what has come before. He is being authorial. And appropriately so, because the story concerns two characters with artistic inclinations and all the attendant confusion and doubt and desire. Such a shift fixes the action, stilling it. In the final moments, life is held fast.

WRITING POSSIBILITIES

1. You are working on a story you can't seem to end. Maybe it's time to freeze time, to change tense. Of course you should not do this just for the sake of making an interesting move, but maybe just once, it's the right way to go. The quote uses the present tense of dialogue to make the move, so let's begin with:

You're still a good man.

Yes. I think so. He drew a finger across the coffee ring on the table-cloth, trying to . . . (Continue.)

I'm the evil one. Hoover said. What's to say?

Not much. What's done is close to done.

Now the room has . . . (Continue.)

2. A writer coming from behind the veil of fiction is a bold move. It breaks the spell, fading out on the characters as the writer takes center stage. Let's focus on such a move. Ted says, *They're necessary. Who else can absolve us of our sordid pasts?* With this question, the door cracks open for someone to answer, and not necessarily Bernie, because it is a rhetorical question. Write five such questions. Two examples: Who else can right our wrongs? Maybe there just are no good choices?

3. Follow up on one of your rhetorical questions. Begin: Now the day has the last light of the sun. . . . (Continue.)

4. Following the quote there are slightly more than fifty words to the end of this story. In those words the writer comes forth even more. How would you end this story in just fifty words? The writer doesn't move into the future tense, but is that a possibility? The fifty words are just plain smart talk about words and writing. Write one more sentence about the room and then begin with the following words from the story's end: Now it begins . . . Remember that words are . . . (Continue.)

TIMES TO COME

READING

. . . He would kneel before Riley as we must all, he thought, kneel before one another.

Of course the chapter now ending for Professor Brooke was not ending for everyone else. Throughout that winter he found, in his mailbox at the university, anonymous love poems in envelopes with no return address.

And Brooke's wife, unpacking his clothes, smelled perfume on his necktie.

FROM THE STORY "AN EPISODE IN THE LIFE OF PROFESSOR BROOKE," BY TOBIAS WOLFF

LESSON

This transition begins the ending of Wolff's story. Until these lines, time has been very tight, very chronological. The feel of time changes completely with the line *Throughout that winter* . . . Time expands. We see farther into the future than we've previously been allowed. It can be a dramatic effect to place two kinds of times closely together this way, and if it is used for an ending, we get the impression of being allowed to stay with these characters a little bit longer than we might have otherwise. Notice this is done without the use of the future tense and without the use of a line break. The writer has told the story he wants us to know, so that he can tell us the rest of the story. If this were science, we'd call it "the cause," and only with the passing of time do we see "the effect." Simply put, our narrative time rarely comes to us with the dependability and regularity of the clock. As writers we want to stay true to events, and if the events are in need of movement in time, we need ways to make those moves.

WRITING POSSIBILITIES

1. There are so many delightful phrases we use every day to mark the passing of time. Note Wolff's second paragraph. Try five versions of this yourself. For example: But the sad affair now ending for _____ was not the ending for all involved. All that summer he . . .

2. Try a rewrite using the simple future tense to accomplish the same effect. What's different? Begin: He will kneel before Riley as we must all, he thought, kneel before one another. . . . Throughout that winter he will find . . .

3. Wolff shifts the way he handles time in this passage from very tight to very loose. This passage also marks the beginning of his ending. Try reversing his shift to open a story. Begin with a paragraph of very loose time and move into a chronological story. Begin with: Throughout that winter . . . (Continue.)

THE PAST THROUGH NONFICTION

READING

Before 1940 the tangible evidence of twentieth-century man's passage here consisted of very little—the hard tracery of travel corridors; the widely scattered, relatively insignificant evidence of mining operations; and the fair expanse of irrigated fields at the desert's periphery. In the space of a hundred years or so the wagon roads were paved, railroads were laid down, and canals and high-tension lines were built to bring water and electricity across the desert to Los Angeles from the Colorado River. The dark mouths of gold, talc, and tin mines yawned from the bony flanks of desert ranges. Dust-encrusted chemical plants stood at work on the lonely edges of dry lake beds. And crops of grapes, lettuce, dates, alfalfa, and cotton covered the Coachella and Imperial valleys, north and south of the Salton Sea, and the Palo Verde Valley along the Colorado.

FROM THE BOOK *CROSSING OPEN GROUND*, BY BARRY LOPEZ

LESSON

With every word, every sentence, every paragraph, the writer makes decisions, such as how to sketch in my edges, covering what I need to establish the necessary foundation so that I might then continue to sharpen and hone. All of these decisions are made, of course, in the name of narrating a compelling drama.

Lopez has taken it upon himself to commit a swath of history to the page. This is an ambitious way to establish a foundation for the drama that is to come. The intention is to convey how rapidly man has come to take over this particular landscape. The images are precise and singular, as if etched on the face of the land, and yet personified, as if animate, increasing the sense of motion that pervades the passage. Many of the words either function as verbs or have the appearance or sound of verbs. Many words mark time: *Before 1940, twentieth-century, passage, consisted, tracery, scattered, mining operations, irrigated, hundred years, were paved, were laid, were built to bring water, yawned, ranges, dust-encrusted, stood, work, covered.* His direction-giving serves the same purpose: *across, to, from, north, south.* Lopez, in the first sentence, designates travel, mining and irrigation as being the most revealing aspects to follow and then gives each its due in the almost breathtaking sweep of a hundred years.

WRITING POSSIBILITIES

1. To get a feel for how few working verbs there are in the quote, rewrite it in the present tense. Only five words change, and three of them are the same. What are those five words?

2. A phrase like *In the space of a hundred years* is an interesting one. It encompasses both time and place, the heart of this piece. List five such phrases that can signify two reference points. Two examples: In the course of your day; In the sweep of a year.

3. Imagine it isn't a place you want to account for through a stretch of time, but a process. What might that process be? The making of steel? Maybe it's a history. The ten-thousand-year history of agriculture? The history of your family as the opening to your own life story or that of a fictional character? Begin this way and continue: Before I was born in 1940 the tangible evidence of my family's waltz through time consists of very little—the odd habit of collecting clocks and timepieces, the widely scattered, relatively insignificant evidence of world travel; and the justified execution of two or three for thievery. In the space of two hundred years or so . . . (Continue with a sentence on the evolution of the clocks and timepieces, a sentence extrapolating on world travel and a sentence detailing the thievery.)

FORETELLING

READING

. . . He embraced the old Indian and said that he would return, to which One Stab only said, "I know it," as he rigged a lead line for Tristan's horse.

The voyage never really ended, except as it does for everyone: in this man's life, on a snowy hillside in Alberta late in December in 1977 at the age of eighty-four (a grandson found him beside the carcass of a deer he had been gutting, his hand frozen around the skinning knife One Stab had given him that day in Great Falls—the grandson hung the deer in the tamarack and carried the old man home, his snowshoes sinking only a little deeper in the snow).

FROM THE NOVELLA LEGENDS OF THE FALL, BY JIM HARRISON

LESSON

Foretelling is a dramatic move for a writer, a way of giving away some details of your ending without giving away your story. Here is a case where Harrison uses the past tense to tell about future events for Tristan. What to make of the parenthetical aside? Where to use foretelling? These are decisions for the writer to make. The fate of the hero does come to be known. It adds to the larger-than-life qualities we already know him to possess. Foretelling the nature of his death only enhances him in life.

Note also that the death comes long after the story. We suspect the character, given the time of events (he's a young man at the beginning of World War I), may be dead anyway. It's like reading about Daniel Boone or Calamity Jane or George Washington. We know they are not around anymore. So the foretelling is bold and dramatic and lends even more authority to writer and character. At the same time, it is a move that touches what we already must know. Note, too, the piece of dialogue preceding the paragraph that foretells. Already this world is filled with prescience.

WRITING POSSIBILITIES

1. Let's imagine a character from the past, someone whose story we are telling. Perhaps our character is a woman named Judith McGill, a pioneer who traveled the Oregon Trail. Review the quote for leads. Let's begin with:

She embraced _____ and said _____, to which _____ only said, "I know it," as he _____.

The _____ never really ended, except where it does for everyone . . . (Continue the small single story that details the end of Judith McGill.)

2. Imagine you are working on a piece of nonfiction—profiling a ski jumper. As a reporter you spend time with a person. There is no need to hold back what is to come. Begin:

He embraced his father and said that together they'd lick the world, to which Jake Sr. only said, "I know it," as he palmed the blocks of wax.

But they never really got that far together. A few months later, Jake Sr. would go off a road near Stowe, Vermont, and . . . (Continue.)

3. Rewrite the quote moving from past tense to future tense for the second paragraph. Which one works best, your rewrite or the original?

LINE BREAKS

READING

After he stood the ironing board in its alcove on the porch, he sat down again and, when she came into the kitchen, he said, "Well, what else went on between you and Mitchell Anderson that night?"

"Nothing," she said. "I was thinking about something else."
"What?"
"About the children, the dress I want Dorothea to have for next Easter. And about the class I'm going to have tomorrow. I was thinking of seeing how they'd go for a little Rimbaud," and she laughed.

FROM "WILL YOU PLEASE BE QUIET, PLEASE?" BY RAYMOND CARVER

LESSON

Line breaks move us through time and space. Perhaps we want to move ahead in time, or go from the ocean back home to Pittsburgh. In this quote the move through time is small. The writer has been so bold as to leave a space for the time it takes to have a single thought, a single emotion, a gasp or a something like a double-take of the interior. The writer does this several times in the story, and the effect is that of time slowing down, time jumping only to return where it started. There is, in the accrued use of these breaks, the building of dread or fear or pain. It's like having a chill run through you, or a tickle in your throat. On the one hand, it's disconcerting. The writer is using the line break against its own tradition, its own expectation, and for that we feel pinned by what we are experiencing as moment by moment we are ever deeper inside something we cannot and would not stop. On the other hand, the line break displaces one time in their lives together to another time.

WRITING POSSIBILITIES

1. Imagine yourself writing a story in which a confession is imminent. Perhaps you even have such a story in progress. Consider using this specialized line break as Carver does. Remember to keep the action tight. Begin:

After he rinsed his glass out in the sink, he stood by the stove and, when she came into the kitchen, he said, "_____." (Something powerful has been on his mind. What does he ask of her?)

"_____," she said. "I was thinking _____."

"What?"

"About _____, the _____. And about the _____ . . . (Continue.)

2. The second time the writer uses this kind of line break, she speaks and then he replies. How might this go? Perhaps:

She said, "What is this about? Why are we at each other? What's the point in pushing this?"

"_____." (What does he now say?)

3. Carver uses a simple prompt, *He said, "Go on, Marian,"* to keep the information coming. What is it we say to each other? What are five other possibilities? Two examples:

He said, "Just tell me what happened, _____."

He said, "Keep going, _____."

PART V
POINT OF VIEW

FIRST PERSON

READING

. . . I pushed open the creaky door and saw my mother spooned up against my father's back, as she always was, and Mr. DeCuervo spooned up against her, his arm over the covers, his other hand resting on the top of her head.

I stood up and looked and then backed out of the bedroom. They hadn't moved, the three of them breathing deeply, in unison. What was that, I thought, what did I see? I wanted to go back and take another look, to see it again, to make it disappear, to watch them carefully, until I understood.

FROM THE STORY "LOVE IS NOT A PIE," BY AMY BLOOM

LESSON

The primary function of the first person is to witness, to think about that witnessing and then to narrate. It's that simple. In the first sentence, the "I" tells us what is seen. It seems easy enough, but do not underestimate how critical are the words *as she always was, and.* These words are pivotal. They cast backward and forward as if this condition is permanent. Appreciate also how Bloom uses the conjunction *and*, not *but*. The drama is not emphasized in the telling but rather in the not telling. This, too, is a function of first person point of view; what she sees tells us about her.

A paragraph break leaves the scene singular and undisturbed. Then three beats: the narrator stands, looks and backs out, taking the image with her like a memento. She questions herself, wants verification as to her own sight, and finally wants the power of her sight to deliver her one way or another. This is also a function of Bloom's first person character. We readers are privy to her thoughts, and her thoughts can endear us, repel us, deliver understanding or sympathy.

WRITING POSSIBILITIES

1. To start, you need something a first person character can see and think about: a car accident, a snake eating a frog, two people kissing who shouldn't be kissing, Santa Claus in July, someone getting dressed with the shades up, someone alone and crying. Make a list.

2. Now see what isn't meant for you. Select one of the events suggested, or use your own, but be sure to turn the sentence with a phrase like Bloom's *as she always was, and.* For example: as I expected, and . . . ; as usual, and . . . ; like every other time, and . . .

3. Now it's time to think about what has been seen. Bloom's question is natural, but still it has many versions: What was that, I wondered,

what did I see? Or: What's that all about, I thought, what could it possibly be? Write a question of your own.

4. Then comes the thinking, the action that creates the boundaries of the mind, not for the sake of conclusion so much as for verification, followed by the range of responses. For example:

I turned down the alley and my father was there waiting for me, leaned up against the wall as I anticipated, and he did not see me and I could see the tears running down his face.

I stopped and turned away and into the dark shade of the building. I wanted to come around the corner again and see if it really was my father and if he really was crying, or if it was someone else and maybe the tears were just a trick of light.

FIRST PERSON NONFICTION

READING

I am driving and I am driving too fast. This often happens. In one hour, I will get a ticket for going fourteen miles over the speed limit, but this does not matter now. I try not to pay attention to limits anyway. Speed is part of the price for me and my kind. I also do not wear a seat belt. This is not a rational act, which is why it occurs. I have become skeptical of many rational things including the deductive skills of my own mind. I know medically that Sundance is dying from cancer in his bones but I do not believe this and neither, I think, does he. I know it is safer to wear a seat belt and drive more slowly but I do not think dying on the highway is where the danger lies for me or for others. I do not think any danger lies in dying. The grave is not the terror, it is . . . I am far from Los Angeles, I will not tell you where.

There is a woman riding with me, a woman of the Sioux nation.

FROM THE BOOK *BLOOD ORCHID: AN UNNATURAL HISTORY OF AMERICA*, BY CHARLES BOWDEN

LESSON

The use of the first person point of view in nonfiction can be a confidential endeavor. As a writer, you are investing yourself in the story, because the "I" is really you. But the most important concerns are seeing and thinking. There are several ways to do this: as an impartial observer, as a commentator, or as the subject yourself. Bowden uses the third approach; he is acutely aware of himself as a participant in his book and he offers his personal wisdom at every turn.

In this quote, he begins with himself in action, driving, and he tells of his habits, of what they might mean in the grand scope of life. He ventures a sweeping opinion with the line *speed is a part of the price for me and my kind*, a personal revelation with *I have become skeptical of many rational things*, and this passage builds to a conversation with the Sioux woman concerning alcoholism on reservations, and by association, the broader subject of the book—the cool underbelly of American society.

Throughout, time is at Bowden's beck and call. This is different from an autobiography or memoir, however; Bowden sets out in the beginning of this book to tell a story and therein he becomes our closest link to the story. He is involved insofar as he is the writer; he runs this show. He knows that he will get a speeding ticket in the near future. Consider the line: *The grave is not the terror, it is . . . I am far from Los Angeles, I will not tell you where.* He baits us with the secret of life, and then he will not even tell us where he's driving. As readers, we trust the writer to inform us of what we need to know.

WRITING POSSIBILITIES

1. Notice in the quote how Bowden begins with the simple action of driving fast. He then moves from driving fast to not wearing a seat belt, and from there out into the reaches of his brain. List other small actions of your own that can be heavy with meaning. Remember, this is nonfiction. You are obligated to tell true things about yourself. Take a few minutes to think about the actions you perform during a typical day. Come up with five. For example: lighting candles, and then licking your fingers to put them out; locking your doors, and then checking them repeatedly.

2. Take one of your examples and write a paragraph like Bowden's in which simple action is revealing. Use his quote as a frame. For example: I lock my doors whenever I am home and I have a dozen locks. This is necessary. Later today, I will read in the paper about another crime in this neighborhood in this city, and I will get up and check my locks again. I try not to pay attention to newspapers, but I cannot help myself. Caution is part of the price for me and my kind. . . . (Continue.)

3. Broaden your subject. Using the example in exercise two, we could now talk about people with jobs that require caution, people living in cities, women who live alone, the extraordinary surge of crime in Philadelphia, the fine art of picking locks. This is always the task of nonfiction, deciding what to write about. Take your own paragraph from exercise two and brainstorm with it for a while. Where does it take you? You have the beginning of an essay or article. Do some research and keep going.

FIRST PERSON PLURAL

READING

Our own knowledge of Cecilia kept growing after her death, too, with the same unnatural persistence. Though she had spoken only rarely and had had no real friends, everybody possessed his own vivid memories of Cecilia. Some of us had held her for five minutes as a baby while Mrs. Lisbon ran back into the house to get her purse. Some of us had played in the sandbox with her, fighting over a shovel, or had exposed ourselves to her behind the mulberry tree that grew like deformed flesh through the chain link fence. We had stood in line with her for smallpox vaccinations, had held polio sugar cubes under our tongues with her, had taught her to jump rope, to light snakes, had stopped her from picking her scabs on numerous occasions, and had cautioned her against touching her mouth to the drinking fountain at Three Mile Park. A few of us had fallen in love with her, but had kept it to ourselves, knowing that she was the weird sister.

FROM THE NOVEL *THE VIRGIN SUICIDES*, BY JEFFREY EUGENIDES

LESSON

This novel is written in the first person plural, from the perspective of a bunch of neighborhood boys infatuated with a family of sisters who all commit suicide. The story is told after the deaths and from a distance, and the language takes on a nostalgic, legendary tone. We have to notice the literary nod Eugenides gives to William Faulkner's classic short story "A Rose for Emily," which is also written from the first person plural point of view and is about a town's fascination with a mysterious dead woman.

This point of view is useful in unbelievable situations like a family of suicides. There is credibility in numbers, as if to say, we all saw it, so it must have happened. Eugenides' quote unfolds from the line *everybody possessed his own vivid memories of Cecilia*. Even as the phrases and pronouns before and after are plural, this line allows for singularity, diversity among the neighborhood narrators. Each one had his own connection to Cecilia.

WRITING POSSIBILITIES

1. Eugenides uses a group of neighborhood boys who were all witness to the lives of the Lisbon girls and, consequently, their deaths. Come up with five groups like this that can bear witness to an unbelievable (or, at least, unlikely) event. For example: a high school class/the nervous breakdown of a teacher; an office staff/the demonic possession of the boss.

POINT OF VIEW
149

2. Choose your favorite group and list the common occurrences in their lives. For example, a high school class would have algebra, gym and such, but also a class trip, a dance, football games and track practice. These would be occasions for new observations, times when theories might be passed back and forth, clues unfolded.

3. The opening to Faulkner's story "A Rose for Emily" reads: *When Miss Emily Grierson died, our whole town went to her funeral: the men through a sort of respectful affection for a fallen monument, the women mostly out of curiosity to see the inside of her house. . . .* Notice the way he divides *our whole town* into *the men* and *the women*. This has the same effect as Eugenides' line *everybody possessed his own vivid memories of Cecilia.* Come up with a different way to individualize your group. For example, with the office staff, you could have the secretaries and the computer programmers and the corporate executives. You might say that each one of the high school students had a conference with the art teacher, and seventy-five individual theories formed in those few minutes. Come up with your own way to do this and then write a paragraph that gives the details.

FIRST PERSON PLURAL

READING
. . . The stories and the songs blend into one ache.

What more is there to tell? Our bones began to break under the slightest pressure—getting out of bed, climbing stairs. Our hair rinsed out of our scalps. Our fingertips turned black and the black spread along the fingers by the first knuckle while the skin held a wet sheen. Our hands were negatives of hands. The brittle black fingernails were etched with bone white.

But this was after so many of those afternoons at the Un-dark plant with its steady northern light.

FROM THE STORY "IT'S TIME," BY MICHAEL MARTONE

LESSON
This story uses the first person plural for its ending. The storyteller is a woman who in the 1940s painted clockfaces with radium to make the numbers glow in the dark. Radium is a radioactive metallic element, and her work was poisoning her. The storyteller speaks of the stories and songs of the people she worked with blending together, and with that, the story shifts to the plural perspective. The story itself may chronicle only one woman, but the effects of radium fell on thousands.

In essence, they become like ghosts, and it is disturbing to read about such a death in the plural. The writer then shifts out of the plural and continues the one woman's story.

WRITING POSSIBILITIES

1. Imagine another event that would bring about a physical condition such as this. Perhaps chemotherapy or frostbite. List five more.

2. Imagine another event that would bring about a change in the mind, a change in habits. Perhaps trauma or abuse. List five.

3. Imagine a love affair. Maybe a marriage has come apart, and you have been telling that story from the wife's point of view, but she is speaking for her husband also. Use the frame of the quote to make the shift to a plural point of view. For example:

The days and months and years blend into a wash of pain.

What more is there to tell? Our words began to _____. Our time to _____. Our ideas about _____. Our touches _____.

But before all that, there were so many evenings on the back porch. . . . (Continue.)

FIRST PERSON SINGULAR, FIRST PERSON PLURAL

READING

In order to keep the police out of it, I agreed to go see Howie. At first I tried to get someone else to do it, but when I saw how anxious some of the others were to call in the authorities, I got a move on. He really had been a friend to all of us. But the pack instinct, whatever that is, was on alert. I think I felt a little of it myself, sort of like "Let's kill Howie."

FROM THE STORY "DOGS," BY THOMAS MCGUANE

LESSON

McGuane shifts point of view in this short quote, and he does it in a fluid, conversational manner, taking on the voice of the group. It sounds natural, but why? Notice in the first line, the point of view is first person singular. It remains singular for the second line, but McGuane also uses two phrases that anticipate the transition to first person plural: *someone else* and *some of the others*. He refers to a group before he includes himself in one. The next line is *He really had been a friend to all of us.* This makes the shift to the first person plural, and McGuane continues to use phrases such as *the pack instinct* to reference the plural perspective.

WRITING POSSIBILITIES

1. Make a list of phrases like those McGuane uses to smooth the transition from singular to plural first person. Come up with at least ten. Some examples: the rest of them; the crowd; ganging up.

2. Try out a few of your phrases. Remember, mention a group before you make your first person narrator part of it. Finish this example: In order to keep _____ out of it, I agreed to go see _____. At first I tried to get _____ to do it, but when I saw how anxious _____ were to call in _____, I got a move on. . . . (Continue.)

3. Write a paragraph in which you shift from singular to plural. Begin: In an effort to make some peace amongst us all, I ventured a phone call to Cathy Anne. The club secretary wanted to do it herself, but . . .

4. Listen to a conversation, or just pay attention when somebody is talking to you. We shift point of view all the time when we are talking. Consider McGuane's line: *I think I felt a little of it myself, sort of like "Let's kill Howie."* The phrase *sort of like* is a very conversational transition, and McGuane even uses quotes for what follows. Keep a list.

FIRST PERSON MEMOIR

READING

The Bird Refuge has remained a constant. It is a landscape so familiar to me, there have been times I have felt a species long before I saw it. The long-billed curlews that foraged the grasslands seven miles outside the Refuge were trustworthy. I can count on them year after year. And when the six whimbrels joined them—whimbrel entered my mind as an idea. Before I ever saw them mingling with curlews, I recognized them as a new thought in familiar country.

The birds and I share a natural history. It is a matter of rootedness, of living inside a place for so long that the mind and imagination fuse.

Maybe it's the expanse of sky above and water below that soothes my soul. Or maybe it's the anticipation of seeing something new. Whatever the magic of Bear River is—I appreciate this corner of northern Utah, where the numbers of ducks and geese I find resemble those found by early explorers.

Of the 208 species of birds who use the Refuge, sixty-two are known to nest here.

FROM THE MEMOIR *REFUGE*, BY TERRY TEMPEST WILLIAMS

LESSON

Williams' memoir is about growing up in Utah in the then-unknown shadow of nuclear testing. In this passage, she uses words like *constant, familiar, trustworthy, recognized, rootedness, soothes, appreciate.* Such words suggest an intimacy and faith in the place where she grew up, something that endures and helps her to endure the hardships later in her story. Notice the way she continually links herself and the birds: *I have felt a species long before I saw it. . . . I can count on them. . . . whimbrel entered my mind as an idea. . . . The birds and I share a natural history.* Williams and the birds seem almost to overlap in spirit, their affinity for one another is so strong. This connection, of course, is developed by design.

Drawing on a relationship you might have with an animal or plant or mountaintop is a way to develop yourself as a character, a way you might convey your thinking or your sensibilities. This can be an important tool in memoir, the process of linking yourself with your landscape. Use it when you can.

WRITING POSSIBILITIES

1. Think of a place that means something to you, one you feel a special connection with. It might be a natural place like the ocean or your favorite hiking trail, or a particular street corner in New York City. It might be a place you knew well as a child but haven't seen for many years. Take a moment to picture this place clearly in your mind. Now list at least twenty-five things that exist or might occur there.

2. Now list a dozen words that describe this connection you have. Williams' words are *constant, familiar, trustworthy, recognized, rootedness, soothes, appreciate.* Invent your own. For example, in writing about a street corner in Manhattan, a list might begin with *fluctuation, foreign, shifty, mysterious, confused, charged.*

3. Write a passage using Williams' quote as a model and drawing on your lists from exercises one and two. Remember to emphasize your connection to the place.

4. The last line of Wiliams' passage allows her to open her narrative to detail: *Of the 208 species of birds who use the Refuge, sixty-two are known to nest here.* What might follow this? Facts and figures about the nesting habits of birds is one possibility. In your passage from exercise three, use your version of this line as a springboard into some nuts-and-bolts nonfiction about an aspect of your landscape. In New York City, it could be street people. On your favorite hiking trail, the mountain laurels or the wild blueberries. Write a paragraph that follows exercise three in this fashion.

FIRST PERSON MEMOIR

READING

I HAVE A STORY TO TELL. IT IS A STORY OF MURDERS: murders of the flesh, and of the spirit; murders born of heartbreak, of hatred, of retribution. It is the story of where those murders begin, of how they take form and enter our actions, how they transform our lives, how their legacies spill into the world and the history around us. And it is a story of how the claims of violence and murder end—if, indeed, they ever end.

I know this story well, because I have been stuck inside it. I have lived with its causes and effects, its details and indelible lessons, my entire life. I know the dead in this story—I know why they made death for others, and why they sought it for themselves. And if I ever hope to leave this place, I must tell what I know.

So let me begin.

I AM THE BROTHER OF A MAN WHO MURDERED INNOCENT MEN. His name was Gary Gilmore, and he would end up as one of modern America's more epochal criminal figures.

FROM THE MEMOIR *SHOT IN THE HEART*, BY MIKAL GILMORE

LESSON

This is from the opening to Mikal Gilmore's memoir about his family, which included murderer Gary Gilmore. Such a subject naturally lends itself to high drama, and that is the tone Gilmore chooses. The lines in small capitals leap from the page; they work like signs, billboards, a raised voice. Gilmore announces he has a story to tell and then he characterizes what's to come. He says *I know this story well, because I have been stuck inside it.* Here is the reason for Gilmore's memoir. He believes that, if he tells what he knows, he will be set free from the more horrible events of his life. His connection to his story is one of uncomfortable distance. He observed rather than participated in the events that would shape his life. It's almost as if he's been held captive by his life; he's been *stuck inside* the story he watched unfold. This is a possible position for the first person narrator, that of the isolated observer, and for such a dramatic story as Gilmore's, it is an interesting choice.

WRITING POSSIBILITIES

1. A memoir has to be a function of your personal experiences or it's not a memoir, though it's pretty unlikely that any of us has a brother like Gary Gilmore or an experience as dramatic as that in our pasts. Go through your family history—call your mother, your grandfather, your great aunt's second husband. Almost every family has a true-life

dramatic anecdote, secret or strange arrangement. Collect one story from your own family.

2. Now try to claim some of Gilmore's drama for yourself. Rewrite his first paragraph and substitute your own family story. Complete this frame as an example and then write a paragraph of your own: I HAVE A STORY TO TELL. IT IS A STORY OF ACCIDENTS: accidents of the _____, and of the _____; accidents born of _____, of _____, of _____. It is the story of where those accidents happened, of how they _____, how they _____, how their legacies _____. And it is a story of how the claims of accidents _____ —if, indeed, they ever _____.

3. Follow your paragraph from exercise two with a paragraph that explains your relationship to the story you are telling. Begin with Gilmore's sentence: I know this story well, because . . .

Run with this idea. Maybe you don't know the story you are telling all that well because the events it describes happened when you were a child, but you remember the strange ways of your Aunt Anne at the reunion when you were ten; you remember hearing your grandmother yelling at her in the kitchen at three o'clock in the morning when you snuck downstairs for a glass of water; you remember how, for a year, your mother cried every time she saw her sister. Find all the places in your past where you have come across a thread of the story and write those down. Create a personal relationship that way.

FIRST PERSON MEMOIR

READING

On a sunny day in a sunny humor I could sometimes think of death as mere gossip, the ugly rumor behind that locked door over there. This was such a day, the last of July at Narragansett on the Rhode Island shore. . . .

I listen for my father and I hear a stammer. This was explosive and unashamed, not a choking on words but a spray of words. His speech was headlong, edgy, breathless: there was neither room in his mouth nor time in the day to contain what he burned to utter. I have a remnant of that stammer, and I wish I did not; I stammer and blush, my father would stammer and grin. He depended on listener's good will. My father depended excessively on people's good will.

FROM THE MEMOIR *THE DUKE OF DECEPTION*, BY GEOFFREY WOLFF

LESSON

The first two sentences of the quote are the opening to Wolff's memoir about the life of his father, whose nickname is the Duke. These first lines begin a brief section titled "Opening the Door," in which the writer recounts the day he received the news that his father had died. The next section is not titled but is designated as chapter one. It begins *I listen for my father and I hear a stammer.* The writer proceeds to ponder his father's speech, his way of speaking, his stature, his clothing, his likes and dislikes, his talent for deception—an inventory of the man, settling on those aspects he knows as best he can.

Entering memoir—entering memory—we often need a reason; we often need a vehicle to transport us. Often the telling is not linear, does not track from beginning to end. These are memories and they will resemble such as they are rendered onto the page. It isn't until chapter six that the writer tells us of his own birth. Keep in mind that this writer is not merely indulging his own whimsy. His father is a ghost of a character, capable of all sorts of guile and craftiness. He is a son trying to get a fix on his bloodlines. He's writing down the way it was the best he can.

WRITING POSSIBILITIES

1. The writer's first thoughts show the cast of his mind, preface the news to come, and give time, place and speaker. Try an opening like this one. Begin with the frame and then try one of your own: On a (adjective) (noun) in a (adjective) (noun) I could sometimes think of (life, love, sadness, death?). . . . This was one of those days, the last of (month) at (town, state?). . . .

2. Look at the second part of the quote. Imagine yourself in a dark room alone. Fix on a loved one, perhaps someone who has passed away. It's time to conjure him. Is it a sound for you, too? Try a sound.

3. In exercise two we used the same sense as the writer—hearing. What about sight or smell or touch? Try sight. Begin: I look for my _____ and I see (him/her) standing by the fireplace, always the fireplace. This was what you'd call posture, ramrod straight, elbow on the mantle, foot on the hearth, not a slack muscle in his body. . . . (Continue.)

4. Beginning with chapter one, the writer goes on to inventory what he remembers of his father, his codes of life, his despising of black leather, the fact he was a Jew. Think about your subject. Begin to record, in no special order, all you can remember. Begin these simple statements as Wolff begins some of his: I recollect things, . . . ; I remember his . . . ; He was . . . ; He owned . . . ; His pocket watch was . . .

FIRST PERSON MEMOIR

READING

Our car boiled over again just after my mother and I crossed the Continental Divide. While we were waiting for it to cool we heard, from somewhere above us, the bawling of an airhorn. The sound got louder and then a big truck came around the corner and shot past us into the next curve, its trailer shimmying wildly. We stared after it. "Oh, Toby," my mother said, "he's lost his brakes." . . .

It was 1955 and we were driving from Florida to Utah, to get away from a man my mother was afraid of and to get rich on uranium. We were going to change our luck.

We'd left Sarasota in the dead of summer, right after my tenth birthday, and headed West under the low flickering skies that turned black and exploded and cleared just long enough to leave the air gauzy with steam.

FROM THE MEMOIR *THIS BOY'S LIFE*, BY TOBIAS WOLFF

LESSON

Wolff is also a fiction writer and brings to his memoir all of the art and craft, care and attention he uses in his short stories. Because it really happened, it does make a good read, but it still has to be beautifully written. The quote begins with a dramatic event. The first person narrator is driving through the mountains with his mother. The next three paragraphs tell us the story of the truck crash. Then there is a line break. Then he begins again with *It was 1955 and we were driving from Florida to Utah.*

This move begins to establish the writing as memoir. It fulfills the reader's expectation that these are real people in a real place in a real time. And as such, the story begins when the narrator was a child. It makes sense, then, that Wolff begins his memoir with a plural point of view. He is not under his own steam, but carried along with his mother. The line break followed by those first three words *It was 1955* tells us a lot. We know in the simplest, most elegant way: I was a boy then. I am a man now. I am looking back over all these years and there are things I want to tell you. This is a way to begin when you are thinking about your own memoir.

WRITING POSSIBILITIES

1. The advantage of this opening is in how it quickly expands the narrator's point of view. It's as if there are two narrators, the younger one and the older one. The younger narrator gives us the drama of event

and the older one crafts the context. Listed below are some of the words of each. Find others and then create a parallel list in which you rewrite the author's words. Key words are in italics.

Younger narrator: Our car boiled over *again just after* . . . ; *While we were* . . . ; The sound *got* louder and then . . .

Older narrator: *It was* 1955 and we *were* driv*ing* . . . ; We *were going to* . . . ; We*'d* left . . .

2. Consider a very precise and small dramatic moment from your past. Think about it for a long time. Pick and choose from the many. Think about it the way you would if you were writing a short story. Keep it to three paragraphs and then make your line break and begin again.

3. The quote is from a memoir but it also has possibility for a good piece of fiction. The story perhaps contains a powerful telling event from the character's past. Rather than tell it in flashback, consider beginning your story with the event.

SECOND PERSON

READING

Outside Mannheim, West Germany, you are stationed with the 57th. It is November, and Novembers in Germany remind you of the sadness and despair of a fallen woman. Let us also say we know of your fondness for heroin. You want to get off, and two men in your squad need to shoot up. This is how you do it:

There are three floors to your barracks. You get your main buddy, Stoney, and two others, Simmons and Cabot. You go to the top floor where there are storage rooms and broom closets. Generally, this is the kind of place to be avoided. It is too quiet here, too lonely, and if the yams catch you napping they might tear you a new asshole just for the hell of it. But with Stoney to protect you, you're not worried.

FROM THE NOVEL *BUFFALO SOLDIERS*, BY ROBERT O'CONNOR

LESSON

Some people are uncomfortable with the second person point of view. Perhaps it seems too close to them or too much like a device. Here is the second person point of view with a little twist thrown in. Notice the second sentence: *Let us also say we know of your fondness for heroin.* By that *us,* are we to assume this is actually a first person plural point of view? It's a small move that comes in the first paragraph and then does not come back again, but it accomplishes several goals. It further demonstrates the elasticity of the second person point of view. It implies company. It also gives the uncomfortable reader a window out, so he doesn't have to read himself as the protagonist. Follow this idea with the particular vocabulary of this place and experience and you have another escape route for your reader.

WRITING POSSIBILITIES

1. Rewrite the quote in first person. What is gained and what is lost? Try it in third person. What do we do with a sentence like *Let us also say we know of your fondness for heroin*? We might have to give it up. The answers to these questions are your call.

2. Second person can be a lot of fun. It's a particularly mischievous point of view. Okay—without thinking too much about it—you be the character and use your own life in a rewrite of the quote. Begin: Outside _____, you are (verb) (prepositional phrase). It is (month), and _____s in _____ remind you of _____. (Continue.)

Let's go back and consider two of the spaces in the frame, the verb and the prepositional phrase. What are some good possibilities? List ten. Make them all different for the different aspects and settings of your life. For example: stuck in a trailer with a mangy dog; roped to a desk in a nowhere job. Now rewrite the quote several more times using some of those possibilities.

3. What are other versions of the phrase *Let us also say we know?* List ten. Two examples: Let's also assume we know; We should also add we know.

4. What are other versions of the transition the writer uses to end the first paragraph and enter the second? The sentence he uses is *This is how you do it:* ... List ten more of these. Two examples: This is the way it's done: ... ; You do it like this: ...

SECOND PERSON

READING

First, try to be something, anything, else. A movie star/astronaut. A movie star/missionary. A movie star/kindergarten teacher. President of the World. Fail miserably. It is best if you fail at an early age—say, fourteen. Early, critical disillusionment is necessary so that at fifteen you can write long haiku sequences about thwarted desire. It is a pond, a cherry blossom, a wind brushing against sparrow wing leaving for mountain. Count the syllables. Show it to your mom.

FROM THE STORY "HOW TO BECOME A WRITER," BY LORRIE MOORE

LESSON

Part of this story's genius comes from the title and its tone of high salesmanship and unsolicited advice, the same tone as "how to make your first million" or "how to win friends and influence people." When we offer advice, we expect it to be heeded. We tend to speak with authority and direction, sometimes in commands. Moore's sentences are structured as commands with the second person implied. It's as if she is dictating a long and specific list of actions to be carried out. Her first sentence works in response to her title, and it's a funny response: *First, try to be something, anything, else.* This is not what we expect to hear, and Moore continues to work against the grain of expectation.

WRITING POSSIBILITIES

1. As writers, we have to know how things will go in our characters' lives. Sometimes, we also have the same responsibility to say smart things about life for everyone. Try a pass at this kind of authority with a few of the structures Moore uses. You need a subject, something your character knows how to do that maybe no one else does exactly the same way. It could be cooking, hunting, skydiving, raising children, whatever. Complete Moore's sentences to make a paragraph: First, try . . . ; It is best if . . . ; . . . is necessary so that . . .

2. Moore's story is told entirely in the second person—quite an ambitious undertaking. Try using the second person in small doses. Take your paragraph from exercise one and make it a piece of dialogue. How would another character respond to such a list of commands? What other directives might be given? Write a page's worth of an exchange.

3. Take your paragraph from exercise one and try fitting it within a third person narrative or a first person narrative. Start to establish your perspective with a pair of sentences before making the shift with a simple declarative sentence like the one in italics below. For example: Colleen knows she has a way with animals that is beyond understanding. It's as if she can think her own thoughts into their heads, make them do what she wants without lifting a finger. *It's all about concentration, she thinks.* First, try . . .

4. Nonfiction is a place where a second person stance like Moore's might serve you well. There are many times in articles and essays where you find yourself needing to describe a process or a method to your reader. Now you need a true-life subject, but for the purposes of this exercise, keep it simple. Watch someone wash the dinner dishes or get the dog ready for a walk. Describe the series of steps, using the same frames for sentences outlined in exercise one.

SECOND PERSON

READING

You are not the kind of guy who would be at a place like this at this time of the morning. But here you are, and you cannot say that the terrain is entirely unfamiliar, although the details are fuzzy. You are at a nightclub talking to a girl with a shaved head. The club is either Heartbreak or the Lizard Lounge. All might come clear if you could just slip into the bathroom and do a little more Bolivian Marching Powder. Then again, it might not. A small voice inside you insists that this epidemic lack of clarity is a result of too much of that already.

FROM THE NOVEL *BRIGHT LIGHTS, BIG CITY*, BY JAY MCINERNEY

LESSON

The second person point of view is a strange animal. It's almost as if you are creating the kind of narrator who talks to himself in the second person, asks himself questions, coaches himself along from inside his own brain. But, at the same time, you are creating a similar relationship with the reader, who constantly hears his or her name being called with *you*. It works simultaneously as an invitation into the story and a prescription for how the story will affect its reader. It is a point of view choice that maintains tight control over the audience. McInerney's entire novel is written in the second person. Think about natural phrasing of language in conversation—it is rare for someone telling a story to maintain the second person point of view for anything more substantial than small, intimate effect.

WRITING POSSIBILITIES

1. Rewrite the quote in the first person point of view. What happens to the bar scene—the feeling, the tone? Everything seems to be a lot more straightforward and benign, doesn't it? Our version of McInerney stays out of the reader's own mind, and it is less threatening, less powerful, too.

2. What kind of situations would lend themselves to the tension and mood of the second person for an extended time? McInerney puts a man where he wouldn't normally be, fuzzes up his mind and gives him a craving for cocaine. Come up with one of your own. Use the quote as a frame: You are not the kind of (man/woman) who would _____. But here you are, and you cannot say that _____, although the details are _____. You are at . . . (Continue.)

3. Consider McInerney's line: *A small voice inside you insists. . . .* A second person point of view works a lot like a small voice in the

reader's head. Use this line for a transition from a standard first or third person perspective in a story you already have going. Treat it this way: A small voice inside (him/her/me) insists that you . . .

Keep going in the second person for a paragraph. This functions as an interior for your character, a window into his mind. Through this shift, you show the character beginning to talk to himself.

THIRD PERSON HISTORICAL NONFICTION

READING

Early morning. The sky was pale and cloudless except for a smudge of black smoke rising above an oat field over east. The oats had been cut and bundled the week before, the bundles stacked in shocks and lined up in neat rows to dry. Now a dozen wagons slowly drove down the rows. At each shock the driver stopped, wrapped the reins around the wagon post, and began to build a load of bundles on the rack. Two blasts of a steam whistle signaled that the separator was working, and all over the field men and horses quickened their pace, all of them inextricably connected to a whirring machine whose appetite for grain never slackened.

FROM THE BOOK *MAPPING THE FARM*, BY JOHN HILDEBRAND

LESSON

The quote is from a work of nonfiction told mostly in the first person. It takes place in contemporary Minnesota. But the setting in the passage is Minnesota in 1911. Chapter one of this book begins *It is the start of Memorial Day weekend and we are at my wife's family farm, the O'Neill farm south of Rochester, because her father is in the hospital.* Chapter eight begins *The moment John O'Neill stepped outside the front door of St. Bridget's Church on a raw morning in November 1899, friends pounded him on the back and wished him and his bride all the luck in the world.* Chapter eight is where our quote comes from. So what's up? The writer wants to tell a story of the past. Rather than do it the way a historian would, or a writer of history, he takes the risk of moving into the third person. He depends upon an immense amount of research, interviews and imagination. He is after a kind of truth.

WRITING POSSIBILITIES

1. While the lives of particular people in another time may not be known precisely, the things they did can be known with quite a high degree of accuracy. List ten processes from the past that can be learned.

For example: making soap, baking bread, slaughtering a hog, starting a fire in the cookstove.

2. Think about your own memoir of place. Maybe you've wanted to tell the story of a grandparent. You know the year, the location, what was invented and what was not invented. Write an opening paragraph of this memoir. For example: Early evening. All day the sky was white and sunless except for a curl of woodsmoke rising above the sugarhouse in the hollow. The taps had been drilled and set the day before, the buckets hung waist high, some four to a tree. Now a yoke of oxen trundled down the sloppy road, dragging a scoot and with a wooden tank. At each tree the driver stopped, touched at the yoke and emptied buckets into the barrel, all the while chatting with draught animals, a pair of Brown Swiss weighing a ton apiece. . . .

3. Perhaps you are after a piece of historical fiction. Let's pretend the quote is fiction and we have written it. What might come next? Two examples: Roy and his father hastened to keep up. They'd followed the harvest from town to town, sleeping in barns and under tarps, anywhere to keep back the night's cold. And: Roy stayed to the field. He didn't want to be around the steam tractor, not since Eau Claire, where a boiler explosion killed a man and his son.

THIRD PERSON TO
PREVIOUS LIFE THIRD PERSON

READING

Sitting in the shaded cool quiet of St. Paul's Church in Flagstaff, Walter remembers a family picnic. This memory is two years old, but nothing ever fades from it. It takes place in a small park called Hathaway Forest, on Long Island, one Sunday afternoon in early summer. . . .

. . . In his mind are the voices of two years ago, the quality of light on that day, and how the breezes blew, fragrant and warm. He can hear the voices.

"Oh," William says, shortly before they start to eat. "We forgot to say grace."

FROM THE STORY "ALL THE WAY IN FLAGSTAFF, ARIZONA," BY RICHARD BAUSCH

LESSON

Imagine you have a point of view you wish to transport back in time through a character's remembering. Perhaps the character has come to a point in life where he needs to get a fix on his past, needs to dial in the lens of time. A shift like this is almost a shift in point of view. Your character is going back to a moment when he was essentially a different person. Why would he have to do this? Certainly he is of an age when one is apt and able to take a look back.

Bausch uses these two passages to send his character off into powerful and separate memories. Memory comes to this character without device, without triggering mechanism, and this is how memory often works. Memories come to us of their own volition, whether we want them or not. But notice how it is not arbitrary, is not mere happenstance. Bausch positions Walter for memory. In the first instance, it's Saint Paul's Church. In the second instance, it's a quality of voice and light. Because of the work Bausch does in the first memory, he lays the foundation for the second one and allows it to happen even more quickly. The second memory goes immediately to dialogue.

WRITING POSSIBILITIES

1. Recalling the past seems not as necessary to the young as to the elderly. Say your character is as old as eighty-five, as young as thirty-two. Why would each look back? List five characters and five reasons. For example: Bonnie has lost a loved one; Leonard hit the jackpot.

2. Pick a character from your list and give her a place to pause and remember. Give the memory an age, a place of its own like Hathaway Forest in Walter's memory. Notice how Bausch does not stop there, but also gives another place, Long Island, and another, more specific time, one Sunday in early summer.

3. This time, put the place of your memory inside your character's mind. Have your character hear, and taste, and see, perhaps even smell and feel. Notice how Bausch, in the second passage, gives Walter this ability to remember with his senses. Continue with dialogue as if we were truly back in time. Keep writing.

THIRD PERSON FICTIONAL HISTORY

READING

. . . So he will set up a ring around the hills and when Lee's all nicely dug in behind fat rocks, Meade will finally attack, if he can coordinate the army, straight up the hillside, out in the open in that gorgeous field of fire, and we will attack valiantly and be butchered valiantly, and afterward men will thump their chests and say what a brave charge it was.

The vision was brutally clear: he had to wonder at the clarity of it.

Few things in a soldier's life were so clear as this, so black-line etched that he could actually see the blue troops for one long bloody moment, going up the long slope to the stony top as if it were already done and a memory already, an odd, set, stony quality to it, as if tomorrow had occurred and there was nothing you could do about it, the way you sometimes feel before a foolish attack, knowing it will fail but you cannot stop it or even run away but must even take part and help it fail. But never this clearly. There was always some hope. Never this detail. But if we withdraw—there is no good ground south of here. *This* is the place to fight.

FROM THE NOVEL *THE KILLER ANGELS*, BY MICHAEL SHAARA

LESSON

This is a historical novel set during the Civil War. The point of view is third person. The writer travels back in time over a hundred years to find his way into the mind of this soldier. It's a long way back, yet notice how full the thoughts, how intricate the mind's wranglings on the eve of battle. How does the writer do this? Surely there are differences in the psyches of a nineteenth-century and a twentieth-century man.

Of course there are differences, but at the same time there are universals. A soldier on the eve of battle, in any century, wonders about its outcome. The question for the writer becomes, once common ground is established, how far in do you dare to go? With research, the reading of documents and diaries, journals and letters, you build confidence, you acquire a feel for a time period, you learn far more than you will ever use, all for the sake of authentic transport.

WRITING POSSIBILITIES

1. One of the features of this character's interior is the way his mind doubles back on him . . . *knowing it will fail but you cannot stop it or even run away but must even take part and help it fail. But never this clearly.* This is not so exotic an idea. List five fictional and five real-life characters in situations. For example: Sergeant _____ in the early hours of D-Day (historical); my Uncle George in the early hours of D-Day (memoir); Private Joe Bresette in the early hours of D-Day (fiction).

2. Stop thinking about war for a moment. Stop thinking about major historical events. What about real life? The everyday existence of people? This is a little more difficult. The quote brings together men and war. There is something very important to be thinking about. But what about everyday life? Try a list of ten characters in everyday situations. For example: a plainswoman late in pregnancy; a boy in Philadelphia in 1899.

3. Use entries from your list and begin rewriting parts of the quote as a way to learn about your character, as a way to see how certain phrasings can travel in time. Maybe the character will only be in your mind as you change the words of the quote. Here are some starters: (a) The realization was painfully clear: if Ethan didn't return home, she'd have to find a way to have this baby on her own. (b) Few things in a _____ life were so apparent as this, so black and white that he could see the . . . (c) So _____ will set up a _____ around the _____ and when old mister woodchuck pokes his head out. . . . (d) There was nothing you could do about the sun, the way it was there every day and you could not escape it. . . . (e) You feel foolish before a woman gives birth, hoping for the best, hoping it will be all right. You cannot stop it or run away but must even take part. . . .

THIRD PERSON DEAD

READING
Denied speech in life, having died with only monosyllabic goos and gaahs in his vocabulary, Gerald possessed the gift of tongues in death. His ability to communicate and to understand was at the genius level among the dead. He could speak with any resident adult in any language, but more notable was his ability to understand the chattery squirrels and chipmunks, the silent signals of the ants and beetles, and the slithy semaphores of the slugs and worms that moved above and through his earth. He could read the waning flow of energy in the leaves and berries as they fell from the box elder above him.

FROM THE NOVEL *IRONWEED*, BY WILLIAM KENNEDY

LESSON
In this quote, a dead infant receives the power to speak from the grave, literally—being dead gives him the *gift of tongues*. It is a special narrative, though, that can maintain this kind of supernatural storyline without such conventions as flashbacks or other wranglings of chronology.

The point of view is third person, omniscient enough to speak on behalf of the dead, but not distant. The omniscience becomes a means to intimacy. Preceding this passage, Gerald watches his father pass over him in his grave. Other paragraphs lead Francis to Gerald: *Francis found the grave without a search . . . ; Tears oozed from Francis' eyes, and when one of them fell onto his shoetop, he pitched forward onto the grave. . . .* And in another paragraph, Francis talks to Gerald about the day he died. And after that? *Gerald, through an act of silent will, imposed on his father the pressing obligation to perform his final acts of expiation for abandoning the family.* The third person does not have to mean distance. It can access the interiors of the dead if we want. It is as dynamic as your imagination will allow.

WRITING POSSIBILITIES

1. Imagine a character in the grave. Rewrite the quote to create that character, and then try one of your own. Begin: Denied all but a snip of life, having died without vocabulary, without idea, without thought, _____ possessed the gift of wisdom in death. His ability to. . . .

2. A character does not have to be dead to be absent. The character can be away with no prospect of returning, but your third person narrator may want to bring that character into the story in a special way. Imagine a woman has left behind a man forever. Write a paragraph about her. Begin: Denied much of herself in love, having left with only a suitcase and a vaguest notion of escape and a better way to live, _____ possessed a hold on him in her absence. . . .

3. In memoir we may have reason to bring the dead to life. We can do it the same way we did in exercise one. Imagine it is a true person you are bringing forward. Begin with the first person: My great-great uncle, denied life by a horse, having been kicked in the head, possessed a strange hold on me in death. His ability to occupy my mind . . . causing me to imagine him . . .

THIRD PERSON AUTOBIOGRAPHY

READING

Of all this that was being done to complicate his education, he knew only the color yellow. He first found himself sitting on a yellow kitchen floor in strong sunlight. He was three years old when he took this earliest step in education; a lesson of color. The second followed soon; a lesson of taste. On December 3, 1841, he developed scarlet fever. For several days he was as good as dead, reviving only under the careful nursing of his family. When he began to recover strength, about January 1, 1842, his hunger must have been stronger than any other pleasure or pain, for while in after life he retained not the faintest recollection of his illness, he remembered quite clearly his aunt entering the sick-room bearing in her hand a saucer with a baked apple.

FROM *THE EDUCATION OF HENRY ADAMS*, BY HENRY ADAMS

LESSON

Henry Adams wrote this autobiography in the third person. Whether or not a convention of the time, it makes for a curious point of view—the writing of one's own life as if it were someone else's life. Yet, the writing is anything but distant. The images are precise, the steps in his earliest education are delineated, dates are precise and his memory is lucid. Adams says this is how he remembers it and he remembers quite clearly. Of course we will suspend our disbelief. The writer has just told us it's okay.

The writer spends a lot of time considering how he knows and what he knows and when he learned it. This is natural enough given his intentions as expressed in the title of the book. He uses phrases like *he knew, He first found himself, He was three years old when he took this earliest step in education.* The story of your life is often not enough. The telling needs a purpose, a reason, something more than, It's my life and I lived it. This is the story of learning, not just a life.

WRITING POSSIBILITIES

1. The quote offers some very precise images from the writer's earliest memory: *the color yellow, a yellow kitchen floor, in strong sunlight, scarlet fever, a saucer with a baked apple.* Begin a list of ten for your own life.

2. What were your earliest lessons? For Adams we have *a lesson of color* and *a lesson of taste.* What were your first two lessons? What are some of the possibilities? Touch? Temperature? Sound?

3. Is there another way to thematicize a life? Invent five titles like *The Education of Henry Adams,* by Henry Adams, but make it your own name and focus on something other than education. Take some chances. Risk sounding goofy. That's why they make delete keys, erasers and correction fluid. Fill in the blanks: *The _____ of _____,* by _____.

4. Adams uses the simple phrase *he remembered quite clearly.* List five more phrases that quietly build the credibility of the memory. For example: he remembered it as if it were yesterday; the memory was vivid.

5. Exercises one through four lay some solid groundwork. Maybe you are uncomfortable talking about yourself. Often it's even more complex than that. Distance from ourselves is what we need and desire. Think about using the quote above as a way to tell of your life in nonfiction or to use your life for fiction. Either way, give it a try. Begin with whichever is you: He first found himself . . . ; She first found herself . . .

THIRD PERSON DRAMATIC

READING

Lennie said, "Tell how it's gonna be."

George had been listening to the distant sounds. For a moment he was business-like. "Look acrost the river, Lennie, an' I'll tell you so you can almost see it."

Lennie turned his head and looked off across the pool and up the darkening slopes of the Gabilans. "We gonna get a little place," George began. He reached in his side pocket and brought out Carlson's Luger; he snapped off the safety, and the hand and gun lay on the ground behind Lennie's back. He looked at the back of Lennie's head, at the place where the spine and skull were joined.

A man's voice called from up the river, and another man answered.

FROM THE NOVEL *OF MICE AND MEN*, BY JOHN STEINBECK

LESSON

Third person omniscient holds a special place in the hearts of writers. It is a grand premise—to see all, to know all and to orchestrate such onto the page. We have heard this story before in the novel during more hopeful times, something George tells to soothe Lennie, like a piece of candy for a child. Here, it calls up those same feelings. Steinbeck adds urgency to the scene with the sounds of the manhunt in the background. In the second line the sounds are distant. By the last line, the sounds are near. Steinbeck does not narrate their approach, but allows them to gain ground at the edges of the scene while recounting the action of Lennie and George. This makes for high emotions—fear and gravity and a sweet calm all finding a place in the reader in this tragic moment. We realize what is going to happen when George reaches into his pocket. We know what Lennie does not know—that George is going to shoot him.

This is the obvious strength of third person narrative: it can move outside the drama for an all-encompassing vantage point and yet, without hesitation, move in for the most intimate relationships. Nearness and intimacy mark this passage. The narrator recounts each of George's movements with careful detail, but he gives the elements of the execution to someone else. It is Carlson's gun, and *the hand and the gun lay on the ground*, as if they belong to someone other than George.

WRITING POSSIBILITIES

1. Create a character who is more aware of impending doom or sadness or pain than another character. He will act as witness, agent or confidante. Consider a likely situation: the less aware character may be

dying, or must leave, or may have failed. Name your characters and settle on a particular situation. Keep in mind, you are responsible for both.

2. Give one character a favorite story, a memory, an occasion he often thinks about. It could be as simple as a dream she had when she was a child or the memory of a beautiful place. You can give it to either character.

3. Use Steinbeck to map your way. For example, maybe one character is close to death and the other is in attendance:

Mary said, "Tell me how long I have."

John had been listening to the children next door riding their skateboards in the driveway. For a moment he felt cold. "Look at the painting, Mary, and I'll tell you what it will be like. . . ." (Continue.)

Now try another one. From the outset, sense the challenge of intimacy and the responsibilty you bear for the lives of both your characters. This quickly, you are in the midst of third person drama.

NARRATORS

READING

The traffic of the great city went on in the deepening night upon the sleepless river. We looked on, waiting patiently—there was nothing else to do till the end of the flood; but it was only after a long silence, when he said, in a hestitating voice, "I suppose you fellows remember I did once turn fresh-water sailor for a bit," that we knew we were fated, before the ebb began to run, to hear about one of Marlow's inconclusive experiences.

"I don't want to bother you much with what happened to me personally," he began, showing in this remark the weakness of many tellers of tales who seem so often unaware of what their audience would best like to hear; "yet to understand the effect of it on me you ought to know how I got out there, what I saw, how I went up that river to the place where I first met the poor chap. . . ."

FROM THE NOVEL *HEART OF DARKNESS*, BY JOSEPH CONRAD

LESSON

Think about the places you see people reading books—on airplanes, in waiting rooms, curled up on sofas on rainy days. A lot of people read to pass time, and this dates back to telling tales around the fire. Conrad opens his novel with the first person plural point of view, men whose ship cannot travel due to floods, but who cannot go ashore because of the same floods. They need to fill their wait, and how better than with a story? This plural point of view inspires familiarity; we are all waiting and restless and bound again to one of Marlow's rambling tales.

Conrad uses this point of view to frame the story, to give it a legendary quality and allow for its trandscendence into something like a ballad for a mythic hero, but with a twist. These men have heard Marlow's *inconclusive experiences* before, and they are critical of his style, his insistence that he will omit what happened to him personally, in other words, the juicy stuff. Conrad shifts to the first person singular point of view when Marlow begins to tell his own story in direct quotes. We are audience to the source. Marlow turns out to be in audience himself to the story of his main character, Kurtz. The rest of the novel reads with Marlow as a traditional first-person narrator, a witness to his characters' actions and his own experiences.

WRITING POSSIBILITIES

1. Conrad's opening sets up a layered system of narration: Kurtz's story as told by Marlow to a bunch of sailors years later, which is then related by Conrad to us. To begin such a system, you need a captive audience. List ten groups of people who might need a story to pass their time. Notice how Conrad's sailors are familiar with Marlow and his stories. Some similar characters might be: nursing home cronies; a ladies' bridge club in a power outage; a scout troop caught in a thunderstorm.

2. Write a paragraph in the first person plural point of view that puts your chosen group of characters in their given predicament. Begin: Outside, the town had quietly gone to darkness. Who knew when the power would return? We looked on, waiting quietly. . . .

3. Now choose one character to tell a story. Remember, your group is familar with this person, his ways and mannerisms. Maybe he tells terrible stories, or maybe he hardly ever speaks up. Continue with where you left off in exercise two. For example: . . . when she said in a whisper, "I take it you all know that I have done some unintended traveling in my life. . . ."

NARRATORS

READING

Now we have arrived where we began and are in continuous time, a wonderful illusion for those addicted to notions of yesterday, right now and tomorrow.

FROM THE NOVELLA *THE MAN WHO GAVE UP HIS NAME*, BY JIM HARRISON

LESSON

Sometimes a writer momentarily steps from behind the veil of fiction and talks directly to the reader. This is a kind of first person point of view, a narrating voice that can guide the reader, can divulge information, or can bring focus to a scene. In this quote, Harrison offers a discourse on the nature of time. A sentence such as this inserts the writer into the fiction, tells the reader when it is and how time will work from this point forward in the life of the story. This sentence works as a hinge between the backstory, or relevant past of the narrative, and the story's own time. Such shifts can confuse a reader. Harrison's authorial voice organizes this possible sticking point using the first person plural; he writes, *we have arrived where we began.* This plural includes the narrator/author himself; we all, readers and writer, have come to this spot, and this is what we've accomplished. Do not underestimate the practicality of such a sentence. Being lost as a reader is not a pleasant experience, and who better to steer us along than the writer himself?

WRITING POSSIBILITIES

1. Perhaps you have a story in progress where you need to conclude a long backstory. Try an overt move like Harrison's and insert your own point of view as the writer to make this bridge. Start by rewriting Harrison's sentence. Some examples: Now we have arrived back at the beginning . . . ; Now we have entered into the night and . . . ; Now it's time for lunch. . . .

2. You can also use such an opening within the body of a story to place your reader and your character in an unreal time. Write five such openings. For example: Now we are in dream time and . . .

3. Where else can you use your point of view as the writer? A writer's voice might make a good opening, and using the first person plural would draw your readers right along with you. Rewrite Harrison's sentence to begin a story. Begin: Now we begin and are in (a place, a season, a mood?), a wonderful . . . (Continue.)

Complete a paragraph. You could follow this model sentence by introducing your character, an event in your story, or your own description of time.

4. In the opinion of the sentence, continuous time is an addiction, an illusion. That is another capacity of a writer's voice, the power of opinion. Find a scene in one of your stories where your own statement of opinion might help to clarify a transition in time. Be bold. It is your creation. Go to a story in progress in which you feel like you've reached a dead end. Try a move such as Harrison's—come from behind the veil of fiction.

NARRATORS

READING

I had the story, bit by bit, from various people, and, as generally happens in such cases, each time it was a different story.

If you know Starkfield, Massachusetts, you know the post-office. If you know the post-office you must have seen Ethan Frome drive up to it, drop the reins on his hollow-backed bay and drag himself across the brick pavement to the white colonnade: and you must have asked who he was. . . .

It was that night that I found the clue to Ethan Frome, and began to put together this vision of his story. . . .

The village lay under two feet of snow, with drifts at the windy corners. In a sky of iron the points of the dipper hung like icicles and Orion flashed his cold fires.

FROM THE NOVEL *ETHAN FROME*, BY EDITH WHARTON

LESSON

The narrative voice in Wharton's novel is not the writer herself but a storyteller. Notice the phrasing. It has an oral tradition behind it, a spoken sound: such phrases as *bit by bit,* and *as generally happens.* Wharton's first person narrator inhabits the landscape of the story. This storyteller knows the post office in Starkfield, knows various people living there and has enough gumption to gather clues to the town's scandals and secrets. The narrator's tone is not so much authoritative as friendly, even gossipy.

Wharton then shifts into second person, a conversational move that has the effect of placing the reader in the action, as if we had seen Ethan Frome like anyone else in Starkfield. She then shifts back to the first person to divulge her narrator's credibility, the story's roots and processes. Wharton's final move is to enter the traditional third person point of view for the body of the novel. This is in the high style of an old-fashioned storyteller, and it's a concert of points of view that can create a very traditional sound.

WRITING POSSIBILITIES

1. Perhaps you have a story in the third person that would benefit from a traditional first person narrator. This narrator is another character for you to envision. She needs a place in your setting, a connection, however loose, with the events. Create such a narrator and a way for her to get her information. Start the way Wharton does. Write five of these openings. For example: I had the story, all in a rush, from my interior decorator who tells me everything she hears, fact and rumor.

2. Your next move is to the second person for its conversational tone, for the way it will draw readers further into your setting. Build on your sentence from exercise one with a second person paragraph. For example: . . . If you know Louise, my interior decorator, you know her stucco house on Oleander Street. If you know that stucco house, you must have seen the pink flamingoes in the trees last Thursday morning. . . . (Continue.)

3. Now shift into your third person story. A good way to do this is with your first person narrator making a conversational transition, as Wharton's does. To continue with the example from exercise two:

. . . and you must have asked yourself why Louise would allow such a thing.

Well, Louise was very clear to me that she does not allow that sort of thing. Louise told me she was out of town all week. . . .

THIRD PERSON INTO FIRST PERSON

READING

Why don't you finish your water, dear? she said. And gratefully, welcoming this brief respite, he raised the glass. And Lilly, her grip tight on the heavy purse, swung it with all her might.

It's my fault, she told herself; the way I raised him, his age, my age, wrestling and brawling him as though he were a kid brother; my fault, my creation. But what the hell can I do about that, now?

The purse crashed against the glass, shattering it. The purse flew open, and the money spewed out in a green torrent. A torrent splattered and splashed with red.

Lilly looked at it bewilderedly. She looked at the gushing wound in her son's throat. He rose up out of his chair, clutching at it, and an ugly shard of glass oozed out between his fingers.

FROM THE NOVEL *THE GRIFTERS*, BY JIM THOMPSON

LESSON

This passage comes near the end of Thompson's gritty novel about confidence men. The telling is third person, but Thompson works closely in the minds of Lilly and her son, so closely that the second paragraph, except for two words, is in first person. These are Lilly's thoughts. The action comes in four clear movements. In the first paragraph, momentum begins with the swinging purse. Then Thompson steps out of the story's action and into Lilly's mind. The third paragraph re-engages the action as the effects of Lilly's swing are recounted, and finally the focus returns to Lilly and her response to what she sees.

What goes through the mind of someone who kills? In the second paragraph, Lilly takes blame. In the fourth paragraph, Thompson leaves her bewildered. As the action is precise and swift, so, too, is her way of thinking and being.

WRITING POSSIBILITIES
Name two characters of your own and build a scene between them with the action in four movements. One of them will kill the other. Write a paragraph modeled after each exercise that follows. Review the Thompson quote as necessary to recreate the length of each movement.

1. In this first paragraph, the character, Madge, will entice Jack to the stairwell. This will be a three-sentence paragraph, ending with: *And Madge dropped the vase from the top of the stairwell.*

2. The second paragraph will move to Madge's interior: *It's my fault, she told herself. I am always so clumsy, always hurting people I care about. But I can't seem to help myself.*

3. The third paragraph will return to action: *The vase broke on Jack's head, shards scattering across the hardwood floor like rotten ice.*

4. Now for the fourth paragraph. As first sentences: *Madge looked at the mess, flustered. She looked at the gash in Jack's head and thought she saw bone.*

SECOND PERSON INTO FIRST PERSON

READING
Say it is late February and the winter runoff is just beginning, Deep Creek and Twenty-Mile coming high and muddy from the Warner Mountains. A cold, dark morning, spitting rain, and miles of mudslick levee banks to patrol before breakfast, pumps and head gates to check.

Rotten conditions, you might think, and they were when you fooled around and got yourself stuck before daybreak and had to walk out three miles for help. But swear to God, that wasn't it—I never did run clear out of patience with getting the work done. My reasons for leaving had more to do with what might be called varieties of loneliness.

FROM THE ESSAY "LEAVING," BY WILLIAM KITTREDGE

LESSON
It's a good bet you know someone who moves with ease between first and second person when they tell a story. This essay is written in such a way. The writer addresses the audience. The use of the second person

is quite clear. It's you, the reader, he's talking to. You are included. This passage has the pure, familiar tone of conversation, of storytelling at the dinner table, or on Grandpa's knee. Phrases like *Say it is, you might think, swear to God,* and *what might be called,* these are conversational asides, familiar beginnings and middles and fillers and flourishes. But it's even more. It's apparent from the title that something weighs on the writer. He wants to tell us his reasons for leaving, but even he isn't sure of the facts or the reasons. He's not withholding them. He's just working up to them. He's trying to make sense out of what he does not fully understand.

WRITING POSSIBILITIES

1. List ten conversational phrases that connect with the reader. Two examples: Imagine it is . . . ; But I swear on a stack of Bibles . . .

2. The last sentence tells but doesn't tell. It satisfies for the time being, but we anticipate more explanation. What are some other ways to buy time as we are figuring out ourselves on the page? Try five different ways. For example: _____ had to with I am not quite sure what. Call it a feeling of levitation in my soul. _____ had to do with what might be called the vagaries of rural life.

3. Let's rewrite the quote. Your practice title is also "Leaving" or "Not Leaving," whichever best suits you. Begin:

Take late January and the winter snow is just beginning to break records, the Yellow Breeches and the Conodoguinet sprawl to cross the roads and run white with ice and cold. A _____, _____ morning, (weather), and miles of. . . . (Continue.)

4. Try your own essay. Think of a one-word title. The essay will be its explanation. For example: "Staying"; "Returning"; "Disappearing."

THIRD, SECOND, FIRST

READING

Arriving in a "developing nation" is becoming increasingly hazardous. It's got something to do with the fact that "developing" is what the country would like to be doing, not what it is doing. Avoiding disintegration and utter ruin is an ambitious aspiration in over half of the countries on the planet these days. A "developing nation" is a far more ominous prospect than a "Third World country." Will it, you wonder, sitting in your airplane entertaining apocalyptic jet lag, have "developed" an airport, for instance?

Landing in Cairo is thus a very pleasant surprise. For a start, the *new* terminal looks like a giant suite in the Trump Tower. And instead of the brutal interrogations and muggings you usually endure at the hands of North American Customs and Immigration storm troopers, I was greeted with astounding courtesy, then ushered through a couple of brief formalities, and—scarcely ten minutes after landing—found myself seated in a snazzy limo hurtling off down a highway so modern I wondered if I'd flown to the future by mistake.

FROM THE BOOK *RIVER IN THE DESERT,* BY PAUL WILLIAM ROBERTS

LESSON

Gaining credibility as a travel writer can sometimes be difficult, because you are judged on the honesty of your observations. In the quote, we read the opening to chapter one of *River in the Desert.* Roberts employs third, second and first person points of view. He begins this quote by discussing the general ambition of developing countries, passing on information. This is the third person point of view, objective and pseudoscientific and cool, presumably that of the country itself. He then shifts to second person with the question: *Will it, you wonder, sitting in your airplane entertaining apocalyptic jet lag, have "developed" an airport, for instance?*

This move draws readers right into his picture; we are sitting on the plane, about to be sitting in the airport. With the next paragraph, Roberts settles into a first person narrative to bring his personal experiences to bear on the writing. In using all three points of view, the writer opens up the third person objective, extends the second person invitation to the reader, and presents his own first person experiences as support for all he's done.

WRITING POSSIBILITIES

1. The ambition of this opening is to strike up a relationship with us as his readers. The writer is our tour guide. Moving from third to second to first is a way of introducing himself. We will be close to him, but always capable of respectful distance. Try this approach yourself, establishing both distance and intimacy with your reader. Do an opening tour of your hometown. Begin:

Arriving in a _____ is becoming increasingly _____. It has got something to do with the fact that _____ is what the _____ would like to be doing, not what it is doing. Avoiding _____ and _____ is an ambitious aspiration in over half of the _____ on the planet these days. A _____ is a far more _____ prospect than a _____. Will it, you wonder, sitting in your _____ entertaining _____, have _____, for instance? . . . (Continue.)

2. Roberts is not taking us on a package tour. This is not the fare of the Travel Channel, not a travel show on public television. What words indicate this? Collect them into a list. For example: *developing nation*; *increasingly hazardous*.

3. The writer has a personality. It's revealed in his phrasings. Rewrite the quote or your practice paragraph from exercise one, but emphasize your own personality. Would you be apt to use the simile *like a giant suite in the Trump Tower*?

FIRST, SECOND, THIRD

READING

Jack "Big Guy" Fitch is trying to crack his teeth. He swishes a mouthful of ice water, then straightaway throws back slugs of hot coffee.

"Like in Antarctica," he says, where, if you believe what Big Guy tells you, the people are forever cracking their teeth when they come in from the cold and gulp their coffee down.

I believe what Big Guy tells you. I'm his partner in crime, so I'm chewing on the shaved ice too. I mean, someone that good-looking tells you what to do, you pretty much do what he says.

FROM THE STORY "THE MOST GIRL PART OF YOU," BY AMY HEMPEL

LESSON

Hempel uses all three points of view in this passage, but the perspective is that of the first person character. The quote is the opening of the story. For the record, the "I" is the storyteller, Big Guy is her boyfriend, and the reader is "you." But "you" is also the narrator. She, too, is listening to Big Guy, witnessing his actions. In essence, this is straight first person, but think of it this way: imagine a character on stage, moving back and forth between the action of the play and addressing you in the audience. The stage begins to expand, until you feel it slipping under your own feet, and before you know it, you have become part of this play too. The "I" is intent on telling. She stands between us and Big Guy. She walks between us and passes on event and dialogue until finally, by the end of the story, she goes over to him and does not come back.

WRITING POSSIBILITIES

1. Hempel's story opens with a character other than the narrator. Big Guy is obviously vital, but this also sets the pattern for how the narrator will defer to Big Guy, will talk about him before herself. Maybe you

have a similar relationship between two characters in one of your own first person stories. If not, try creating one. These people could be siblings, lovers, enemies. Write a paragraph where you open with a character other than your narrator. Use this frame to get started: (Name) is trying to _____. He. . . . (Continue.)

2. The second person affords us a very natural construction: *if you believe* . . . ; *I believe* . . . This construction also facilitates the shift from third person to first with its natural roots in conversation. Try it yourself. Do three of these, and find one to follow your paragraph from exercise one. Use this frame to get started: "_____," he says, where, if you believe what _____ . . .

I believe _____.

3. The first person narrator and the present tense combine to make an immediate presence of character and action. Add Hempel's inclusion of the reader, and the story unfolds right in front of us. Phrases like *then straightaway, the people are forever,* and *so I'm* contribute to that immediacy. List ten more. For example: so as I was saying, he . . . ; then, just like that, he . . .

THIRD, FIRST, THIRD

READING

When his boys were young, Guy Bishop formed the habit of stopping in their room each night on his way to bed. . . . [third person]

Five months later, Keith disappeared. I was in jump school at Fort Benning when it happened, at the tail end of a training course that proved harder than anything I had ever done. . . . [first person]

Lewis shuffles along the road leading out of Fort Bragg, muttering to himself and trying to hitch a ride, but he is so angry that he glares at all the drivers and they pass him up. [third person]

FROM THE NOVELLA *THE BARRACKS THIEF,* BY TOBIAS WOLFF

LESSON

Wolff's novella begins in the third person. Keith and Phillip are the sons of Guy Bishop. In the second chapter, Wolff switches to first person and the narrator becomes Phillip. Later on, Phillip meets another soldier named Lewis and Lewis gets in trouble. To tell the story of Lewis getting in trouble, Wolff switches back to the third person and then closes out the novel with Phillip as narrator again.

Having a consistent, single-character point of view is considered a rule in writing, but it is a rule that writers often intentionally break.

Wolff allows the story to be told *by* or *through* the person to whom it belongs. Some parts he tells himself and some parts he gives to Phillip. Lives are being lived side by side with our own. No matter, the few times Wolff makes the switch, he does it at the beginning of a chapter. At no time is the reader confused as to who is telling the story. Wolff takes care to introduce the character to the story before he moves to their point of view.

WRITING POSSIBILITIES

1. You can do this too. Try it with a narrative you already have in progress, one with several characters. Choose one of your characters to be a first person narrator, and let the others form a constellation around her story. Once you know who your first person is and have a clear idea of her relationship to the other storytellers, it is easier to arrange the other points of view. Make a map like this of your own.

2. We are going to try a smaller version of Wolff's quotes. Take a paragraph from your first person narrator's perspective and isolate it on a separate sheet of paper. Now choose a third person point of view to precede that paragraph and one to follow it. Wolff's quotes have a timeline to them: the first quote is from Phillip's childhood, the second from his recent past, the third in the present tense. Do this with your own paragraphs. Give each of the three paragraphs a separate sheet of paper.

3. Now tape your pieces of paper together in one long strip. You can see the blank spaces between the paragraphs. Go back through your story and figure out which parts belong to which character and note these moves on your strip of paper. You've just rearranged your story. What do you think?

FIRST PERSON INTO SECOND PERSON

READING

. . . And I wondered, because it seemed funny, what would you think a man was doing if you saw him in the middle of the night, looking in the windows of cars in the parking lot of the Ramada Inn? Would you think he was trying to get his head cleared? Would you think he was trying to get ready for a day when trouble would come down on him? Would you think his girlfriend was leaving him? Would you think he had a daughter? Would you think he was anybody like you?

FROM THE STORY "ROCK SPRINGS," BY RICHARD FORD

LESSON

"Rock Springs" is written in the first person. It's the story of a man who is leaving his life behind and heading to Florida. This moment comes at the end. He has gone into this parking lot looking for a car to steal. This entire passage is written in rhetorical questions. As far as point of view is concerned, this is a significant feature of the writing. It seems as if both Ford and his protagonist are asking us these questions. We have been with him all this time—literally, secretly, along for the ride. We have been content to witness, and now at this precise moment he turns to us and asks us these questions as if he's known all along that we were there. In an instant, we are made complicitous. Changing point of view is always a bold move; in this case, it's a masterful stroke.

WRITING POSSIBILITIES

1. Try this ending. Begin: And I thought, because it was so very odd, what would you think a _____ was doing if you saw (him/her) in the _____, looking in the _____ of _____ in the _____ of _____? Would you think (he/she) was trying to _____? Would you think (he/she) was trying to _____? Would you think _____? Would you think _____? Would you think _____?

2. The first sentence sets up for the refrain *Would you think.* What are some other ways of phrasing this question? List ten. Two examples: Would you wonder . . . ? Might you wonder . . . ?

3. The last question he asks is *Would you think he was anybody like you?* It's like a hand closing on your shoulder. It's as if you can feel his breath as he's saying it. Rewrite the question five times, coaxing it as far from the original as possible, but remember to find a way to always turn it on the reader. For example: Would you think he was like you? Would you have reason to wonder about yourself?

4. The protagonist is asking these questions of the reader. Imagine a situation in which they might be asked of another character. To see how this might work, break the sentences into paragraphs and leave room for a response. Begin:

(Question) "And I wondered, because it seemed funny, what would you think a man was doing if you saw him in the middle of the night, looking in the windows of cars in the parking lot of the Ramada Inn?"

(Answer) "_____."

(Question) "Would you think he was trying to get his head cleared?"

PART VI

VOICE AND LANGUAGE

VOICE

READINGS

In September, after the primary, they rented an old yellow cottage in the timber at the edge of Lake of the Woods. There were many trees, mostly pine and birch, and there was the dock and the boathouse and the narrow dirt road that came through the forest and ended in polished gray rocks at the shore below the cottage.

FROM THE NOVEL *IN THE LAKE OF THE WOODS*, BY TIM O'BRIEN

In the late summer of that year we lived in a house in a village that looked across the river and the plain to the mountains. In the bed of the river there were pebbles and boulders, dry and white in the sun, and the water was clear and swiftly moving and blue in the channels.

FROM THE NOVEL *A FAREWELL TO ARMS*, BY ERNEST HEMINGWAY

LESSON

All writers begin as readers. Our first love was the feel of a book in our hands and sometimes it is the return of that sustaining love that sends us to the blank page to make something new. Coming down through us are the echoes of our past experiences, lived in life and lived on the page. The two quotes above show a lineage we can trace from one writer quietly passed on to another. O'Brien honors Hemingway in the length of his line, with the use of the conjunction, the pairings of words and the ultimate sound of his sentences. It's as if the two quotes breathe with the same air. Voice is this way. We listen and listen and our sound comes to be informed by those who came before us. It is to honor what we inherit as writers by letting the past resonate through our own unique creations. When you think of voice, think of participating in what has come before, while at the same time contributing what is of your own making.

WRITING POSSIBILITIES

1. Begin by melding the two quotes. Exchange details to make a new one. For example: In *the late summer of that year*, after the primary, *we lived in a house in a village that looked across the* Lake of the Woods. There were many trees, mostly pine and birch, and there was the dock and the boathouse and the narrow dirt road that came through the forest and ended in polished gray rocks at the shore below the cottage.

2. Create lines that echo the work of these two writers. Start by using the following frame based on the first quote: In (month), after the (event), they rented an old (color) cottage in the timber at the edge of (name a lake). There were many trees, mostly _____ and _____, and

there was the _____ and the _____ and the _____ that came through the forest and . . .

3. Now do the same for the Hemingway quote as you did for the O'Brien quote in exercise two. Begin: In (season) of that year we lived in a _____ in a village that looked across the river and the _____ to the mountains. In the bed of the river there were . . .

4. O'Brien uses a lake in September and Hemingway uses a river in the summer. Use either quote to frame a passage where you create: the ocean in summer; the mountains in winter; the desert in spring.

5. Try to echo one of your favorite writers. Create a frame as we did in the previous exercises. Limit yourself to a passage of no more than fifty to seventy-five words.

VOICE OF THE CONJURER

READING

. . . Two or three large gaunt-looking dogs followed at her heels.

The old woman was nothing special. She was one of the nameless ones that hardly anyone knows, but she got into my thoughts. I have just suddenly now, after all these years, remembered her and what happened. It is a story. Her name was Grimes, and she lived with her husband and son in a small unpainted house on the bank of a small creek four miles from town.

The husband and son were a tough lot.

FROM THE STORY "DEATH IN THE WOODS," BY SHERWOOD ANDERSON

LESSON

This is the fifth paragraph and the fifth time Anderson sets the conditions of his story. Each time it is as if he begins anew, as if looking for an entry point, the same way a child might sound out a word. In this passage, Anderson moves in and out of intimacy with his own story. He is constantly adjusting his lens to the point where he has to remind himself: It is a story. With each start, he takes on and casts off information.

The old woman begins each opening. Each time she is coming to town with some purpose in mind. It could be the same time or different times. He tells us she is one of the nameless ones and yet, in the same paragraph, tells us her name. In the same sentence, he tells us hardly anyone knew her, but she got into his thoughts. Without preface he tells us she has just now come into his mind. This is Anderson conjuring the story before our eyes. In the final sentences of the passage, he begins to reveal details. He tells us she lived in a small house on the bank of a small creek. His repetition of the word *small* is more akin to an oral tradition than to a literary one. In rewrite, one might avoid the repetition of an adjective. But to maintain the voice of a storyteller, Anderson does not make such a literary choice.

WRITING POSSIBILITIES

1. Listen closely to how bad or sad news is passed on. Perhaps you can remember how such news was conveyed to you, or maybe you have had to recount a tragedy. You did what Anderson has done on the page. In your mind, you edited and rewrote. You kept your thinking to yourself. Try it on the page. Write an opening in which you begin the story several times.

2. Think about a story you can't quite remember. Maybe you have a family story that has several versions. Allow yourself to think on the page. Start a story three or four times. We already do this as writers, but we are in the habit of deleting what we think of as false starts.

3. Go back and build detail. Rewrite your openings in exercises one and two with an eye toward incremental detail, the addition of a single adjective or adverb.

VOICE OF A CHARACTER

READING

In ninth grade I was a great admirer of Jesus Christ. He was everywhere at Sacred Heart: perched over doorways and in corners, peering from calendars and felt wall hangings. I liked his woeful eyebrows and the way his thin, delicate legs crossed at the ankles. The stained-glass windows in our chapel looked like piles of wet candy to me, and from the organ came sounds that seemed to rise from another world, a world of ecstasy and violence.

FROM THE STORY "SACRED HEART," BY JENNIFER EGAN

LESSON

An introduction like this is akin to meeting a precocious, thoughtful child, one whose oddness we mistake for innocence and honesty. Egan opens her story with her character's voice coming forth in no shy way. She tells us she *admires* Jesus Christ, an odd word to use for its everydayness. People admire their dads, admire the President, have secret admirers, but talk of religious figures usually inspires more lofty feelings like reverence or worship. That Egan's character *admires* Jesus Christ makes her significant in one short sentence.

She mentions common, human qualities to explain why she admires Jesus Christ. She ends this passage in the spirit she began with, another odd combination of words, the conjoining of ecstacy and violence. The voice in design is a speaking voice, but it is literary in form.

WRITING POSSIBILITIES

1. Make a list of five people you would not necessarily think of admiring. Write these out as sentences. Some examples: As a boy, I was a great admirer of my postman. I was a great admirer of Buddha.

2. Take another look at Egan's second sentence. Using an example from your list, position the admired person in at least three places.

3. Give the person at least three physical attributes. Egan does this in her fourth sentence.

4. Note how the sound of the organ *seems to rise from a world of ecstasy and violence*. List five words that might take the place of *world*. For example: a state of . . . ; a place of . . .

5. Use your list from exercise two and complete the movement begun in exercise four with a combination of words that do not seem suited for each other. For example: . . . a place of joy and pain; . . . a state of bliss and anxiety.

6. Combine the first five exercises.

NONFICTION BY THE NUMBERS

READING

Like many people I do my life by the numbers, or if not my life exactly, then at least my personal habits—the small, secret hygienes no one, not my wife, not my children, is privy to. Each day I brush from left to right and top to bottom as if I were reading my teeth. I shave the right side of my face before the left. I lather my privates three times and follow the invented, customized rituals of my morning shower with all the formality and inflexibility of a coronation.

FROM THE ESSAY "OUT OF ONE'S TREE," BY STANLEY ELKIN

LESSON

As we seek to lend small and large structures to our work for the sake of clarity and the feel of intention, we might depend on more than logical procession of one idea to another. We might use a natural pattern the reader already knows. Think of it as the equivalent of drawing arrows, or the way road signs work on the highway. In this essay, the writer has found a way to convey the aspects of his life by using numbers. His character, his point of view, his setting, his time and his story find life inside a frame constructed with numbers. He uses numbers as a device, a mechanism that enlivens and animates the writing.

WRITING POSSIBILITIES

1. In the quote, Elkin writes of personal habits. List five other aspects of life that might be explored with numbers. One example might be the planting of your garden.

2. Let's try one by the numbers. Let this be the beginning of your own personal essay. Begin: I like to do my life by the numbers. . . . (Pick one from your list in exercise one and continue.)

3. What other ways might you organize a personal essay? List ten possibilities. For example: by the clock; by the week.

4. Select one from exercise three and try a new method of organizing elements. For example: Like a lot of people, I live my life by the clock. Not so much the obvious up by six, lunch at noon and all the rest, but the little bits of time like a must-have cup of coffee by quarter after eight and a long moment of silence before going to bed. . . .

5. So far we have limited ourselves to numbers, but what about colors, or food, or weather? List ten more of these and then select one and try a new opening. For example: My life, I am pleased to say, is made meaningful by the television. On television is where I have learned everything I need to know. . . .

FICTION BY THE NUMBERS

READING

Number One, Lance.

But first let me make this clear: it's more than a headline in a bright-colored tabloid, BABY FOUND IN WOMB WITH WOODEN LEG. Or a blurb on the third page of a quality newspaper: WOMAN WEDS FOR 34TH TIME (I'm in Love with Love, says Blushing Bride). It was seven times, something any of us might do if our lives were higgledy-piggledy enough, like Amelia's, or if God had given us what he gave her, a soul too nerveless to stand the sight of much: anything frail or newborn; blood spilled, real or imagined. . . .

FROM THE STORY "MY SISTER HAD SEVEN HUSBANDS," BY DEBRA MONROE

LESSON

Numbers can sometimes be the map we need to guide the reader, a way for our narrators to order the often confusing the world they wish to convey. This narrator has decided to tell her sister's story through her seven marriages, but notice how from the start the storyteller is not bound by this frame. She begins with *Number One, Lance. But first let me . . .* At the outset she begins to digress, to make lateral moves, exercising the strength of her imagination and the range of her experience. Using numbers in this story seems to afford the teller more license rather than less. The teller can move afield, depending upon numbers as a means by which to return.

WRITING POSSIBILITIES

1. Rewrite the title ten times with the intention of finding your own story to tell. For example: "My Brother Had Four Wives," "My Cat Had Nine Lives," "I Died Three Times."

2. Select one from your list in exercise one and begin a story. For example: The first time was in the desert.

But first let me make this clear: (here is where you address the ambition of your title).

3. The writer uses the numbers to frame the story, but within such a frame is every opportunity for the storyteller to tell with imagination and distinct voice. For instance: *It was seven times, something any of us might do if our lives were higgledy-piggledy enough, like Amelia's, or if God had given us what he gave her, a soul too nerveless to stand the sight of much: anything frail or newborn; blood spilled, real or imagined. . . .* This sentence expands the title beyond the edges of its frame. Try this. Begin: It was (number) times, a thing any of us might do if _____, like (name), or if God had _____, a _____: anything _____; _____, _____.

VOICE OF AN AUTHOR

READING

So he went on down there. He went there in his truck.

It rained.

Mrs. Finn was in the kitchen, kneading dough for her daily bread. Around her waist was a calico apron the mice had long since chewed through.

FROM THE STORY "HE HAS BEEN TO MACY'S," BY NOY HOLLAND

LESSON

This story is from a first collection titled *The Spectacle of the Body*. This writer is on the way to owning a sentence, a line, a way of writing. At times it is strange and dreamy and sometimes downright confusing, but then at that very moment a clutch of words makes you forget you were lost. Think of this as writing that is close to the mind at work, writing that comes to the page before it can be told. It seems to be a sound unfiltered, a sound closer to the consciousness that created it than it is to the reader's expectation. The language takes chances as it tries itself out.

The quote above is the opening of the story. In terms of the entire collection, it is quite tame. But see how the story begins with the word *So*. Does this indicate consequence? Conjunction? Is it simply colloquial? Note the sentence/paragraph *It rained*. It seems to be an affectation, maybe a whimsy, but shortly we come upon *kneading dough for her daily bread*. Of a sudden the rain becomes more, a hint of the biblical. Do not mistake a voice like this to be without design and intention for all its appearance to the contrary.

WRITING POSSIBILITIES

1. Begin with a conjunction: and, but, or, nor, for, so, yet. Write ten sets of sentences that work like the first two sentences in the quote. For example: (a) And he came on Tuesday. He came there on his motorcycle. (b) But she had to leave. She had to leave before it was too late.

2. Savor the simplicity of the next one-sentence paragraph *It rained*. Try ten of these yourself. Two examples: It snowed. It got dark.

3. Move on to the last two sentences. Do ten of these. For example: Mary was on the porch, shucking corn for dinner. On her feet were red sneakers, the laces long since frayed away. Mr. Finn was in the kitchen, fixing the pipes under the sink for the water to travel. On his head he wore a green cap that said John Deere.

4. From exercises one, two and three you now have at least thirty entries, maybe even the beginnings of thirty stories. Start to make combinations from your list. With the few examples given above, we might devise something like:

And he came on Tuesday. He came there on his motorcycle.

It got dark.

Mr. Finn was in the kitchen, fixing the pipes under the sink for the water to travel. On his head he wore a green cap that said John Deere.

5. Where to go from here? Holland's next line begins a new paragraph: *The last stretch, he walked, leaving his truck....* (Continue.)

VOICE OF A CHARACTER NARRATOR

READING

. . . He had a young-looking face but his hair was bone white. You could tell by his eyes that he was plastered to the hairline, but otherwise he looked like any other nice young guy in a dinner jacket who had been spending too much money in a joint that exists for that purpose and for no other.

There was a girl beside him. Her hair was a lovely shade of dark red and she had a distant smile on her lips and over her shoulders she had a blue mink that almost made the Rolls-Royce look like just another automobile. It didn't quite. Nothing can.

FROM THE NOVEL *THE LONG GOODBYE*, BY RAYMOND CHANDLER

LESSON

Chandler has used perhaps the most difficult way to introduce a character. He depends upon appearance, physical features. But another character, the narrator, comes to us in an even more difficult way—via the sound of his voice. If we were there, we could see what he sees. This is simple enough, but it really isn't about what is seen. It's how he sees, and how he tells of what he sees, that makes us want to read.

Notice how the character's hair is *bone white* and how in the next sentence he is *plastered to the hairline.* Chandler is writing with a twinkle in his eye. He is playing off the white hair and the white of plaster, and "plastered" meaning drunk. The colors are red, white and blue. There is opulence in the dinner jacket and the mink and the Rolls-Royce, but it is not left alone. The storyteller brings an attitude that shapes what he sees. He is the hard-boiled detective, the unimpressed observer. He slants and shapes what he describes: the *young-looking face*, but the *bone white* hair; drunk but nice. Our narrators are not necessarily like us. They may have ways of observing and telling that are not like us at all.

WRITING POSSIBILITIES

1. Chandler is making observations of his characters rather than describing them. He is telling us the story of how they appear to him. He uses phrases like *you could tell* and *he looked like.* Use these phrases yourself in a brief character description. Begin with one of the following: He looked to me like someone who . . . ; She appeared to have . . . ; At first glance, he was. . . .

2. Realize that the words of description reveal the person who is doing the describing as well as the person described. From this point on, think of language as something that goes two ways. It is not so

much that someone is handsome or homely, but who is saying they are handsome or homely? Realize your character's opinions reflect on the character. Write a paragraph in which one character describes another, making sure that the description reflects clearly on the character who is describing.

3. To use the word *but* does not cancel or challenge a prior description, but makes it more complex. Write a paragraph using the word *but*. Begin with one of the following: She was pretty as the day is long, but her eyes gave up her age . . . ; He wore a new suit of clothes and at first he looked like a businessman, but his hands were raw and calloused. . . .

DREAM LANGUAGE

READING

The voice stops. The burned man looks straight ahead in his morphine focus.

The plane is now in his eye. The slow voice carries it with effort above the earth, the engine missing turns as if losing a stitch, her shroud unfurling in the noisy air of the cockpit, noise terrible after his days of walking in silence. He looks down and sees oil pouring onto his knees. A branch breaks free of her shirt. Acacia and bone. How high is he above the land? How low is he in the sky?

The undercarriage brushes the top of a palm and he pivots up, and the oil slides over the seat, her body slipping down into it. There is a spark from a short, and the twigs at her knee catch fire. He pulls her back into the seat beside him. He thrusts his hands up against the cockpit glass and it will not shift. Begins punching the glass, cracking it, finally breaking it, and the oil and the fire slop and spin everywhere. How low is he in the sky? She collapses—acacia twigs, leaves, the branches that were shaped into arms uncoiling around him. Limbs begin disappearing in the suck of air. The odour of morphine on his tongue.

FROM THE NOVEL *THE ENGLISH PATIENT*, BY MICHAEL ONDAATJE

LESSON

There is language meant to be heard and language meant to be read and also, there are the languages of the mind. These are internal and listened to only by ourselves. So, too, with our characters, and as writers it is our task to represent the mind's experience on the page. This character, the English Patient, is a man too injured to move, burned beyond recognition and dependent on morphine to dull his pain. His identity is kept a mystery throughout the novel, both to us and to the characters around him. Ondaatje uses this dream as a necessary revelation in the novel's plot. The English Patient is remembering in the guise of a dream.

Ondaatje uses the urgent present tense and unfamiliar slant of language, words as if through gauze, to describe the memory's events. This is a dream not only in sleep, but affected by medication. This is not only a dream of image, but a dream of the mind—the English Patient is remembering the workings of his mind when he was a pilot and able to move. This dream delivers this character beyond his current capacity. He sees his way into this dream with a *morphine focus*, and the phrase *the plane is now in his eye*. Memory is personal, selective, amorphous and emotional. It is even more so in the sleep of the medicated.

WRITING POSSIBILITIES

1. Think of dreams you have had when you weren't asleep, perhaps daydreams or fever dreams. These are experiences with dreamlike qualities. Call them dreams in the half-sleep. Do you dream differently when you are, say, asleep in a boat rather than on land, when you've had a few drinks or are dozing in the sun? List five more conditions for dream experiences like these.

2. Be so bold as to use a dream to reveal something about your character that he or she is incapable of revealing any other way. Bring your character to this moment the way Ondaatje does. For example: The sound ceases. Sian looks straight ahead in his whiskey haze. The swerving automobile is now all he can see. . . .

3. What can reveal a dream to someone who watches another sleeping—movements, sleep talk, teeth grinding? Select an example from exercise one and write from the observer's point of view. For example: Sian was clenching his fists again, tangling up bed sheet and blanket. She didn't know what she could do to help. She knew it was the accident and he was going through it all over again. . . .

THE SOUND OF A SETTING

READING

Only the dimming lights of the receding harbor were visible in an ink-black sky. We could feel the heavy storm clouds overhead about to burst into rain, and it was suffocating, in spite of the wind and cold.

FROM THE STORY "AT SEA: A SAILOR'S STORY," BY ANTON CHEKHOV

LESSON

This is the opening to Chekhov's story. A small good lesson can be learned by looking closely at the first sentence. There is no action, yet the sentence seems so full of hushed movement, because of the words *dimming* and *receding*. Chekhov puts objects in motion instead of beginning with a dramatic scene full of characters in motion. He is following a sound and we cannot help but go along.

The same goes for the second sentence. Technically, there are two verbs, *feel* and *was*, and still no actual movement. And yet, there is movement by its absence and its imminence, by the sound of the *s* in so many of the words. Movement flows from the *about to burst* phrase. To risk a point, one could say that in this opening nothing is happening, which runs counter to so much of what we are told to do as writers. But it is clear that much is happening, much at stake by the way the words hold our ear, and it is accomplished through the descriptive words: *dimming, receding* and *suffocating*. This is an opening to be heard as well as seen.

WRITING POSSIBILITIES

1. Consider how the appearance of motion can create motion. It's just as easy to set a thing moving with an adjective as with a verb and what you are achieving is twofold, motion within stillness. For example: the waning moon (as opposed to the moon waned), the setting sun (as opposed to the sun set). Make twenty sets using action words as adjectives, the -ed and -ing form of a word. For example: the rushing water, the blowing wind, the warming sun, the hurried pace.

2. Rewrite a line of Chekhov using two of your sets from exercise one. Echoing—and doing justice to—such a classic opening is nearly impossible, but try as best you can. For example: Only the sound of falling rain and running water could be heard.

3. The verb *be* and its forms—*is, was, were, am, are*—can make powerful declarations and define simple relationships. You can use them to hold together a setting as Chekhov did. For example: The shining light was drawing us in its direction . . . ; the sliding door was coming to a close before we could get there. . . .

4. Use Chekhov's *about* construction to create a sense of imminence. Do ten sets. A few examples: The tree was about to fall . . . ; I was about at the end of my rope . . . ; We were about there when. . . .

5. Combine the above exercises to create an opening like Chekhov's. Use the following frame: Only the ____ing ____ of the ____ ing ____ were visible in an ink-black sky. We could feel the ____ about to ____, and it was ____, in spite of the ____ and ____.

LANGUAGE OF SETTING

READING

Along the western slopes of the Oregon Coastal Range . . . come look: the hysterical crashing of tributaries as they merge into the Wakonda Auga River . . .

The first little washes flashing like thick rushing winds through sheep sorrel and clover, ghost fern and nettle, sheering, cutting . . . forming branches. Then, through bearberry and salmonberry, blueberry and blackberry, the branches crashing into creeks, into streams. Finally, in the foothills, through tamarack and sugar pine, shittim bark and silver spruce—and the green and blue mosaic of Douglas fir—the actual river falls five hundred feet . . . and look: opens out upon the fields.

FROM THE NOVEL *SOMETIMES A GREAT NOTION,* BY KEN KESEY

LESSON

A way to craft the language of setting is to step back and paint a larger picture. Think about maps and ranges and the whole run of a river, what you can't see from one spot on the earth. Geography is as familiar to us as times tables and spelling, another way our readers can locate themselves in our stories. To open a setting this way, Kesey names his state—Oregon—and the specific land formation he wants us to think of—the western slopes of the Coastal Range. He takes us down through the tributaries of the Wakonda Auga River. We could follow his progress with our finger on a map. Phrases such as *come look* and, again, *look* address the reader. They function as a gentle hand on the shoulder, a guide through this vast place.

Kesey uses the -ing form of his verbs for action: *flashing, sheering, cutting*; and he uses it to name things: *crashing of the tributaries*; and he uses it for description: *rushing winds*. Note, too, the specificity of the nouns: his shrubs and trees are not merely underbrush, but *blueberry and blackberry, tamarack* and *silver spruce*. These natural features bring the geography of this setting into three dimensions.

WRITING POSSIBILITIES

1. Create a list of ten phrases that direct the reader to join you in viewing a panorama. Examples are: look at this . . . ; come see . . . ; it's like this. . . .

2. The -ing form of a verb conveys continuous action. Kesey uses the -ing form to make verbs, but also to make nouns and adjectives. The use of the same construction for all three creates a feeling of near hypermotion. Everything is moving: the river itself, the sound it makes, even the way it seems. Fill in these blanks: (noun) the _____ing was

poor . . . ; (verb) the _____ing of the wood took all day . . . ; (adjective) the _____ing light and the _____ing darkness . . . Come up with ten -ing verb phrases of your own for each part of speech.

3. Use the names of trees, flowers, birds, animals, rocks and minerals to evoke a place. As a writer, you are obliged to know these names, whatever your world of reference. It lends authority to your work. Consider the atlas a valuable resource. In the same way you'd browse through a dictionary, browse through the index of an atlas. Make a list of twenty place names you like. Try Arabia, North Carolina, or French Asylum, Pennsylvania. Don't limit yourself to the names of cities and towns. Include the names of rivers, lakes, streams, mountains.

LANGUAGE OF THE GROTESQUE

READING
. . . Ollie grasped the handle and with a heave slid the door open.

As Howard remembered the event later, it was as if the moment Ollie opened the door, they were spacemen on an alien, hostile planet. The sunlight, he decided, caused the feeling, illuminating the snow-covered fields like a vast sheet of rippling, white-hot steel, the hills beyond dark and grim. In fact, as Howard remembered, he had watched Turtle begin his pantomime before he had seen the cow, though it lay in frozen gore nearly at his feet. He had been fascinated with the hunchback—on his knees, tongue out, eyes bulging, cheeks taut—and he believed that at that second he had guessed the truth before he had actually seen it, though of course you couldn't be sure about such things. It was Ollie's awed voice saying "My Jesus" that had taken his eyes from the hunchback to the steer, cut in half with a chain saw. What he last remembered, the image that stayed deep in his mind, to rise up in dreams and odd waking moments, was the hunchback's completing his imitation, his face beside the severed steer, their expressions identical, and his thought at the time, how marvelous the human mind, and Ollie's words, "My Jesus . . . my Jesus . . . my sweet Jesus, what a sense of humor that boy has got."

FROM THE NOVEL *THE DOGS OF MARCH*, BY ERNEST HEBERT

LESSON
In this passage we only glimpse what is so very unsettling. We learn that one way of crafting such a terrible scene is by not writing it at all, but by depending upon the thoughts and perceptions of our characters.

Consider the number of worlds we pass through: memory, decision, emotion, fascination, belief, speculation, truth, dream. There is the out-of-doors, the passing through to the interior of the barn. Each character inhabits a separate place and perceives in a particular manner. It's as if the scene were orchestrated rather than written. Even before Howard witnesses the carcass, he is pulling away on our behalf while at the same time fixing it forever in memory. The final observation is Ollie's, his *awed voice* lending a touch of the sacred by invoking the name of Jesus as if a hymn or a benediction and then concluding with the idea of it all being humorous. Consider this a lesson in what not to write, a lesson in the judicious use of words. The scene works because we learn what we need to, which is not so much singular image but how that image settles into our characters.

WRITING POSSIBILITIES

1. Imagine a scene such as the one in the quote: three very different people come to a strange moment. List five sets. For example: Bill, Roger and the tattooed man come across a body while fishing; Suzie, Kimberlee and the new girl find a litter of frozen kittens in the shed.

2. Go to sentences two, three and four of the quote. This language precedes the *frozen gore nearly at our feet*. First Hebert unmoors the reader with talk of aliens. Then he delivers an image of strange beauty. Then, beginning with *In fact,* he leads us to what we are to see. Try this yourself. Maintain Hebert's length of line. Begin: As _____ remembered the event later, it was as if _____. The _____, he decided, caused _____. In fact, as _____ remembered, _____. _____ had been fascinated with the _____ — _____ —and (he/she) believed that at that second (he/she) had guessed the truth before. . . . It was _____'s awed voice saying . . .

3. Pick another set from your list in exercise one and begin again. Let this be the opening of a story.

LANGUAGE OF EVENT

READING
She could hear the distant sound of the calliope and she saw in her head all the tents raised up in a kind of gold sawdust light and the diamond ring of the ferris wheel going around and around up in the air and down again and the screeking merry-go-round going around and around on the ground.

FROM THE STORY "A TEMPLE OF THE HOLY GHOST," BY FLANNERY O'CONNOR

LESSON

Familiar events such as holidays, birthdays, fairs and weddings are difficult to make new because the words we use to describe such events are so common, but sometimes we can turn this to our advantage. We can send our character into a familiar world and allow her to see it differently. This quote can be read for how time, setting, point of view, narrative and character all cross the same threshold. In fact, this quote is but one sentence and to remove a single facet would diminish its power. Notice how O'Connor uses her character's eyes and ears to make us experience this familiar event in a whole new light. After all, this character is a whole new person to the world, bound to be unique.

Notice the phrase *she saw in her head*. We don't usually think of someone seeing in their heads. It is almost as if she were imagining the scene she is seeing. Though the scene is described with precise detail, it takes on a dreamlike, almost surreal quality. O'Connor uses the word *and* five times, the word *around* four times. This unites the images and keeps them in motion. Consider the phrase: *a kind of gold sawdust light and the diamond ring of the ferris wheel*. O'Connor links related images, going from *gold* to *diamond* to *ring* to *wheel*. These images connect the sentence, and they add a metallic shimmer to the scene as a whole.

WRITING POSSIBILITIES

1. Write a short passage in which a character approaches an event such as a circus, a funeral, a wedding, a birthday party, an anniversary, a concert, a Thanksgiving dinner. Use the phrases O'Connor uses, *she could hear* and *she saw*. Include the other senses: He could feel . . . ; She could taste . . . ; He could hear it and it sounded like . . . ; The smell reminded me of . . .

2. Events follow a pattern, and our minds deliver these events to us as static pictures, but do not forget they are in constant motion. O'Connor describes the tents as *raised up*, the ferris wheel is going *around* and *up* and *down*, the merry-go-round is going *around and around*. Revise or expand your passage from exercise one to include movement. For example: The dancers moved round and round, weaving . . . ; The party-goers laughed and drank under the raised tent, under the high July sun . . . ; We stood by the lowering of the black casket. . . .

3. Notice how the merry-go-round is also *screeking*. Invent a word that names a sound like *screeking* does. A wooden chair on a wooden floor? Walking through sand? The sound of a deep fry? Add this word to your description, but try not to call attention to your coinage. Use it as you would any other descriptive word.

4. A small thing to do. Note the phrase *gold sawdust light*. As an exercise, find words with which to replace *sawdust*. Perhaps *evening, winter* or *pine*. Now think of words to precede *gold light*. Perhaps *wet, scaly, white, brittle*. These are difficult exercises because O'Connor has laid claim to that phrase and no change quite measures up. To rethink in even a small way becomes difficult, but these small movements give life to the whole. The exercise allows you to stretch your vocabulary and your imagination, to make the phrase your own.

VOICE OF SOUND

READING

No noises after dark, at least none like the sounds in a town, the hoarse calling of trains, the rattle of wheels and clack of hoofs and squeak of a dry axle in the street, the unfamiliar roar of an automobile coming around a corner and diminishing, softening, disappearing again down another street you could imagine, tree-lined, pooled with shadows, perhaps a single light in the gable of some house, and the dark pitch of roofs cutting off the stars. Nothing here but the soft continuous murmur like a sigh from the trees crowding the clearing, nothing but the padded blow of an erratic, tree-broken wind on the canvas roof, the faint rustle of needles falling from the fir at the back corner of the tent and skating down the canvas incline. No noises but inanimate creakings and rustlings that you strained to hear and were never satisfied with, stealthy noises that eluded identification and kept you straining for their repetition, noises too soft to be comforting, noises without the surety and satisfaction of trains calling or freight cars jarring as they coupled in the yards beyond the dark.

FROM THE NOVEL *THE BIG ROCK CANDY MOUNTAIN*, BY WALLACE STEGNER

LESSON

Elsa has been scalded by water. She is now listening to the world outside as she recuperates. Is this setting? Is it character? Point of view? It's clearly all of these. It's the writer doing what only writers can do: making words fit together in an absolutely beautiful way.

The quote is three long sentences. They begin *No noises . . . , Nothing . . . , No noises. . . .*, and then each of the negatives is contradicted within the next few words. How else to unlock this quote as being representative of a writer's voice? We could talk about sibilance (the *s* sound), consonance (terminal consonant sounds) and assonance (repeated vowel sounds), could analyze and dissect, but that's no fun.

Too much like work. Do this—wait until nightfall and turn down the lights and read the quote again and again. Read it aloud in a whisper. Read it slowly. Read it in a corner or a closet where your reading might gain resonance as it is faintly echoed back to you. This, too, is what writers do.

WRITING POSSIBILITIES

1. Let's experience this quote simply by changing *noises* to *sights* and proceeding from there. Be diligent and maintain Stegner's length of phrase. Begin: No sights after dark, at least none like the sights in a town, the _____, the _____ and _____ and _____, the _____ of _____ coming around a corner and _____ down another street you could imagine, _____, _____, perhaps a _____, and the _____. Nothing here but the _____ like a _____ from the _____, nothing but the _____ . . . (Conclude this sentence and continue.)

2. This time let's rewrite by reversing the negative constructions. Rewrite the quote for what is present, whether it be of eye or ear. Begin with: Some noises after dark, the sounds in a town . . . ; Something here, a soft continuous murmur . . . ; Some noises, inanimate creakings and rustlings . . .

3. Break away from the quote this time. What is another condition that may exist outside us? For example: No rain after so many days, at least none like what's needed, the rain that soaks . . . ; Nothing of rain . . . ; No rain but . . .

A TELLING VOICE

READING

Pretty soon I wanted to smoke, and asked the widow to let me. But she wouldn't. She said it was a mean practice and wasn't clean, and I must try to not do it any more. That is just the way with some people. They get down on a thing when they don't know nothing about it. Here she was a bothering about Moses, which was no kin to her, and no use to anybody, being gone, you see, yet finding a power of fault with me for doing a thing that had some good in it. And she took snuff too; of course that was all right, because she done it herself.

FROM THE NOVEL HUCKLEBERRY FINN, BY MARK TWAIN

LESSON

Here's a fine example of Huck doing what we expect all great characters to do with their thinking time: cogitating on the various aspects of life. He is mulling over what he's been told, what he's heard and seen and he's trying to make it all match. Remember, this is a young boy, but remember, too, it's Huck, the young boy sprung from the mind of Mark Twain. What more is there to say? When you create a Huck Finn, you are creating a voice. Huck is precocious and willful in his ideas. When he thinks something, he believes it to be true. We can give this sort of confidence to our characters and make it part of their charm so that they are pleasures to live with.

Coincidentally, Huck shares Twain's shrewd, mischievous eye for human frailty. And that eye has a twinkle in it. Characters who have the voice of a natural born storyteller, characters who are smart, give us aid and comfort as we log the hours it takes to do this work. Huck as a talker, as a teller, has a sound all his own, and it is a sound we never want to stop.

WRITING POSSIBILITIES

1. Create a character who sounds like Huck and give him a situation to mull over. Two examples: Marjorie doesn't know why she can't wear makeup when Mom does. Milton doesn't know why he has to go to church when his father doesn't. Write a sentence in which he states that situation.

2. Consider Twain's sentence: *That is just the way with some people.* This is an example of Huck's little wisdoms. Come up with five of your own and use your best one to follow the sentence in exercise one.

3. Now it's time to take your character through some thinking. Be generous with her way of thinking. For example: I decided I wanted to wear makeup and asked my mother about it. She said, no way. She said I was too young and too pretty already which didn't make sense to me because I thought she was already pretty too. . . . (Continue.)

4. Let's separate Huck from his voice. Let's give it to a storyteller who is telling us about Huck. Rewrite the passage. Begin: Pretty soon Huck wanted to smoke, and asked the widow to let him. But she wouldn't. She said it was a mean practice and wasn't clean, and he must try . . . (Continue.)

5. In exercise four we separated Huck from his voice. You wouldn't have thought it, but the voice still holds up. Perhaps it isn't quite as compelling, but you can't deny that it is still pretty strong. Now try something as strange as this voice in second person, present tense. Rewrite the quote. Begin: Pretty soon you want to smoke, and ask the widow to let you. But she won't. She says it's a mean practice and isn't clean, and you . . . (Continue.)

Here again, the voice seems to survive. It seems to exist as something more than the sum of its parts.

VOICE OF ENTRY

READING

We dash the black river, its flats smooth as stone. Not a ship, not a dinghy, not one cry of white. The water lies broken, cracked from the wind. This great estuary is wide, endless. The river is brackish, blue with the cold. It passes beneath us blurring. The sea birds hang above it, they wheel, disappear. We flash the wide river, a dream of the past. The deeps fall behind, the bottom is paling the surface, we rush by the shallows, boats beached for winter, desolate piers. And on wings like the gulls, soar up, turn, look back.

The day is white as paper. The windows are chilled. The quarries lie empty, the silver mine drowned. The Hudson is vast here, vast and unmoving. . . .

FROM THE NOVEL *LIGHT YEARS*, BY JAMES SALTER

LESSON

This is the opening to Salter's novel. A voice is taking us into the drama. From such an opening you might expect the novel to be first person. In a very strict sense, it is. The first person plural is used in the first several paragraphs, and then not again until the very end. An "I" is present in the "We." That "I" might be the author taking us on this tour. What to make of this? Simply put, behind every piece of writing is a writer, whether revealed or not. Perhaps by using *we*, he includes the reader along with himself. We are doing these things with him, but we are present only in the frame of his story. He is positioning us as audience to his story. We are brought close, but kept at a safe distance from where we might see and listen. Think of it as being in an airplane. Think of it also as cinematic. Even think of it as if we are figures in a Chagall painting floating over the town, or like Peter Pan and we are flying. The precedents and antecedents are many. No matter. For a moment, the writer calls on our attention, settles us in and the play of the narrative drama commences in the present tense—here and now and that's where we are.

WRITING POSSIBILITIES

1. Reread the quote, omitting the first person plural *we*. For instance: Dash the black river. . . . Flash the wide river. . . .

Notice how the *we* is still there, only now it is silent and implied, almost an imperative.

2. Read into the quote for the commas. The length of line, the way it is broken and then continued is a feature of this writer's way of telling. The effect is one of incantation. The lines are being weighed or

measured, as if they are ingredients. Try this. Begin: We dash the _____, its _____ _____ as _____. _____, _____, _____. . . . (Continue.)

3. In the second paragraph, don't overlook the work that the word *here* does—*The Hudson is vast here, vast and unmoving.* . . . The word *there* would not work. It does not have anywhere near the proximity, the intimacy, the immediacy. Try a single sentence like this. Begin: The _____ is _____ here, _____ and _____.

4. Combine the elements of exercises one, two, and three into your own opening, maybe a novel or a piece of nonfiction. Begin: We . . .

5. How then does the writer move into the third person? He follows the quote above with history and image of place and then departs from the first person plural in the sixth and seventh paragraphs. He does it this way:

We strolled in the garden, eating the small, bitter apples. The trees were dry and gnarled. The lights in the kitchen were on.

A car comes up the driveway, back from the city. . . .

Rewrite the transition for your own opening. Perhaps it comes as soon as the third paragraph for you. Begin: We _____, _____ the _____. The _____ were _____ and _____. The lights _____.

A car _____ . . . (Continue.)

VOICE OF PLACE

READING

A Georgia peach, a real Georgia peach, a backyard great-grand-mother's-orchard peach, is as thickly furred as a sweater, and so fluent and sweet that once you bite through the flannel, it brings tears to your eyes. The voices of the coastal people were like half-wild and lovely local peaches, compared to the bald, dry, homogeneous peaches displayed at a slant in the national chain supermarkets.

"Come in! Come in! Let's have some gossip and slander!" cried an old man living near the sea, whenever a passerby roamed within sight of his porch. "I believe these young ladies of today might clothe themselves more modestly," he said. "Of course, I am getting on and it has been many years since I was conversant with the wherewithal and nomenclature of the female."

For most of this century the McIntosh County black people lived much as they had since emancipation.

FROM THE BOOK *PRAYING FOR SHEETROCK*, BY MELISSA FAY GREENE

LESSON

Writers must try to contain the spirit of a place and a time and its people, but these can never be fully collected or catalogued. Each depends on whole sciences—geology, sociology, psychology—and each would fill a book. The quote does amazing service in the pursuit of a corner of the earth. The peach makes for place and bends around to the people, the people to language and language to history. The moves are bold and the embrace is wide-armed.

This writer has but a few hundred pages to tell a grand story. She depends on her imagination to make connections that provide in an instant a feeling, a sensitivity, a perception that otherwise would take reams of data and still never come to be coherent and full. Greene's *Praying for Sheetrock* is the story of a place and its people and the struggle of a people for equality, but the eye and hand of the storyteller are those of the poet or fiction writer who rely more often on imagination than on fact. But of course by now it is silly to make such distinctions. Of all writing, we require a hand that is felicitous, a mind that is sharp, and an eye that sees what we cannot.

WRITING POSSIBILITIES

1. Start where you live. Brace yourself for some silliness, but can you capture your place in one of its foods? What would some of those likenesses be? Come up with five that are local to you and then five more from places you know well. For example: Maple syrup, real New Hampshire maple syrup . . .

2. Take the word *peach*. The first sentence immerses us in the peach experience. Try a sentence like that. Use the following frame: _____, a real _____, a _____, is _____ as a _____, and so _____ and _____ that once you. . . . (Continue.)

3. Notice how the word *fluent* sits quietly in the first sentence. The taste of a peach being *fluent*? It leads us to the next sentence, *The voices of the coastal people . . . Fluent* begets *voices* and the reference to voice leads to the sound of voice. Did you write a word that can work this way? If not, go back and change one of your words.

4. The sound of the old man's voice in the second paragraph works like music in a movie. A snatch of speech such as this is tailor-made to creating a vivid and specific sense of place. In the making of nonfiction, collect these small speeches the way you collect images with your camera. Write them in a notebook.

5. The quote ends with a third kind of writing, not speech or description, but something that sounds like fact. Now write a new three-paragraph movement concluding with such a sentence.

VOICE TO VOICE

READING

Ray, you are a doctor and you are in a hospital in Mobile, except now you are a patient but you're still me. Say what? You say you want to know who I am?

I have a boat on the water. I have magnificent children. I have a wife who turns her beauty on and off like a light switch.

But I can think myself out of this. My mind can do it. It did it before, can do it again, as when I was pilot of the jet when I was taking the obnoxious rich people in their Lear from Montreal to New York to Charlotte to Pensacola to New Orleans to Mexico City to the Yucatán to Tuscaloosa, Alabama, because they had a old friend there.

You can do it, mind and heart. You can give it the throttle and pick up your tail and ease it on. You can do it, Ray.

FROM THE NOVELLA *RAY*, BY BARRY HANNAH

LESSON

We have here a voice on the edge of control. Sometimes such voices are in our heads and want to come out. This is a high, adamant voice and will not be denied. Such voices can be stagelike, or stereotyped, or simply uninteresting, have nothing to say. Style over substance. But this voice has capacity and range. The storytelling is in first person, but he often refers to himself in the third person. He has discussions with himself, carries on dialogues.

Consider the middle paragraphs, a sentence like *I have a wife who turns her beauty on and off like a light switch*. This sentence is like a signature. It shows this writer's delight, bravado, and deliberate use of language. Ray is a doctor and was the pilot of a jet. He tells us this. He has a boat and magnificent children. He believes in his mind and heart. There is no one else like Ray. How can we not keep reading?

WRITING POSSIBILITIES

1. Let's try out a voice like the one in the quote: exciting, excitable and excited, maybe not quite normal. Rewrite the beginning of the quote using the following frame:

(Name), you are a _____ and you are in a _____ in (city), except now you are _____ but you're still me. Say what? You say you want to know who I am?

I have _____. I have _____. I have a (husband/wife) who _____.

2. Now change the word *have* to the word *think*. Do three sentences you might substitute to make the quote a bit more your own. For

example: I think children should be seen and not heard. I think France is a beautiful country. . . . (Continue.)

3. The third paragraph continues with Ray's voice and, at the same time, begins to sketch in backstory. Let's try a single paragraph like this. Begin: My brain can do it. It did it before, can do it again, as when . . . (Continue a bit of history for your character.)

4. Let's try the whole quote in this exercise. Begin again with a new name, new character:

(Name), you are a _____ and you are in a _____ in (city), except now you are _____ but you're still me. Say what? You say you want to know who I am?

I know that _____. I know that _____. I know my (husband/wife) to be _____ . . . (Continue.)

FIRST PERSON, A CHILD

READING

"If it runs, a Bean will shoot it! If it falls, a Bean will eat it," Daddy says, and his lip curls. A million times Daddy says, "Earlene, don't go over on the Beans' side of the right-of-way. Not ever!"

Daddy's bedroom is pine-paneled . . . the real kind. Daddy done it all. He filled the nail holes with MIRACLE WOOD. One weekend after we was all settled in, Daddy gets up on a chair and opens a can of MIRACLE WOOD. He works it into the nail holes with a putty knife. He needs the chair 'cause he's probably the littlest man in Egypt, Maine.

FROM THE NOVEL *THE BEANS OF EGYPT, MAINE*, BY CAROLYN CHUTE

LESSON

Earlene is the storyteller for part of this novel, though when she grows older, the point of view moves into the third person. Children are difficult characters to create as it is, but to turn over a significant part of the storytelling to a child and especially a child like Earlene is a particular challenge. She is too young to write, is not contemplative, is not precocious in a bookish sense, is not privileged, is not contrived to be more than she can be, and yet her words ring so true. She makes observations and remembers what she is told.

It is the writer's ear and experience and talent that gets her onto the page without device or sentiment, without patronizing or condescending. Earlene gives us all that we require from any storyteller—a sound we can hear in our heads telling us something we do not know. She is coming to us with the news of what it is to be a poor child in Egypt, Maine, living next door to the Bean family.

WRITING POSSIBILITIES

1. It is our natural inclination with children to interact, to join in and converse, to correct them and improve them, and before we know it, we are the talkers and they are the listeners. Begin to add to your drawer of notes the sayings of children. Share the room with children at play; hide behind a newspaper, your note pad in your lap, and listen.

2. Imagine a child quoting you. How would that child sound saying your words? Do ten of these. For example: "When the going gets tough, the tough get going!" Daddy says, and he means it. Over and over again Daddy says, "If you don't like the heat, stay out of the kitchen!" Daddy knows because he's a small businessman and coaches my softball team.

3. How would a child describe you? Do ten sentences like: *He needs the chair 'cause he's probably the littlest man in Egypt, Maine.* For example: He needs a hat 'cause he's probably the baldest man in Jim Thorpe, Pennsylvania.

4. Go to the second paragraph. The child narrator creates setting. Rewrite this paragraph using the following frame: Daddy's _____ is _____ . . . the _____. Daddy _____. He _____ with _____. One weekend after we _____, Daddy _____ and _____. He . . . (Continue.)

VOICE IN NONFICTION

READING

. . . The Swedes have known a Swedish autumn before; I have not.

Travel returns us in just this way to sharpness of notice; and to be saturated in the sight of what is entirely new—the sun at an unaccustomed slope, stretched across the northland, separate from the infiltrating dusk that always seems about to fall through clear gray Stockholm—is to revisit the enigmatically lit puppet-stage outlines of childhood: those mental photographs and dreaming woodcuts or engravings that we retain from our earliest years. What we remember from childhood we remember forever—permanent ghosts, stamped, imprinted, eternally seen. Travelers regain this ghost-seizing brightness, eeriness, firstness.

FROM THE ESSAY "THE SHOCK OF TEAPOTS," BY CYNTHIA OZICK

LESSON

In this quote, you sense the writer at work. It's as if you can see her; she is wielding a baton and the alphabet is her orchestra. The words are seated in chairs on the stage, following her cues. There is the sense that they are arranged on the page rather than written. As readers we simultaneously watch and participate; we are inside and outside by way of phrases like: *Travel returns us, we retain, we remember, we remember forever.*

The quote is not only about travel to a place, but about the nature of travel itself. It is wise. Ozick writes *Travel returns us in just this way to sharpness of notice,* and surely it does if we allow it to do so. The essay is perceptive, both in the eye and the intellect, and still the quote is not content to be only about travel, but about childhood and memory and how travel can touch the same within us, how they are the same and different. The writer calls upon all that is within her to transport you to this place while she uses this journey to evoke a number of complex issues.

WRITING POSSIBILITIES

1. When was the last time you wrote a good travel letter? Rewrite the quote as if it were your own and you were writing to a best friend. Begin: Travel returns me in just this way to sharpness of notice. . . . (Continue.)

2. Think about a place you visited recently or one you anticipate visiting. Write letters about these places. Allow them to be contemplative and reflective rather than newsy. Use carbon paper so you can keep a copy and then mail them to a friend, or mail them to yourself. Make it a point to begin several sentences as in the quote. Some examples: Travel (verb) me in just this way . . . ; What (I/we) remember . . . ; Travelers . . .

3. How much of Sweden is in the quote? The answer: *the sun at an unaccustomed slope, stretched across the northland, separate from the infiltrating dusk that always seems about to fall through clear gray Stockholm.* . . . Of course there is more to come, but for now, where you are at this moment, what can you say of the sun? Begin: the sun, nowhere to be seen in the gray vault of wet sky that covers South Georgia in January, rain, and 27 degrees . . . ; the sun gone early this daylight saving time at the seventy-seventh meridian, October 30th.

4. Now let's attend to the last two sentences of the quote. Write your own ending to the sentences that begin: What we remember from childhood we remember forever. . . . Travelers regain this _____ _____ness, _____ness, _____ness.

VOICE IN NONFICTION

READING

" . . . *Just like a tree that's planted by the wa-a-ter, oh . . . I shall not be moved!"*

There are moments when you stand on the brink of a new experience and understand that you have no choice about it. Either you walk into the experience or you turn away from it, but you know that no matter what you choose, you will have altered your life in a permanent way. Either way, there will be consequences.

I walked on in.

A dozen or so men and women were clapping hands and stomping feet.

FROM THE BOOK *SALVATION ON SAND MOUNTAIN*, BY DENNIS COVINGTON

LESSON

The quote is a fine example of many elements coming together—the subject's voice, the writer's voice, narrative and setting, all in that order. Think of this as travel to experience, rather than travel to place, although the place is quite extraordinary. It is the world of snake handling, religion and redemption in southern Appalachia. The place is physical and spiritual and draws the writer in as he explores this corner of America. The quote comes from early in the book as he recounts the first time he went to a snake-handling service. As the book opens, the writer crosses the tracks, approaches the church and feels the music, then hears the voices of the singers. These are the people he has come to learn about. He takes a moment before entering to come forward and talk to the reader. He uses the second person, but of course he is telling us about himself as well. There is then a brief line of first person narrative and just like that begins Covington's immersion in the experience that will become this book.

WRITING POSSIBILITIES

1. Look at the second paragraph, the one where the writer comes forward, especially these words: . . . *no matter what you choose, you will have altered your life in a permanent way. Either way, there will be consequences. . . .* Are you ready for such a risk? Not necessarily one of danger, but one where you step outside yourself and into a world that is so very alien to your experience? Rewrite those lines as you anticipate such a moment. Begin: Sometimes in life you . . .

2. A hymn, a bit of philosophy, narrative and scene. Simple enough, but what wisdom can you put forth on the nature of new experiences? This is not mere reportage. It demands that the writer tell of himself.

The second paragraph is critical because it is where he first comes forward. In the spirit of the quote, what can you say about learning; a challenge; adversity; resistance; a particular event?

3. Select an event and simulate the writer's experience. Perhaps it's a bullfight, or boxing match, or Las Vegas, or the Grand Canyon. You might begin with any sound. Perhaps it's your first dive off a reef or your visit to a tent revival. Begin with the attendant sound:

Sometimes you come to a place in life where . . . (Continue.)

I . . . (Replace *walked on in* with the appropriate three or four words. Now set the scene.)

VOICE IN NONFICTION

READING

It had been like dying, that sliding down the mountain pass. It had been like the death of someone, irrational, that sliding down the mountain pass and into the region of dread. It was like the slipping into fever, or falling down that hole in sleep from which you wake yourself whimpering. We had crossed the mountains that day, and now we were in a strange place—a hotel in central Washington, in a town near Yakima. The eclipse we had traveled here to see would occur early the next morning.

FROM THE ESSAY "TOTAL ECLIPSE," BY ANNIE DILLARD

LESSON

The writer is on her way to witness an event where the natural world rivals anything the imagination of the fiction writer or poet or painter might conjure—a total eclipse. For the essayist, the intention is to observe, to tell of the self. It's an idea as simple as show and tell.

The piece opens with a simile and continues that way, goes on to read as if it could be a piece of fiction written in the first person. Even the last sentence, one so clearly of fact and promise, a sentence so unlike those that precede it, could still be something told us by a character in a short story. The voice of a writer, the way she uses language, is identifiable, is discrete, whether the piece is intended to be fiction or nonfiction. The making of prose, no matter its category, no matter its intention, can still be an artistic creation, felicitous, elegant and compelling. From here we travel to the site from which we view the eclipse. The writing ranges from fact of eclipse to fact of eclipse history to fact of eclipse experience, and then we leave. The writer's experience becomes our own.

WRITING POSSIBILITIES

1. Imagine you are the writer on your way to an event in the natural world. What are ten events you might witness? For example: a place of famous sunsets; a place of bats or ants or prairie dogs.

2. The -ing form of the word serves as a noun while seeming like a verb. Words such as *dying, sliding, slipping* are followed by *falling, whimpering* and *morning*. Rewrite the following phrases three times: *that sliding down the mountain pass*; *the slipping into fever*; *It had been like dying*. For example: *that sliding down the mountain pass*—the driving through the black night.

3. Twice the writer expands upon lines she has written. The first time is *that sliding down the mountain pass . . . that sliding down the mountain pass and into the region of dread*. And the second time is *It was like the slipping into fever, or falling down that hole in sleep from which you wake yourself whimpering*. Try these yourself. Key words are in italics. Try to use them or words like them.

. . . that sliding down the mountain pass . . . that sliding down the mountain pass *and* into the region of dread.

. . . that _____ . . . that _____ and . . .

It was like the slipping into fever, *or* falling down *that* hole *in* sleep *from which* you wake yourself whimpering.

It was like the _____, or _____.

4. Let us begin with the conditions of our arrival. Select one from your exercises and proceed with the following frame, maintaining the writer's length of line: It had been like _____, the _____. It had been like _____, _____, that (repeat second fill-in) and _____. It was like the _____ing, or _____ing. We had _____ed, and now we were _____ — a hotel in _____, in a town near _____. The _____ we had traveled here to see would occur early the next morning.

VOICE—DIGNIFIED

READING

As a young intern assigned to the pathology laboratory of a Catholic hospital run by a monastic order, I was ill prepared for some of the routines. The nuns administered the place with exemplary efficiency. At each key post an overseer or coordinator (may the youthful levity of those who said "spy" be forgiven) saw to it that cleanliness, order, punctuality, and systematic avoidance of waste prevail throughout the establishment.

FROM THE ESSAY "MICROCOSM IN A BOTTLE," BY F. GONZALES-CRUSSI

LESSON

The writer of this quote is a doctor and professor of pathology. His collection of essays on the preservation of body parts is personal and reflective. Given the subject matter, the hand that brings them to the page is elegant and respectful, yet capable of wit. We enter his world through him, a world we could easily turn away from because it is the world of the dead one capable of stirring fear in all of us.

With this writer, though, we know we are in good, capable hands. From the first sentence we feel safe. Notice how he withholds subject and verb until he tells us who he is and where he is, and when he does give us subject and verb, it is to say how *ill prepared* he felt. The next sentence introduces the *efficiency* of the nuns, and of course, their unspoken sacredness. The third sentence gives way to wit inside the parenthetical and further supports the idea that, however squeamish we may be, we are entering a place of order and respect. And we quickly come to respect the people who work here. We will be safe in the company of the dead.

WRITING POSSIBILITIES

1. Maybe there has been profound pain in your family and you want to write of it in a dignified way and from a comfortable distance. Rewrite the quote using your personal experience. Begin with: As a young man assigned by my family to care for an elderly uncle in his last months on earth, I was ill prepared for the days to come. The visiting nurse (may she ever hold secret my unreasonable squeamishness at the sight of needles) administered all necessary medications, and at designated hours of the day, family members stopped in to clean, cook . . . (Continue.)

2. Begin a list of explorations outside your private experience. Perhaps your job is odd or bumps up against another occupation that is fascinating. Perhaps a relative or friend has a job that is a possibility for writing. Your list of places might include an emergency room, a nursing home, even an abattoir. If possible, come up with a list of five such places, where workers must deal on a regular basis with human pain and suffering.

3. Attend to the quote not so much for its subject matter as for the way it sounds. Imagine it to be a piece of fiction. What's the storyteller like? How do you see him? Does he have a moustache or not? Does he wear glasses? Does he have good posture? Write a sentence that could follow the quote if it were a piece of fiction. For example: Being a particular man, I had no problem whatsoever complying with the rules. . . . (Continue.)

VOICE—HUMOROUS

READING

. . . I found the seat and whiled away the hour until game time by perusing a compendium called *Inside the Astrodome*. Reading it made me feel a little like Jonah probably felt when he was inside the whale. The book contained a letter from the President, another from the governor, a quote from Coleridge (guess which), a detailed comparison of the Astrodome and the Roman Colosseum, and page after page of staggering statistics. The stadium's iceplant, for example, can produce 36,000 pounds of ice a day—no one in this climate can fail to be impressed with such a figure.

FROM THE ESSAY "LOVE, DEATH & THE ASTRODOME," BY LARRY MCMURTRY

LESSON

The writer has come to the Astrodome in Houston, Texas. It is an outsized construction, and what better way to render it than to appear monumentally unimpressed? The sound behind the words is tongue-firmly-planted-in-cheek. The storyteller is smiling, his eye gone to twinkle. He is playing off and at the same time outsizing the Astrodome itself. He's having fun with Texas-size ambitions that gave the world the Astrodome, outdoing it by posturing as one who is unimpressed. Every nook and cranny of America has a way it fancies itself to be. This is all directed at those capable of enduring, perhaps even enjoying, a good teasing.

WRITING POSSIBILITIES

1. Is there an outsized structure or event somewhere near you that you might take on in the spirit of the quote above? List ten, including structures or features of nature. But don't forget other possibilities such as high school football, a chili cooking competition, a fishing derby.

2. Select an example from your list in exercise one. Maybe something real, or something imagined for the purpose of the exercise. Let's begin with: I found a seat and killed some time by perusing a nifty little pamphlet called *Mad Dog Football—The Run to Greatness*. Reading it made me feel a little like I was the pathetic underachiever I always suspected. The book contained a letter from the Mayor, another from the Governor (recently indicted), a quote from the Bible, a detailed history of Mad Dog football, and list upon list of indecipherable statistics. The team's Gatorade intake, for example . . . (Continue.)

3. Consider using the sound of this quote to begin a piece of fiction. Imagine we are writing about a family reunion. Our storyteller is the one in the family who's been away, perhaps estranged. Let's not think

it out too far in advance. Let's try a beginning such as: I found a chair in the shade and whiled away the time reading a fresh mimeograph called *Two Hundred Years of the Nudds in America*. Reading it made me feel a little like Daniel in the lion's den. I was a long lost Nudd, now come home but thinking I should have stayed long lost. . . . (Continue.)

4. Consider other ideas. Perhaps you have a character on vacation, experiencing a place as large as the Astrodome or as small as a vineyard open to the public. As with the writing of fiction, you generate your own ideas and go after them.

VOICE—ACERBIC

READING
I have now seen sucrose beaches and water a very bright blue. I have seen an all-red leisure suit with flared lapels. I have smelled suntan lotion spread over 2,100 pounds of hot flesh. I have been addressed as "Mon" in three different nations. I have seen 500 upscale Americans dance the Electric Slide. I have seen sunsets that looked computer-enhanced. I have (very briefly) joined a conga line.

FROM THE ESSAY "SHIPPING OUT," BY DAVID FOSTER WALLACE

LESSON
The tone of this piece could be described as acerbic, sarcastic. Behind the tone is something larger, and that is voice. Voice keeps the piece from becoming that of a complainer. Voice brings to light later moments of self-deprecation, the writer's sense that he is not of this place, does not belong here and is here only because it would give rise to humor, ill-fitted as he is to the situation. Think of the entire piece as the sincere performance of a most disconcerted individual. The method is simple enough. The writer begins at the end, begins with his conclusion. He winnows events down to their most telling components, using numbers for their truth and power, using the refrain *I have* to enter each sentence, as if it were a device with which to barely contain his consternation. The opening suggests a narrator at wit's end, and we expect to discover what has taxed him so.

WRITING POSSIBILITIES
1. In the essay, the writer continues for almost thirty sentences with this tone, sometimes using *I now know*. . . . List a dozen other such phrases. For example: I have felt . . . ; I have tasted . . . ; I saw . . . ; He saw . . .

2. Imagine you have been to an event. A wedding? A family reunion? Some roadside attraction? A gathering of unsettling proportion? Begin: I have now seen _____ and _____. I have seen _____. I have smelled _____. I have been _____. I have seen _____. I have seen _____. I have (very briefly) _____. (Continue for as many as thirty sentences.)

3. Now take the event from exercise two and turn it around. Make it a thing of delight and amazement and wonderment.

4. How to move on? As noted in exercise one, the writer goes on for almost thirty sentences with essentially the same beginning. He then writes: *To be specific: voluntarily and for pay, I underwent a 7-Night Caribbean (7NC) Cruise. . . .* That's how he moves on, by saying specifically what it is he's telling about and proceeding from there. Select an event, real or imagined. Try taking it up to twenty-five sentences and then make your next move with a sentence starting like: To be precise: . . . ; To be exact: . . .

VOICE OF NARRATIVE

READING

Something was done about it.

Isabelle Holly, the widow who owned the building and suffered this—what shall we call it?—knew there was going to be trouble in the house when she saw Miss Domingo come in the front door one evening with a medium-sized box labeled EXPLOSIVES.

The widow Holly did not wait for eventualities that night. She went right out on the street, dressed as she was, in a pair of rayon bloomers and a brassière. She had hardly gotten around the corner when the whole block shook with a terrible detonation.

FROM THE STORY "THE COMING OF SOMETHING TO THE WIDOW HOLLY,"
BY TENNESSEE WILLIAMS

LESSON

As writers we establish a relationship with our projects. We find ourselves living in degrees of proximity. This is not to be mistaken for point of view, a more technical and definable element. The question is, how close will we be to our work? It is not something we calculate so much as something that comes to us, a way to sound as narrator, a way to be as if we were also a character.

What Williams is telling us are the elements of a good scene, an event worth recounting, but *how* he is telling it makes all the difference.

He writes as an intimate, as a citizen of this place, a close neighbor, a confidante. He writes as someone who is privy to the goings-on and whose sensibility is perhaps more of their ken than that of the reader at large, but for all his loyalties, the telling is old-fashioned yarn-spinning bent on eliciting gasps and laughs and sweet delight.

WRITING POSSIBILITIES

1. Begin with a pair of names, an unlikely combination. Write ten sets. For example: the hermit Francis Pope and Immaculata Trooskin; the hairdresser Keow Swinehart and Miss Oberacker.

2. How might the lives of the characters in exercise one cross in an unfriendly way? List an intersection for each. For example: Immaculata Trooskin has inherited the land where the hermit Francis Pope has his shack.

3. Now, rewrite the quote using your characters. For example:

Something was done about it.

Francis Pope, the hermit who dwelled in the shack down by the scenic overlook and witnessed this—what shall we call it?—knew there was going to be hell to pay when he saw Immaculata Trooskin come down the wooded lane one evening atop a medium-sized bulldozer. . . . (Continue.)

4. Take another pair from your list. Rewrite the quote again, but with a bit more distance, using your own mannerisms. For example:

It would not stand.

Jinho Smith, the ecdysiast who owned the pink feather boa and endured this what you might call professional affront, knew something was up when she saw Mr. Pavloski. . . . (Continue.)

WORDS OF TIME AND MEMORY

READING

. . . But it had never crossed my mind that they would try to stop you from going barefoot in June, no matter if there had been a gully-washer and a cold spell.

Nobody had ever tried to stop me in June as long as I could remember, and when you are nine years old, what you remember seems forever; for you remember everything and everything is important and stands big and full and fills up Time and is so solid that you can walk around and around it like a tree and look at it.

FROM THE STORY "BLACKBERRY WINTER," BY ROBERT PENN WARREN

LESSON

Time as a consideration can be a simple matter of deciding upon a tense, whether past or present, or occasionally future. But more than that, the act of recounting, of remembering, can make time itself a subject of narrative as it is a subject of philosophy. In this way, the language of time is opened to us and in so doing, it opens our character. The act of remembering posits thoughts of time in the mind of a character, especially a first person character. We fashion time as a way of helping us remember. Maybe it's a time line, our thoughts clipped along the rope like laundry.

In this quote, the storyteller begins with a simple memory of going barefoot in June. Remembering this anecdote turns memory onto itself, and the storyteller's thoughts move from the memory of the anecdote to the nature of memory itself and back to something as solid as a tree. The movement in time and the idea of time are the subjects of this quote. As your first person narrators conjure up memory, it is only natural that the memory and the act of remembering will find themselves in the language of the dance of time.

WRITING POSSIBILITIES

1. This is a long-term assignment that could yield a number of stories or essays. First, make a list of your memories of each of the twelve months. For example: sugar-on-snow in March; a kind of cold that comes in November; the hard dusty ground of August.

2. Now make another list as you did in exercise one, only this time, do it for the days of the week. Let both your months list and your days-of-the-week list be ongoing. Add to them regularly as new memories emerge. For example: Sunday night was always Ed Sullivan; Saturday morning is when we washed my father's car.

3. Robert Penn Warren writes *when you are nine years old, what you remember seems forever.* Now take your months and days-of-the-week lists and, wherever you can, give an age to the memory.

4. From each one of your lists, choose a time, memory and age that have taken hold of your curiosity. Use these as the elements for a short story. Since you're writing fiction, feel free to imagine characters and events, using your memories only as a starting point. Fit them into the first sentence and keep writing. For example: When you are twelve years old, and it's August in North Carolina, what you remember is peach juice running down your thin sunburned arm. Your brother calls from the porch. "Gerald, get on up here."

5. Use your list again and begin with the slenderest of frames: When _____, and it's _____, what _____. . . .

THE SOUND OF A LINE BREAK

READING

Leaning from the waist, throwing his good two hundred pounds behind it, Kenny brought the brush hook down.

***

"Hogs'll eat just about anything," Tobe Fogus had told me as he emptied the bucket into one of the feed troughs on the lot behind his house.

. . . It was easier to believe that Booze was dead.

***

It was a killing blow, well aimed.

FROM THE STORY "BOOZE," BY PINCKNEY BENEDICT

LESSON

"Booze" is a story about a giant hog that has escaped into the countryside. The boys have come across the hog and are determined to kill it because it has been a terror. At the moment Kenny brings down the brush hook, Benedict breaks off from that action and goes into a long backstory. Concluding the backstory, he breaks away and returns to where we left off.

This is a daring move for a writer, to leave behind the moment of tension so carefully developed. Such a move, of course, risks losing the reader. But follow the steps, the sounds inside the words: Lean*ing* . . . throw*ing* . . . *** any*thing* . . . ha*d* tol*d* . . . emptie*d* . . . wa*s* . . . wa*s* . . . *** . . . wa*s* . . . kill*ing* . . . aime*d*. Apparent is the stitch of -ing and -d and -s that surrounds this move in time. Whether by intent or not, it is there. Benedict knows he is asking the reader to leave a most dramatic moment. He uses every skill he has to make that move, however abrupt, as seamless as possible. How much to demand of your reader? How can you ever really know? The truth is, you don't know. You take your chances with the parts of words seeking to make connections in the ear of the reader. You hope that these are enough to suggest a connection and that your reader sees the need for such a move rather than feels manipulated.

WRITING POSSIBILITIES

1. Let's try to imitate what Benedict has done in the quote. Think of a narrative in which you might perform the following steps: suspend the moment of action; strike a line break; tell the backstory; strike a line break; return to the suspended action.

Think of it as two separate but connected stories: the story of now and the story of back then. List five moments of suspended action.

For example: striking a match, leaning to kiss, hitting a baseball.

2. Let's rewrite the quote using a possibility from exercise one. Begin:

Striding forward in the box, powering his strong muscles into it, Roger brought the bat around.

***

"Boys'll do just about anything to play ball," Stumpy had told me as he emptied the rubbish into one of the cans in the alley behind his joint. . . .

. . . It was easier to imagine the game was as good as lost.

***

It was a stunning blow, well timed.

VOICE OF BEGINNING

READINGS

I am an invisible man. No, I am not a spook like those who haunted Edgar Allan Poe; nor am I one of your Hollywood-movie ectoplasms. I am a man of substance, of flesh and bone, fiber and liquids—and I might even be said to possess a mind. I am invisible, understand, simply because people refuse to see me. Like the bodiless heads you see sometimes in circus sideshows, it is as though I have been surrounded by mirrors of hard, distorting glass. When they approach me they see only my surroundings, themselves, or figments of their imagination—indeed, everything and anything except me.

FROM THE NOVEL *INVISIBLE MAN*, BY RALPH ELLISON

Call me Ishmael. Some years ago—never mind how long precisely—having little or no money in my purse, and nothing particular to interest me on shore, I thought I would sail about a little and see the watery part of the world.

FROM THE NOVEL *MOBY DICK*, BY HERMAN MELVILLE

LESSON

In the first lesson of chapter one we began with a storyteller. The quote was the opening to Herman Melville's *Moby Dick*. We could as easily end with the same quote because voice threads its way through all the best writing. It is like the temperature or tone or soul of the writer's words, whether fiction or nonfiction. Voice is the sense that there is someone behind the work making decisions, a pilot guiding the language. As far as that goes, any quote in this book could be read for voice alone.

The "I" in Ellison's novel is Ishmael turned inside out and brought forward one hundred years. He is voice. He is the sound of something we cannot see because of our own incapacities. Both novels are considered Great American Novels for their ambition, urgency of intent, power of language, and ability to grasp and hold something deep inside us. Notice how elusive and secretive are two of the world's greatest protagonists. Both withhold, both challenge. Neither can escape himself, neither can come forward from behind the veil, and yet they both deliver so much. Both deny us information. Both direct our curiosity. Both are precise and particular. Both give and take, all for the purpose of telling their stories.

WRITING POSSIBILITIES

1. The Invisible Man introduces himself: *I am an invisible man.* What story is in your heart that must be told? What words will represent that story? This can be fiction or perhaps memoir. Either way, work through as many possibilities for *invisible* as you need to until you find the right first sentence. It may even take a few days. Begin: I am (a, an, the?) (adjective) (man/woman). I am an ugly man. (True, but who cares?) I am a useless man. (No, not quite.) I am a culpable man. (Interesting.) Continue. This one should not be easy; it may even be impossible. Be patient with yourself, and keep in mind that even a failed attempt is a learning experience. The time is not wasted.

2. Select your best from exercise one and proceed with a rewrite of the quote, or continue with this one: I am a guilty man. No, I am not a criminal, like those who steal and kill and haunt the dark night; nor am I one of your . . .

3. Concentrate on the second sentence. Sometimes it's easier to say what we are not, rather than what we are. For example: . . . I am not evil, like those who cannot hear or see or feel what they do; nor am I someone who hears and sees and feels all that he should. Begin: . . . I am not a _____, like those who _____; nor am I _____.

4. Let's try the rest of the quote. Attempt to maintain the same length of line as in the quote. Begin: . . . I am a (man/woman) of _____, of _____ and _____, _____ and _____ —and I might even _____. I am _____, understand, simply because _____. Like _____, it is as though I _____. When they _____ me, they _____, _____, or _____ — indeed, _____.

5. Now let's try to put it all together. This may be the beginning of your own Great American Novel. We're certainly trying for a bit of

epic grandeur—a work of large ambition and large themes. Each sentence has been isolated and sketched in. As a warm-up exercise, add to the sentences where you can. Continue with:

I am a silent man.

No, I am not without a tongue or larynx or vocal cords; nor am I without education or the words of the educated. . . .

I am a man of letters, of intellect and insight, experience and age—and I might even be said to possess wisdom.

But I am silent, you should know, simply because . . .

Like the . . .

When they speak to me, they . . .

Now start from scratch with just those two simple words to get you on your way—I am . . .

ABOUT THE AUTHOR

Robert Olmstead is the author of three novels—*America by Land* (Random House, 1993), *Soft Water* (Vintage, 1988) and *A Trail of Heart's Blood Wherever We Go* (Random House, 1990)—as well as a collection of short stories, *River Dogs* (Vintage, 1987), and a memoir, *Stay Here With Me* (Metropolitan Books, 1996). His work has appeared in STORY, *Granta, Cutbank, Black Warrior Review, Epoch, Ploughshares, Graywolf, Weber Studies, American Literature, Spin* and *Sports Afield*. He has received fellowships from the Guggenheim Foundation and the National Endowment for the Arts, as well as the Pennsylvania Council for the Arts.

LESSON INDEX

INDEX